THE
CONFESSIONS
OF
SAINT
AUGUSTINE

THE
CONFESSIONS
OF
SAINT
AUGUSTINE

Whitaker House

Publisher's note:
This Whitaker House edition of Augustine's *Confessions*
is a revision of the highly respected Edward B. Pusey
English translation. This version has been edited for
content and also updated for the modern reader.
Words, expressions, and sentence structure have
been revised for clarity and readability.

All Scripture quotations are taken from the King James
Version (KJV) of the Holy Bible.

THE CONFESSIONS OF SAINT AUGUSTINE

ISBN: 0-88368-382-2
Printed in the United States of America
© 1996 by Whitaker House

Whitaker House
30 Hunt Valley Circle
New Kensington, PA 15068
www.whitakerhouse.com

---

4 5 6 7 8 9 10 11 12 13 **UI** 11 10 09 08 07 06 05 04

Contents

Introduction

Aurelius Augustinus, better known as Saint Augustine, was born of poor parents in the small town of Thagaste in Numidia, North Africa, A.D. 354. His father, Patricius, a pagan who lived somewhat of a loose life, was converted to Christianity before his death; his mother Monnica, on account of her personal piety and her influence on her son, is one of the most revered women in the history of the Christian church.

Augustine was educated at the University of Carthage and, according to his own account, belonged to a group of rowdy friends and joined in their intemperate living. While there he entered into a fourteen-year relationship with a young woman who became the mother of his son, Adeodatus. He also joined the heretical sect of the Manicheans, who professed to have received from their founder a higher form of truth than was taught by Christ.

At the close of his university career, which had been brilliant in spite of distractions, he returned to his native town, and first there, and later in Carthage and Rome, he practiced as a teacher of rhetoric, training young lawyers in the art of debating. By the time he was about twenty-seven he had begun to have doubts as to the validity of the Manichean faith, but it was not until

387, while he was professor of rhetoric in the University of Milan, that he was converted to Christianity and received baptism. He then gave up his profession and became an ascetic, studying the foundations of faith; writing, chiefly against his former sect; and conversing with a group of disciples, first at Rome and then in his native town.

When he was on a visit to Hippo, not far from Thagaste, he went into the priesthood, and in 395 he became Bishop of Hippo, an office which he filled for the remaining thirty-five years of his life. Though he took a leading part in the activities of the African Church through all this time, and gradually became one of the most distinguished ecclesiastical figures in the Roman Empire, the care of his diocese and the writing of his books formed his chief occupations. He continued to lead a life of extreme simplicity and self-denial, and in his pastoral establishment he trained a large number of disciples who became leaders in the church. The strength of his hold on these younger men was due not merely to his intellectual ascendancy but also to the charm and sweetness of his disposition.

A large part of his literary activity was devoted to controversy with the heretics of his time. His two most important books are *The City of God* and the *Confessions*. The former of these was provoked by the attacks upon Christianity which were roused by the disasters that began to fall upon the Western Empire in the beginning of the fifth century. Augustine replies to these by pointing out the failure of the heathen gods in former times to protect the people who trusted in them, and he goes on to expose the evil influence of the belief in the old mythology, in a detailed examination of its traditions and mysteries. The second part of the book deals with the history of the "City of Man," founded upon love of self, and of the "City of God," founded upon love of God and contempt of self. This work is a vast storehouse of the knowledge of the time, and it is a monument not only to Augustine's great learning but also to the keenest metaphysical mind of the age.

The Confessions speaks for itself. The earliest of autobiographies, it remains unsurpassed as a sincere and intimate record of a great and pious soul laid bare before God.

Book One

Confessions of the greatness and unsearchableness of God, of God's mercies in infancy and boyhood, and of human willfulness. Of Augustine's own sins of idleness, of the abuse of his studies, and of God's gifts up to his fifteenth year.

G reat are You, Lord, and greatly to be praised. Great is Your power, and Your wisdom infinite (Ps. 145:3; 147:5). And man wants to praise You; man, but a particle of Your creation; man that bears about him his mortality, the witness of his sin, the witness that You "resisteth the proud" (James 4:6; 1 Pet. 5:5). Yet man wants to praise You, he, but a particle of Your creation. You awaken us to delight in Your praise, for You made us for Yourself, and our hearts are restless until they rest in You.

Grant me, Lord, to know and understand which is first: to call on You or to praise You? And, again, to know You or to call on You? Who can call on You, not knowing You? For he that does not know You may call on You as something other than You are. Or, is it rather that we call on You so that we may know You? But "how then shall they call on him in whom they have not believed?...how shall they [believe] without a preacher?" (Rom. 10:14). And, "they shall praise

11

the LORD that seek him" (Ps. 22:26). For they who seek will find Him (Matt. 7:7), and they who find will praise Him. I will seek You, Lord, by calling on You, and will call on You, believing in You, for to us have You been preached. My faith, Lord, will call on You, my faith which You have given me, by which You have inspired me, through the Incarnation of Your Son, through the ministry of the preacher, St. Ambrose.

And how shall I call upon my God, my God and Lord, since, when I call for Him, I shall be calling Him to myself? And what room is there within me, where my God can come into me? Where can God come into me, God who made heaven and earth? Is there, indeed, O Lord my God, nothing in me that can contain You? Do heaven and earth then, which You have made and wherein You have made me, contain You? Or, because nothing which exists could exist without You, does therefore whatever exists contain You? Since, then, I too exist, why do I seek that You should enter into me, who would not exist were You not in me? Why? Because I am not now in hell, and yet You are there also. For if I go down into hell, "thou art there" (Ps. 139:8). I could not exist then, my God, could not exist at all, were You not in me. Or, rather, I would not exist unless I were in You of whom are all things, by whom are all things, and in whom are all things (Rom. 11:36). Even so, Lord, even so. Where do I call You, since I am in You? Or from where can You enter into me? Where can I go beyond heaven and earth that thus my God should come into me, He

12

who has said, "Do not I fill heaven and earth?" (Jer. 23:24).

Do the heaven and earth then contain You since You fill them? Or do You fill them and yet overflow since they do not contain You? And where, when the heaven and the earth are filled, do You pour forth the remainder of Yourself? Or do You have no need that anything should contain You, who contain all things, since what You fill, You fill by containing it? For the vessels which You fill do not uphold You, since though they were broken, You were not poured out. And when You are poured out on us, You are not cast down, but You uplift us; You are not dissipated, but You gather us. But You who fill all things, do You fill them with Your whole self? Or, since all things cannot contain You wholly, do they contain part of You? And all at once the same part? Or each its own part, the greater more, the smaller less? And is, then, one part of You greater, another less? Or, are You wholly everywhere, while nothing contains You wholly?

What are You then, my God? What but the Lord God? "For who is God save the LORD?" (Ps. 18:31). Or who is God save our God? Most high, most good, most potent, most omnipotent; most merciful, yet most just; most hidden, yet most present; most beautiful, yet most strong; stable, yet incomprehensible; unchangeable, yet all-changing; never new, never old; all-renewing and bringing age upon the proud, and they did not know it; ever working, ever at rest; still gathering, yet nothing lacking; supporting, filling, and overspreading;

creating, nourishing, and maturing; seeking, yet having all things. You love, without passion; are jealous, without anxiety; repent, yet grieve not; are angry, yet serene; change Your words, Your purpose unchanged; receive again what You find, yet never lost; never in need, yet rejoicing in gains; never covetous, yet exacting interest. You receive over and above so that You may owe, and who has anything that is not Yours? You pay debts, owing nothing; remit debts, losing nothing. And what have I now said, my God, my life, my holy joy? Or what does any man say when he speaks of You? Yet woe to him who does not speak, since even the most eloquent are mute.

Oh, that I might repose on You! Oh, that You would enter into my heart and inebriate it, that I may forget my ills and embrace You, my sole good! What are You to me? In Your pity, teach me to utter it. Or what am I to You that You demand my love, and, if I do not give it, are angry with me and threaten me with grievous woes? Is it then a slight woe not to love You? Oh, for Your mercies' sake, tell me, Lord my God, what You are to me. "Say unto my soul, I am thy salvation" (Ps. 35:3). So speak, that I may hear. Behold, Lord, my heart is before You; open the ears of it, and "say unto my soul, I am thy salvation." After this voice let me run and take hold on You. Do not hide Your face from me. Let me die—for fear that I die—only let me see Your face.

Narrow is the mansion of my soul; enlarge it so that You may enter in. It is ruinous; repair it, Lord. It has that within which must offend Your eyes; I confess and know it. But who will cleanse it? Or to whom should I cry, except You? Lord, "cleanse thou me from [my] secret faults" (Ps. 19:12), and spare Your servant from the power of the enemy. "I believed, therefore have I spoken" (Ps. 116:10). Lord, You know. Have I not confessed against myself "my sins to thee," and You, my God, have forgiven "the iniquity of my sin" (Ps. 32:5)? I do not contend in judgment with You (see Job 9:3), You who are the truth; I am afraid of deceiving myself for fear that my iniquity will lie to itself. Therefore, I do not contend in judgment with You, for "if thou, LORD, shouldest mark iniquities, O Lord, who shall stand?" (Ps. 130:3).

Yet allow me to speak to Your mercy, me, "dust and ashes" (Gen. 18:27). Yet allow me to speak, since I speak to Your mercy and not to scornful man. You too, perhaps, despise me, yet You will "return and have compassion on [me]" (Jer. 12:15). For what would I say, O Lord my God, but that I do not know from where I came into this dying life—shall I call it?—or living death. Then immediately did the comforts of Your compassion take me up, as I heard, for I do not remember it, from the parents of my flesh, out of whose substance You did at some time fashion me. Thus there I received the comforts of woman's milk. For neither my mother nor my nurses stored their own breasts for me, but You did bestow the food of my infancy through them, according to Your ordinance, by which You distribute Your riches through the hidden springs of all things.

You also gave me to desire no more than You gave, and to my nurses willingly to give me what You gave them. For they, with a heaven-taught affection, willingly gave me what they abounded with from You. Therefore, this my good from them was good for them. Indeed, it was not from them but through them, for from You, God, are all good things, and from my God is all my health. This I have since learned, when You, through these Your gifts, inside me and outside, were proclaiming Yourself to me. Then I knew only to suck, to repose in what pleased, and to cry at what offended my flesh, nothing more.

Afterwards I began to smile, first in sleep, then waking. So it was told to me of myself, and I believed it, for we see the like in other infants, though of myself I do not remember it. Thus, little by little, I became conscious of where I was and began to want to express my wishes to those who could content them. But I could not express them because the wishes were inside of me, and they outside; nor could they by their senses enter into my spirit. So I flung about at random, limbs and voices, making the few signs I could and such as I could, like—though in truth very little like—what I wished. And when I was not immediately obeyed, my wishes being harmful to me or unintelligible, then I was indignant with my elders for not submitting to me, with those owing me no service, for not serving me, and avenged myself on them by tears. Such I have learned infants to be from observing them. That I was myself such, they, all unconscious, have shown me better than my nurses who knew it.

And, behold! My infancy died long ago, and I live. But You, Lord, live forever, and in You nothing dies, for before the foundation of the worlds and before all that can be called "before," You are, and You are God and Lord of all which You have created. The first causes of all things unabiding and of all things changeable abide in You, fixed forever. The springs abide in You unchangeable, and the eternal reasons of all things unreasoning and temporal live in You. Tell me, Lord, as Your suppliant, all-pitying, tell me, Your pitiable one, tell me, did my infancy succeed another age of mine that died before it? Was it that which I spent within my mother's womb? For of that I have heard something and have myself seen women with child; and again, before that life, God, my joy, was I anywhere or anybody? This I have none to tell me, neither father or mother, nor experience of others, nor my own memory. Do You mock me for asking this and bid me to praise You and acknowledge You for that which I do know?

I acknowledge You, Lord of heaven and earth, and praise You for my first rudiments of being and my infancy, of which I remember nothing, for You have appointed that man should from others guess much about himself and believe much on the strength of weak females. Even then I had being and life, and, at my infancy's close, I could seek for signs by which to make known to others my feelings. Where could such a being come from, except from You, Lord? Will any be his own designer? Or can there elsewhere be derived any vein, which may stream essence and life into us, except from

17

You, Lord, in whom essence and life are one? For You Yourself are supremely essence and life.

You are most high and are not changed (see Malachi 3:6), neither does today come to a close in You. Yet in You does it come to a close because all such things also are in You. For they had no way to pass away unless You upheld them. And since "thy years shall have no end" (Ps. 102:27), Your years are one today. How many of ours and our fathers' years have flowed away through Your "today" and from it received the measure and the mold of such being as they had, and still others will flow away and so receive the mold of their degree of being. But "thou art the same" (Ps. 102:27), and all things of tomorrow and all beyond and all of yesterday and all behind it, You have done today. What is it to me if any do not comprehend this? Let him also rejoice and say, "What thing is this?" (See Exodus 16:15.) Let him rejoice even thus and be content by not discovering it to discover You, rather than by discovering it, not to discover You.

Hear, O God. Alas, for man's sin! So says man, and You pity him, for You made him, but sin in him You did not make. Who reminds me of the sins of my infancy? For in Your sight none is pure from sin (see Job 25:4), not even the infant whose life is but a day upon the earth. Who reminds me? Does not each little infant in whom I see what I do not remember of myself? What then was my sin? Was it that I hung upon the breast and cried? Should I now do so for food suitable to my age, I would justly be laughed at and reproved. What I

18

then did was worthy of reproof, but since I could not understand reproof, custom and reason forbade me to be reproved. For when we are grown, we root out and cast away those habits.

Now, no man, though he prunes, wittingly casts away what is good. Or was it then good, even for a while, to cry for what, if given, would hurt? Or bitterly to resent that people free and my own elders, the very authors of my birth, did not serve me? That many besides, wiser than me, did not obey the nod of my good pleasure? To do my best to strike and hurt because commands were not obeyed, which would have been obeyed only to my hurt? The weakness then of an infant's limbs, not its will, is its innocence. I myself have seen and even known an envious baby; it could not speak, yet it turned pale and looked bitterly on its foster brother. Who does not know this? Mothers and nurses tell you that they appease these things by I do not know what remedies. Is that, too, innocence, when the fountain of milk is flowing in rich abundance, not to allow one to share it, one who is in extreme need and whose very life as yet depends on that? We bear gently with all this, not as being no or slight evils, but because they will disappear as years increase. For, though tolerated now, the very same tempers are utterly intolerable when found in riper years.

You, then, Lord my God—who gave life to this my infancy, furnishing thus with senses, as we see, the frame You gave, compacting its limbs, ornamenting its proportions, and for its general good and safety, implanting in it all vital functions—You commanded me to praise You in these things, to confess to You, and "to sing praises unto thy name, O most High" (Ps. 92:1). For You are God, almighty and good, even if You had done nothing but only this which none could do but You, whose unity is the mold of all things, who out of Your own fairness makes all things fair and orders all things by Your law. This age, then, Lord, of which I have no remembrance, which I take on others' words and guess from other infants that I have observed, true though the guess be, I am loath to include in this life of mine which I live in this world. Much like the time I spent in my mother's womb, is it hid from me in the shadows of forgetfulness. But if "I was shapen in iniquity, and in sin did my mother conceive me" (Ps. 51:5), where, I beseech You, my God, where, Lord, or when, was I, Your servant, guiltless? But, behold! That period I pass by, and what have I now to do with that of which I can recall no vestige?

Moving on from infancy, I came to boyhood, or rather it came to me, displacing infancy. Nor did that depart—for where did it go?—and yet it was no more. For I was no longer a speechless infant, but a speaking boy. This I remember, and I have since observed how I learned to speak. It was not that my elders taught me words in any set method, as, soon after, they did with other learning. I, rather, longing by cries and babblings and various motions of my limbs to express my thoughts that I might have my will, and yet unable to express all I willed, or to whom I willed, did myself, by the understanding which You, my God, gave me, practice the sounds in my memory. When they named anything, and turned towards it as they spoke, I saw and remembered that they called what they pointed out by the name they uttered. That they meant this thing and no other was plain from the motion of their body, the natural language, as it were, of all nations, expressed by the countenance, glances of the eye, gestures of the limbs, and tones of the voice, indicating the affections of the mind as it pursues, possesses, rejects, or shuns. Thus by constantly hearing words, as they occurred in various sentences, I understood gradually what they stood for, and after having imitated these signs with my mouth, I thereby could express my will through language. Thus I exchanged with those about me these current signs of our wills and so launched deeper into the stormy intercourse of human life, though still depending on parental authority and the beck of elders.

Oh God, my God, what miseries and mockeries did I now experience when I was taught that it was proper for a boy to be obedient to his teacher, in order that in this world I might prosper and excel in rhetoric through which I should receive the "praise of men" (John 12:43) and deceitful riches. Next, I was put in school to get learning, in which I, poor wretch, did not know what use there was. Yet, if I was idle in learning, I was beaten. This was considered right by our forefathers, and many who followed the same course before us framed for us weary paths through which we were obliged to pass, multiplying toil and grief upon the sons of Adam. But, Lord, we found that men called upon

You, and we learned from them to think of You, according to our ability to comprehend, as of some great One who, though hidden from our senses, could hear and help us. In this way I began, as a boy, to pray to You, my aid and refuge. In praying to You, I broke the chains of my tongue. Though I was small, I prayed to You with no small earnestness, that I might not be beaten at school. And when You did not hear me, my elders, my own parents who did not wish me any harm, mocked my beatings which were then so great and grievous to me.

Is there anyone, Lord, who is so noble of soul and who is devoted to You with such intensity and love—for there is a kind of thick-witted person who is able in some way to do this—but is there anyone who, from cleaving devoutly to You, is endued with so great a spirit that he can think lightly of the racks and hooks and other torments, against which, throughout all lands, men call on You with extreme dread? Does anyone mock at those who are most bitterly feared, as our parents mocked the torments which we suffered in boyhood from our masters? We did not fear our torments less, and we did not pray less to You to escape them. Yet we sinned, in writing, reading, or studying less than was demanded of us. We did not want, Lord, memory or capacity of what Your will provided in proportion to our age, but our sole delight was play. For this we were punished by those who yet themselves were doing the same. But elder folks' idleness is called "business." The idleness of boys, which is really the same, is punished by those elders, and no one sympathizes with either boys or men. Will any of sound discretion approve of my being beaten as a boy because, by playing at ball, I made less progress in studies that would only lead me to play more unbecomingly when I became a man? And did not the one who beat me do the same thing for which I was beaten? And was not he, if defeated in some trifling discussion with his fellow-tutor, more embittered and jealous than I when beaten at ball by a play-fellow?

And yet, I sinned in this, Lord God, the creator and orderer of all things in nature—but of sin the orderer only. Oh, Lord my God, I sinned in transgressing the commands of my parents and those of my masters. For what they, with whatever motive, would have had me learn, I might afterwards have put to good use. I disobeyed, not from a better choice, but from love of play: loving the pride of victory in my contests and to have my ears tickled with lying fables that they might itch the more. The same curiosity was flashing from my eyes more and more for the shows and games of my elders. Those who give these shows are held in such esteem that almost all parents wish their children to become like them. Yet, they are very willing that their children should be beaten if those very games detain them from the studies which would enable them to become the givers of them. Look with pity, Lord, on these things, and deliver us who call upon You now; deliver those too who do not yet call on You, so that they may call on You and You may deliver them.

As a boy I had already heard of an eternal life, promised us through the humility of the Lord our God who stooped to our pride. Even from the womb of my mother who greatly hoped in You, I was sealed with the mark of His cross and salted with His salt.[1] You saw, Lord, how while I was yet a boy I was once seized by a sudden stomach ailment and was near to death. You saw, my God, for You were my keeper, with what eagerness and what faith I sought, from the pious care of my mother and Your church, the baptism of Your Christ, my God and Lord. Upon which the mother of my flesh was much troubled, since, with a heart pure in Your faith, she even more lovingly "travail[ed] in birth" (Gal. 4:19) for my salvation. She would in eager haste have provided for my consecration and cleansing by the health-giving sacraments, confessing You, Lord Jesus, for the remission of sins, if I had not suddenly recovered. And so, in case I would again be polluted, should I live, my cleansing was deferred because the defilements of sin would, after that washing, bring greater and more perilous guilt. I then already believed, as did my mother and the whole household except my father. Yet he did not prevail over the power of my mother's piety in me, so that I should not believe as he did not yet believe. For it was my mother's earnest care that You, my God, rather than he, should be my father, and in this You did

---

[1] A rite in the western churches, on admission as a catechumen, previous to baptism, denoting the purity and uncorruptedness required of Christians.

aid her to prevail over her husband whom she, the better, obeyed, therein also obeying You who have so commanded.

I beseech You, my God, I would like to know, if You so will, for what purpose my baptism was then deferred? Was it for my good that the rein was laid loose, as it were, upon me for me to sin? Or was it not laid loose? If not, why does it still echo in my ears on all sides, "Let him alone, let him do as he will, for he is not yet baptized"? Yet regarding bodily health, no one says, "Let him be worse wounded, for he is not yet healed." How much better then if I had been at once healed, and then, by my friends' diligence and my own, my soul's recovered health had been kept safe in Your keeping, You who gave it. Better, truly. But how many and how great the waves of temptation seemed to hang over me after my boyhood! These my mother foresaw, but she preferred to expose to them the clay out of which I might afterwards be molded, rather than the very cast when made.

In boyhood itself, however, so much less dreaded for me than youth, I did not love study and hated to be forced to it. Yet I was forced, and this was good for me. But, I did not do well, for, unless forced, I would not have learned anything. But no one does well against his will, even though what he does is done well. Yet neither did they who forced me do well. What was well came to me from You, my God. They were without regard as to how I should make use of what they forced me to learn, except to satiate the insatiate desires of a wealthy beggary and a shameful glory. But You, by

25

whom the very hairs of our heads are numbered (Matt. 10:30), did use for my good the error of all who urged me to learn. And my own error, that of not wanting to learn, You used for my punishment—a fit penalty for so small a boy and yet so great a sinner. So by those who did not do well, You did well for me, and by my own sin You did justly punish me. For You have commanded, and so it is, that every inordinate desire should be its own punishment.

But why did I so much hate the Greek which I studied as a boy? I do not yet fully know. Latin I loved—not what my first masters taught me but what the so-called grammarians taught me. Those first lessons of reading, writing, and arithmetic, I thought were as great a burden and penalty as any Greek. And yet where did this come from, except from the sin and vanity of this life because I was "flesh; a wind that passeth away, and cometh not again" (Ps. 78:39)? For those first lessons were certainly better because they were more certain. By them I obtained, and still retain, the power of reading what I find written and writing what I will. In the others, I was forced to learn the wanderings of one Aeneas, while not considering my own wanderings, and to weep for dead Dido because she killed herself for love. All the while, with dry eyes, I endured my miserable self dying among these things, far from You, my God, my life.

What is more miserable than a wretched being who does not pity himself, weeping over Dido who died out of love for Aeneas, but not weeping over his own death for lack of loving You, O God?

Light of my heart, Bread of my inmost soul, Power who gives strength to my mind, who quickens my thoughts, I did not love You. I committed fornication against You, and all around me as I was fornicating there echoed, "Well done! Well done!" For the friendship of this world is fornication against You (James 4:4), and "Well done! Well done!" echoes on until one is ashamed therefore to be a man. All this I did not weep for, I who wept for Dido slain, and "seeking by the sword a stroke and wound extreme," I myself sought all the while a worse extreme, I the worst and lowest of Your creatures, having forsaken You though I was dust returning to dust. And if forbidden to read all this, I was grieved that I could not read what grieved me. Madness like this is thought a higher and a richer learning than that by which I learned to read and write.

But now, my God, cry aloud in my soul, and let Your truth tell me, "Not so, not so. Far better was that first study." For, behold, I would readily forget the wanderings of Aeneas and all the rest rather than how to read and write. But over the entrance of the grammar school a veil is drawn! This is not so much an emblem of "nothing hidden," as it is a cloak of error. Do not let those whom I no longer fear cry out against me while I confess to You, my God, whatever my soul will and acquiesce in the condemnation of my evil ways that I may love Your good ways. Do not let either buyers or sellers of grammar-learning cry out against me. For if I question them whether it is true that Aeneas came one time to Carthage, as

27

the poet tells, the less learned will reply that they do not know, the more learned that he never did. But should I ask with what letters the name "Aeneas" is written, everyone who has learned this will answer me rightly, according to the symbols which men have agreed upon. If again, I should ask which might be forgotten with the least detriment to the concerns of life, reading and writing, or these poetic fictions, who does not foresee what all must answer who have not wholly forgotten themselves? I sinned, then, when as a boy I preferred those empty studies to those that are more profitable, or rather, loved the one and hated the other. "One and one, two," "two and two, four." This was to me a hateful singsong. "The wooden horse lined with armed men," and "the burning of Troy," and "Creusa's shade and sad similitude," were the choice spectacles of my vanity.

Why then did I hate the Greek classics which have similar tales? For Homer also curiously wove similar fictions and is most sweetly vain, yet he was bitter to my boyish taste. And so I suppose would Virgil be to Grecian children when forced to learn him as I was Homer. Difficulty, in truth, the difficulty of a foreign language, dashed, as it were, with gall all the sweetness of the Grecian fables. Not one word of it did I understand, and to make me understand I was urged vehemently with cruel threats and punishments.

There was also a time in which I knew no Latin, but this I learned, without fear or suffering, by mere observation amid the caresses of my nursery and the jests of friends, smiling and playfully encouraging me. This I learned without any pressure of punishment to urge me on. For my heart urged me to give birth to its conceptions, which I could only do by learning words not of those who taught, but of those who talked with me; in whose ears also I gave birth to the thoughts, whatever I conceived. There is no doubt, then, that a free curiosity has more force in our learning these things than a frightful enforcement. Yet this enforcement restrains the rovings of that freedom, according to Your laws, my God. Your laws, administered from the master's cane to the martyr's trials, being able to temper in us something that is wholesome out of something that is bitter, bringing us back to Yourself from that deathly pleasure which lures us from You.

Hear, Lord, my prayer. Do not let my soul faint under Your discipline. Do not let me faint in confessing to You all Your mercies, by which You have drawn me out of all my most evil ways so that You might become a delight to me above all the allurements which I once pursued, that I may most entirely love You and clasp Your hand with all my affections. You may yet rescue me from every temptation, even to the end. Behold, Lord, my King and my God, it is for Your service that I speak, write, read, think. For You did grant me Your discipline while I was learning vanities, and my sin of delighting in those vanities You have forgiven. In them, indeed, I learned many a useful word, but words may as well be learned in things that are not vain. That is the safe path for the steps of youth.

But woe is the torrent of human custom! Who will stand against it? How long will it not be dried up? How long will the sons of Eve roll into that huge and hideous ocean which even they who climb the cross scarcely overpass? Did not I read in it of Jove the thunderer and the adulterer? Both, doubtless, he could not be, but it was so the false thunder might resemble and pander to real adultery. And now which of our gowned masters lends a sober ear to one who from their own school cries out, "These were Homer's fictions, transferring things human to the gods; would he had brought down things divine to us!" Yet more truly had he said, "These are indeed his fictions, but attributing a divine nature to wicked men, that crimes might be no longer crimes, and whoever commits them might seem to imitate not abandoned men, but the celestial gods."

And yet, you hellish torrent, into you are cast the sons of men who pay rich fees for obtaining such learning. A great solemnity is made of it when this is going on in the forum within sight of laws appointing a salary beside the scholar's payments. This torrent lashes the rocks and roars, "Hence words are learned, hence eloquence most necessary to gain your ends, or maintain opinions." As if we would never have known such works as "golden shower," "lap," "beguile," "temples of the heavens," or others in that passage, unless Terence had brought a lewd youth upon the stage, setting up Jupiter as his example of seduction.

Viewing a picture, where the tale was drawn,
Of Jove's descending in a golden shower
To Danae's lap, a woman to beguile.

30

And then mark how he excites himself to lust as by celestial authority:

> And what God? Great Jove,
> Who shakes heaven's highest temples with his
>   thunder,
> And I, poor mortal man, not do the same!
> I did it, and with all my heart I did it.

Not one bit more easily are the words learned for all this vileness, but by their means the vileness is committed with less shame. Not that I blame the words, for they are, as it were, choice and precious vessels; rather, I would blame that wine of error which is drunk to us in them by intoxicated teachers. If we, too, do not drink, we are beaten and have no sober judge to whom we may appeal. Yet, my God, in whose presence I now without hurt may remember this, all this wretchedly I learned willingly with great delight, and for this was pronounced a promising student.

Bear with me, my God, while I say something of my intelligence, Your gift, and on what feebleness I wasted it. For a task was set before me, troublesome enough to my soul, upon terms of praise of shame and fear of being beaten, to speak the words of Juno as she raged and mourned that she could not, "This Trojan prince from Latium turn." These words I had heard that Juno never uttered, but we were forced to go astray in the footsteps of these poetic fictions and to say in prose much what the poet expressed in verse. The one whose speaking was clothed in the most fitting language, maintaining the dignity of the character, in which the passions of rage and grief were most preeminent, was most applauded. What is it to me, my true life, my God, that my speech was applauded above so many of my own age and class? Is not all this smoke and wind? And was there nothing else on which to exercise my wit and tongue? Your praises, Lord, Your praises might have kept firm the yet tender shoot of my heart by the prop of Your Scriptures, if it had not trailed away amid these empty trifles, a defiled prey for the fowls of the air. For in more ways than one do men sacrifice to the rebellious angels.

But is it surprising that I was thus carried away to vanities and went from Your presence, my God, when men like this were set before me as models: men who, if in discussing some action of theirs—in itself not evil—committed some barbarism or grammatical error and were embarrassed when criticized? But they, when using rich and adorned and well-ordered speech while talking about their own immoral life, were delighted when they were praised? These things You see, Lord, and You hold back Your anger. "Longsuffering, and plenteous in mercy and truth" (Ps. 86:15). But, will You hold Your peace forever?

Yet even now You draw out of this horrible gulf the soul that seeks You, that thirsts for Your pleasures, whose heart says to You, "Thy face, LORD, will I seek" (Ps. 27:8). For evil desires mean separation from You. (See Romans 1:21.) It is not by walking or a change of location that men leave You or return to You. Or did Your younger son seek out horses or chariots or ships, fly with visible wings, or journey on foot so that he might in a far country waste in riotous living all You gave him at his departure? You were a loving Father when You gave, and even more loving to him when he returned empty. So then it is in lustful, that is, in evil desires that we are truly removed from Your face.

Behold, Lord God, behold patiently as You are accustomed, how carefully the sons of men observe the established rules of grammar received from those who spoke before them, neglecting the eternal covenant of everlasting salvation received from You. A teacher or learner of the hereditary laws of pronunciation seems to offend men more by speaking without the aspirate, leaving off the "h" in "human" and mispronouncing it as "*uman* being" in defiance of the laws of grammar, than if he, a "human being," hated a "human being" in defiance of You. As if any enemy could be more hurtful to him than his own seething hatred toward his adversary. Or as if he could more deeply wound someone he is persecuting than he could wound his own soul by his own hatred.

Assuredly no science of letters can be so innate as the record of a person's conscience that he is doing to another what from another he would be loath to suffer. How deep are Your ways, God, You the only great One, who sit silent on high and by an unwearied law, dispensing the punishment of blindness for lawless desires. In quest of the fame of eloquence, a man standing before a human judge, surrounded by a human throng, declaiming against his enemy with fiercest hatred, will take heed most watchfully, lest, by an error of the tongue, he murder the word "human being," but takes no heed, lest, through the fury of his spirit, he murder the real human being.

This was the world at whose gate I lay unhappy in my boyhood; this was the stage where I had feared more to make an error in speech than, after having committed one, to envy those who had not. These things I speak and confess to You, my God, for which I received praise from men, whom I then thought it all virtue to please. For I did not see the abyss of vileness where I was "cut off from before thine eyes" (Ps. 31:22). Before them, what could be more foul than I was already, displeasing even such as myself? With innumerable lies I deceived my tutor, my masters, and my parents, because of my love of play, my eagerness to see vain shows, and my restlessness to imitate them!

I was also enslaved by greediness and stole from my parents' cellar and table, so that I could barter with other boys for their games, which they enjoyed as much as I did. In this play, too, I often tried to win unfairly, but in doing so I conquered myself through my vain desire for preeminence. The behaviors I refused to put up with or which I fiercely reprimanded in others were the same offenses I was committing toward others. If I was detected and was upbraided, I chose rather to quarrel than to yield.

Is this the innocence of boyhood? Not so, Lord, not so; I cry for Your mercy, my God. These very sins, as we grow older, these very sins are transferred from tutors and masters, from nuts and balls and sparrows, to magistrates and kings, to gold and manors and slaves, just as severer punishments replace the cane. It was the low stature then of childhood which You, our King, did command as a symbol of humility when You said, "of such is the kingdom of heaven" (Matt. 19:14).

Yet, Lord, my thanks were due to You, the Creator and Governor of the universe, most excellent and most good, even if You had destined for me boyhood only. Even then I was alive. I lived and felt and had an implanted providence over my own well-being—a trace of Your mysterious unity out of which I was derived. By the inward sense, I guarded the rest of my senses, and in these minute pursuits and in my thoughts on things minute, I learned to delight in truth. I hated to be deceived, had a vigorous memory, was gifted with speech, was soothed by friendship, and avoided pain, baseness, and ignorance. In so small a creature, what of this was not wonderful, not admirable? But all are gifts from my God; it was not I who gave them to me. These are good, and these together are who I am. Good, then, is He who made me; He is my good, and before Him I will exalt Him for every good that I had as a boy. For it was my sin that I sought pleasures, sublimities, and truths in His creatures—myself and others—and not in Him. Therefore, I fell headlong into sorrows, confusions, and errors. Thanks be to You, my joy and my glory and my confidence; my God, thanks be to You for Your gifts, but do preserve them in me. For in doing so You will preserve me, and those things which You have given me will be enlarged and perfected. And, I myself shall be with You since You have given me the gift of life.

Book Two

The object of these Confessions. Further ills of idleness developed in his sixteenth year. Evils of ill society, which betrayed him into theft.

I will now call to mind my past foulness and the carnal corruptions of my soul, not because I love them but that I may love You, my God. Out of love for Your love I do it, reviewing my most wicked ways from my most bitter memories so that You may grow sweet to me—Your sweetness never failing, Your blissful and assured sweetness gathering me again out of my debauchery in which I was torn piecemeal. While I was turned from You, the One Good, I lost myself among a multiplicity of things. I had burned earlier in my youth to be satiated with worldly things, and I dared to grow wild again with these various and shadowy loves. My beauty wasted away, and I stank in Your eyes, pleasing myself and wanting to find favor in the eyes of men.

What was it that I delighted in but to love and to be loved? But I did not keep my love within the bright boundary of friendship, of mind to mind. Out of the muddy desire of my flesh and the passions of youth, mists fumed up which clouded and overcast my heart so that I could not discern the clear brightness of love from the fog of lustfulness.

Both did confusedly boil within me and hurry my unstayed youth over the precipice of unholy desires, and they sank me in a gulf of depravity. Your wrath had gathered over me, but I did not know it. I had grown deaf by the clanking of the chain of my mortality, the punishment of the pride of my soul, and I strayed further from You. You let me alone, and I was tossed about and wasted and dissipated. I boiled over in my fornications, and You held Your peace, You, my belated joy! You then held Your peace, and I wandered further and further from You into more and more fruitless seed-plots of sorrows with a proud dejectedness and a restless weariness.

Oh, that someone had then tempered my confusion and exposed the fleeting beauties of these that have the least important place in Your creation and had put the proper boundaries on their pleasurableness! Then the tides of my youth might have cast themselves upon the marriage shore, if they could not be calmed, and been kept within the object of a family, as Your law prescribes, Lord, who in this way forms the offspring of our mortal bodies. For you are able, with a gentle hand, to blunt the thorns which were excluded from Your paradise. Your omnipotence is not far from us, even when we are far from You. Otherwise, I ought to have more carefully heeded the voice from the clouds: "Nevertheless such shall have trouble in the flesh: but I spare you" (1 Cor. 7:28); "It is good for a man not to touch a woman" (1 Cor. 7:1); and, "He that is unmarried careth for the things that belong to the Lord, how he may please the Lord: But he that is married careth for the things that are of the world, how he may please his wife" (1 Cor. 7:32–33).

To these words I should have listened more attentively and, being chaste "for the kingdom of heaven's sake" (Matt 19:12), had more happily awaited Your embraces. However, I, poor wretch, foamed like a troubled sea, followed the rushing of my own tide, forsook You, and exceeded all Your limits, yet I did not escape Your scourges. For what mortal can? You were ever with me, mercifully rigorous, and sprinkling with most bitter alloy all my unlawful pleasures, so that I might seek pleasures without alloy. But I could not discover where to find such pure pleasures, save in You, Lord, who teaches by sorrow and wounds us to heal and kills us, lest we die apart from You. Where was I, and how far was I exiled from the delights of Your house in my sixteenth year when the madness of lust, to which human shamelessness gives free license, though unlicensed by Your laws, took the rule over me and I resigned myself wholly to it? My friends, meanwhile, took no care to prevent my downfall through marriage; their only care was that I should learn to speak excellently and be a persuasive orator.

That year my studies were interrupted when I returned from Madaura, a neighbor city, where I had journeyed to learn grammar and rhetoric. The expenses for a further journey to Carthage were being provided for me, more from my father's resolve than by his financial means, since he was but a poor freeman of Thagaste. To whom do I tell this? Not to You, my God, but before You to my own kind, even to that small portion of mankind as may light upon these writings of mine. And to what purpose? That whoever reads this may think out of what depths we are to cry to You (Ps. 130:1). What is nearer to Your ears than a confessing heart and a life of faith? Who did not praise my father because beyond the ability of his means he furnished his son with everything needed for a far journey for his studies' sake? For many far abler citizens did no such thing for their children. But yet this same father had no concern how I grew towards You or how chaste I was. He cared only that I become abundant in speech, however barren I was to Your culture, God, You who are the only true and good Lord of Your field, my heart.

While in my sixteenth year I lived with my parents, leaving all school for awhile—a season of idleness brought about by the narrowness of my parents' fortunes. The briers of unclean desires grew profusely over my head, and there was no hand to root them out. When my father saw me at the baths, now growing towards manhood and endued with a restless youthfulness, he, anticipating his descendants, gladly told it to my mother, rejoicing in that tumult of the senses in which the world forgets You, its Creator, and becomes enamored of Your creature instead of Yourself through the fumes of that invisible wine of its self-will, turning aside and bowing down to the very basest things. But in my mother's breast You had already begun Your temple and the foundation of Your holy habitation, whereas my father was as yet but a catechumen, and that but recently. She then was startled with a holy fear and trembling and, though I was not as yet baptized, feared for me because of those crooked ways in which they walk who turn their back and not their face to You.

Woe is me, and dare I say that You held Your peace, my God, while I wandered further from You? But did You then indeed hold Your peace toward me? Whose but Yours were these words which through my mother, Your faithful one, You sang in my ears?

Yet nothing of what she said sank into my heart so that I would obey it. For she wished and, I remember, in private warned me with great anxiety, "not to commit fornication, but especially never to defile another man's wife." This seemed to me womanish advice which I should be embarrassed to obey. But it was Yours, and I did not know it. I thought You were silent and that it was only she who spoke. By her words, You were not silent to me. In despising her, I despised You, though I was her son, "thy servant, and the son of thine handmaid" (Ps. 116:16). But I did not know it and ran headlong with such blindness that among my equals I was ashamed to be less shameful than they when I heard them boast of their wickedness. The more they boasted, the more they were degraded, and I took pleasure, not only in the pleasure of the deed, but in the praise. What is more worthy of dispraise but vice? But I made myself seem worse than I was, that I might not be belittled. When in anything I had not sinned as had the most licentious ones, I would say that I had done what I actually had not done, so that I might not seem contemptible in comparison, as I was innocent or of less account, the more chaste.

Behold with what companions I walked the streets of Babylon and wallowed in its mire, as if in a bed of spices and precious ointments. And that I might cleave the faster to its very center, the invisible enemy trod me down and seduced me because I was easy to seduce. Even my mother, who had by now fled "out of the midst of Babylon" (Jer. 51:6), went more slowly in the skirts of that city as she advised me to chastity. She did not heed what she had heard about me from her husband, what she felt to be unhealthy in the present and dangerous for the future. She did not restrain me within the sanctity of married love when she could not persuade me to deny my desires.

She did not heed this, for she was afraid that a wife should prove a clog and hindrance to my hopes. These hopes were not of the world to come, which my mother reposed in You, but the hope of learning which both my parents were too desirous I should attain: my father, because he had next to no thought of You, and of me he had nothing but vain conceits; my mother, because she reasoned that those usual courses of learning would not be a hindrance, but would be a help towards attaining You. These were the attitudes of my parents as well as I can remember. They slackened the reins of morality on me, beyond proper restraint and strict discipline, allowing me to spend my time in sport, even to licentiousness in doing whatever I wanted. My life was covered with a mist, blocking me, my God, from the brightness of Your truth, and my iniquity burst out as if from very fatness. (See Psalm 73:7.)

Theft is punished by Your law, Lord, and the law written in the hearts of men, which iniquity itself does not efface. For what thief will tolerate another thief? Not even a rich thief will put up with another who steals from need. Yet I lusted to thieve and did it, not compelled by hunger or poverty but because I had had my fill of well-doing and was a glutton for evildoing. I stole things of which I already had enough, and of much better quality. And I did not care to enjoy what I stole but took pleasure in the theft and in sin itself.

There was a pear tree near our vineyard, laden with fruit, tempting neither for color nor taste. To shake and rob this, some lewd young fellows of us went late one night, having according to our mischievous custom prolonged our sports in the streets until then, and took huge loads, not for our eating, but to fling to the very hogs, having only tasted them. And this we liked to do only because it was disliked by others.

Behold my heart, God, behold my heart, which You had pity upon in the bottom of the bottomless pit. Now behold, let my heart tell You what it sought there: that I should be gratuitously evil, not being tempted with anything but evil itself. It was foul, and I loved it. I loved to perish; I loved my own fault, not that for which I was faulty, but my fault itself, foul soul, falling from Your firmament to utter destruction, not seeking anything through the shame but the shame itself!

There is an attractiveness in beautiful bodies, in gold and silver, and in all things; there is an attraction and power in bodily touch, and all the senses have their proper places when suitably moderated. Worldly honor also has its grace and the power of conquering and of authority, where the thirst for revenge also springs. But yet, to obtain all these, we may not depart from You, Lord, nor decline from Your law. The life also which here we live has its own enchantment, through a certain beauty and harmony in its relation to all things beautiful here below. Human friendship also is endeared with a sweet tie by reason of the unity formed of many souls. Through all these and the like, sin can be committed, if through an excessive appetite toward earthly things we forsake the better and higher: You, our Lord God, Your truth, and Your law. These lower things have their delights, but not like my God who made all things, for in Him do the righteous delight, and He is the joy of the upright in heart (Ps. 64:10).

When, therefore, we ask why a crime was committed, we do not believe the explanation given unless it appears that the culprit might have had some desire to obtain some of those things which we call lower goods, or else feared losing them. They are beautiful and comely; although compared with those higher and beatific goods, they are abject and low. A man has murdered another. Why? He loved this man's wife or his estate, or robbed for his own livelihood, or feared the man would rob him of these things, or, having been wronged, burned with revenge. Would any commit murder without any reason, delighting simply in murdering? Who would believe it? As for that furious and savage man, of whom it is said that he was gratuitously evil and cruel, a reason is still given: "lest" (says he) "through idleness, hand or heart should grow inactive." And to what end? That, through that guilty action, he might, having taken the city, attain to honors, empire, and riches, and be freed from fear of the laws and his embarrassment over personal needs and the awareness of his own villainies. So then, not even Catiline himself loved his own villainies but something else for whose sake he did them.

What, then, did I being wretched so love in the theft of mine, the deed of darkness, in that sixteenth year of my age? Lovely you were not, because you were theft. But are you anything, that thus I speak to you? Fair were the pears we stole because they were Your creation, You, fairest of all, Creator of all, good God, God, the sovereign Good and my true good. Fair were those pears, but it was not them that my wretched soul desired, for I had plenty of better ones. Those I gathered, only that I might steal. For, when gathered, I flung them away; my only feast in this action being my own sin which I was pleased to enjoy. For if any of those pears came within my mouth, what sweetened it was the sin. And now, Lord my God, I inquire what in that theft delighted me, and behold it has no loveliness; I mean, not such loveliness as in justice and wisdom, nor such as is in the mind and memory and senses and animated life of man, nor yet as the stars are glorious and beautiful in

44

their orbs nor as the earth or sea, full of embryo-life, replacing by its birth that which decays, no, nor even that false and shadowy beauty which belongs to deceiving vices.

So does pride imitate exaltedness; whereas You alone are God, exalted over all. What does ambition seek, but honors and glory? Whereas You alone are to be honored above all and are glorious forever. The cruelty of the powerful would gladly be feared, but who is to be feared but God alone, out of whose power can anything be forced or withdrawn? When or where or whither or by whom? The tendernesses of the wanton would gladly be counted love, yet is nothing more tender than Your charity, nor is anything loved more healthily than Your truth, bright and beautiful above all? Curiosity makes a pretense of desiring knowledge, whereas You supremely know all.

Ignorance, and foolishness itself, is cloaked under the name of simplicity and harmlessness because nothing is found more single than You. And what is less injurious, since they which injure the sinner are his own works? Sloth would gladly be at rest, but what more secure rest can be found besides in the Lord? Luxury aims at being called plenty and abundance, but You are the fullness and never-failing plenteousness of incorruptible pleasures. Wastefulness presents a shadow of generosity, but You are the most overflowing giver of all good. Covetousness would possess many things, and You possess all things. Envy fights for excellency; what is more excellent than You? Anger seeks revenge; who revenges more justly than

You? Fear startles at things unaccustomed and sudden which endanger things beloved, and takes forethought for their safety. But to You, what is unaccustomed or sudden, or who separates from You what You love? (See Romans 8:39.) Or where but with You is unshaken safety? Grief pines away for things lost, the delight of its desires, because it would have nothing taken from it, as nothing can be taken from You.

Thus does the soul commit fornication when it turns from You, seeking outside of You what it does not find pure and untainted until it returns to You. Thus all who remove far from You pervertedly imitate You and lift themselves up against You. But even by thus imitating You, they presuppose You to be the Creator of all nature, in which there is no place where we can fully remove ourselves from You. What then did I love in that theft? How did I even corruptly and pervertedly imitate my Lord? Did I wish, even through theft, to do contrary to Your law because I could not do it by power, so that as a prisoner, I might mimic a maimed liberty by doing with impunity things not permitted me, a darkened likeness of Your omnipotence? Behold Your servant, fleeing from his Lord and obtaining a shadow. (See Jonah 4:6.) Oh, rottenness, oh, monstrousness of life, and depth of death, could I like what I should not, only because I should not?

"What shall I render unto the LORD" (Ps. 116:12), so that, while my memory recalls these things, my soul is not frightened by them? I will love You, Lord, and thank You and confess Your name because You have forgiven me for these great and heinous deeds. I attribute it to Your grace and to Your mercy that You have melted away my sins as if they were ice. To Your grace I also credit whatever I have not done of evil, for what might I not have done, I who even loved a sin for its own sake? All I confess to have been forgiven me, both what evils I committed by own willfulness and what by Your guidance I did not commit.

What man is he who, weighing his own sin, dares to attribute his purity and innocence to his own strength, so that he should love You less, as if he had less need of Your mercy by which You forgive the sins of those who turn to You? Whoever was called by You, followed Your voice, and avoided those things which he here reads about me as I recall and confess them of myself, let him not scorn me, who, being sick, was cured by that Physician through whose aid it was that he himself was not, or rather was less, sick. For this let him love You as much, and more, since he sees through You that I have been recovered from such deep sickness of sin, and since he sees himself to have been preserved by You from the same plague of sin.

"What fruit had [I, wretched man!] then in those things whereof [I am] now ashamed?" (Rom. 6:21). Especially in that theft which I loved for theft's sake. It too was nothing, and therefore how much more miserable was I who loved it. Yet I never would have done it alone; the way I was then, I remember, I never would have done it alone. Did I then also love the company of the accomplices with whom I did it? I then loved nothing else but the theft; I did love "nothing" else, for that circumstance of the company was also "nothing." What is this matter, in truth? Who can teach me except He who enlightens my heart and discovers its dark corners? What is it that has come into my mind to examine and discuss and consider? For if I had then loved the pears I stole and wished to enjoy them, I might have done it alone, had the bare act of the theft sufficed to give me my pleasure; nor would I have needed to inflame the itching of my desires by the excitement of accomplices. But since my pleasure was not in those pears, it was in the offense itself, which the company of fellow sinners brought about.

What, then, was this feeling? Truly, it was too foul, and woe was me who had it. But yet what was it? "Who can understand his errors?" (Ps. 19:12). The game we were playing tickled us: that we were deceiving those who were unaware of what we were doing and would very much have disliked it. Why then was my delight of the kind that I did not do it alone? Because none ordinarily laugh alone? Ordinarily no one does; yet laughter sometimes masters men alone and singly when no one is with them, if anything very ludicrous presents itself to their senses or mind. Yet I would not have done this alone; alone I never would have done it. Behold my God, before You, the vivid remembrance of my soul. Alone, I never would have committed a theft in which what I stole did not please me except that I stole, nor would I have liked doing it alone, nor would I have done it alone. Friendship too unfriendly, you incomprehensible seducer of the soul, you greediness to do mischief out of mirth and wantonness—you thirst for others' loss without lusting after my own gain or revenge, but when it is said, "Let's go, let's do it," we are ashamed not to be shameless.

Who can disentangle that twisted and intricate knottiness? It is foul; I hate to think on it, to look on it. But I long for You, Righteousness and Innocence, beautiful and comely to all pure eyes and of a satisfaction unsatiable. With You is rest entire and life serene. Whoever enters into You, enters "into the joy of [his] Lord" (Matt. 25:21) and will not fear and will do excellently in the All-Excellent. I sank away from You; I wandered, my God, too far astray from You, my strength, in these days of my youth, and I became in my own eyes a barren land.

Book Three

His residence at Carthage from his seventeenth to his nineteenth year. Source of his turmoil. Love of shows. Advance in studies, and love of wisdom. Distaste for Scripture. Led astray to the Manicheans. Refutation of some of their tenets. Grief of his mother Monnica at his heresy, and prayers for his conversion. Her vision from God, and answer through a bishop.

To Carthage I came, where all around me a cauldron of unholy loves rang in my ears. I did not love yet, yet I loved to love. Out of a deep-seated want, I hated myself for not wanting more. I sought what I might love, in love with loving, and I hated safety and a way without snares. Within me was a famine of that inward food—Yourself, my God—yet through that famine I was not hungry but was without all longing for imperishable sustenance, not because I was filled with it, but because the more empty I was, the more I loathed it. For this reason my soul was sick and full of sores; it miserably cast itself forth, desiring to be scraped by the touch of sensual things. Yet if these did not have a soul, they would not be objects of love.

To love, then, and to be beloved, was sweet to me, but it was more sweet when I was able to have the person I loved. I defiled, therefore, the spring of friendship with the filth of desire, and I clouded its brightness with the hell of lustfulness. Though in this way I was foul and unseemly, I would gladly, through exceeding vanity, be fine and courtly. I fell headlong, then, into the love in which I longed to be ensnared. My God, my Mercy, with how much bitterness did You sprinkle that sweetness out of Your great goodness to me? I was loved, and secretly entered into sexual union, but my joy was fettered with sorrow-bringing bonds that I might be plagued with the iron-burning rods of jealousy and suspicions and fears and angers and quarrels.

Stage plays also carried me away, full of images of my miseries and of fuel for my fire. Why is it that man desires to be made sad watching depressing and tragic things which he himself would by no means suffer? Yet he desires as a spectator to feel sorrow at them, and this very sorrow is his pleasure. What is this but a miserable madness? For the more involved a man is with these performances, the less free he is from such emotions. However, when he suffers in his own life, it is considered misery; when he has compassion for others, then it is mercy. But what sort of compassion is this for feigned and staged sufferings? For the spectator is not called on to relieve, but only to grieve, and the more he applauds the actor of these fictions, the more he grieves. And if the calamities of those people, whether historical or mere fictional, are so acted that the spectator is not moved to tears, he goes away disgusted and criticizing;

but, if he is moved to passion, he stays engrossed and weeps for joy.

Do we love griefs too much? Truly, all desire joy. And whereas no man likes to be miserable, is he therefore pleased to be merciful? Since mercy cannot exist without suffering, is this the reason we love suffering? This also springs from that vein of friendship. But where does that vein go? Where does it flow? Why does it run into that torrent of pitch[1] bubbling forth those monstrous tides of foul lustfulness, into which it is willfully changed and transformed, being of its own will fallen and corrupted from its heavenly clearness? Will compassion then be put away? By no means. Griefs too are sometimes loved. But beware of uncleanness, my soul, under the guardianship of my God, the God of my fathers, who is to be praised and exalted above all forever; beware of uncleanness.

I have not stopped being sympathetic toward others; but then, in the theaters, I rejoiced with lovers when they wickedly enjoyed one another, although this was imaginary only for the play. When they lost one another, I sorrowed with them as if I were very compassionate, yet I delighted in both love and loss. Now I have much more pity for someone in his wickedness than for someone who is thought to suffer hardship by missing some pernicious pleasure and the loss of some shameful

---

[1] He alludes to the sea of Sodom, which is said to bubble out a pitchy slime. Other rivers running into it are there lost in it and, like the lake itself, remain unmovable. This is why it is also called the Dead Sea.

happiness. This certainly is the truer mercy, but it does not delight in grief. Though he who grieves for the miserable is commended for his service of love, it would be better if he, who is genuinely compassionate, had nothing to grieve for. For if good will is given with evil intent (which can never be) then may he, who truly and sincerely sympathizes, wish there might be something sorrowful so that he might have pity! Some sorrow may then be allowed, but none should be loved. You have this mercy, Lord God, You who love souls far more purely than we and who have more inexhaustible pity on them, yet You are wounded with no sorrowfulness. "And who is sufficient for these things?" (2 Cor. 2:16).

But I, wretched as I was, then loved to grieve and sought out things to grieve over, as long as it was another's grief and as long as it was artificial and acted out. What pleased and attracted me most strongly was acting which brought tears to my eyes. Is it any wonder that I, an unhappy sheep, straying from Your flock and impatient of Your keeping, became infected with a foul disease? From this came my love of griefs, not the kind that would deeply affect me, for I did not want to suffer the things I enjoyed watching, but the kind that, after hearing their fictions, should lightly scratch the surface upon which, as on poisoned nails, there followed inflamed swelling, abscess, and a putrefied sore. My life being such, was it indeed life, my God?

Your faithful mercy hovered over me from afar. I found myself consumed with many grievous sins, pursuing a sacrilegious curiosity, that having forsaken You, it might bring me to the treacherous abyss and the beguiling service of devils to whom I sacrificed my evil actions. In all these things You scourged me! I dared even, while Your rituals were celebrated within the walls of Your Church, to desire and to procure a business deserving death for its fruits. Because of this, You chastised me with grievous punishments, though nothing near to what I deserved—You, my exceeding mercy, my God, my refuge from those terrible destroyers among whom I wandered pigheaded, withdrawing further from You, loving my own ways and not Yours, loving an aimless liberty.

Those studies also, which were considered commendable, were those which would lead to a successful career in law, and the craftier they were, the more they were praised. Such is men's blindness, glorying even in their blindness. Now, I was the top student in the rhetoric school in which I proudly delighted, and I swelled with arrogance. Though, Lord, You know, I was far quieter than and altogether removed from the subverting of those "Subverters,"[2] for this fateful and devilish name was the very badge of honor among those with whom I lived, and I was shamelessly ashamed

---

[2] This appears to have been a name which a pestilent and savage set of people gave themselves, licentious both in speech and action. Augustine names them again elsewhere, where they seem to have consisted mainly of Carthaginian students, whose savage life is mentioned by him.

that I was not as bad as they were. With them I lived and was sometimes delighted with their friendship, even though I hated their actions, that is, their subvertings, with which they wantonly persecuted the modesty of strangers, which they disturbed through unwarranted jeering, and on which they fed their malicious mirth. Nothing can be more like the very actions of devils than these. What then could they be more truly called than subverters? They themselves were subverted and altogether perverted first; the deceiving spirits were secretly ridiculing them and seducing them in what they themselves delighted to jeer at and to deceive others with.

Among such as these, in that unsettled period of my life, I studied books of eloquence, through which I developed a desire for fame out of a damnable and conceited ambition, a delight in human vanity. In the ordinary course of study, I fell upon a certain book of Cicero, whose speech almost all admire, though not his heart. This book of his, called *Hortensius*, contains an exhortation to philosophy. But this book altered my outlook and turned my prayers to Yourself, Lord, and made me have other purposes and desires. Every vain hope at once became worthless to me, and I longed with an incredibly burning desire for an immortality of wisdom and began now to arise that I might return to You. I did not study that book to perfect my speaking ability, which was what I seemed to be purchasing with my mother's finances in my nineteenth year, my father having died two years before; it was not its style that influenced me, but its contents.

How did I burn then, my God, how did I burn to re-ascend from earthly things to You, and I did not know what You would do with me! With You is wisdom. But the love of wisdom is called "philosophy" in Greek, with which that book inflamed me. There are some that seduce through philosophy under a great and smooth and honorable name, coloring and disguising their own errors, and almost all who in that and former ages were such, are criticized and set forth in that book. There also that wholesome advice of Your Spirit is made plain by Your good and devout servant:

> Beware lest any man spoil you through philosophy and vain deceit, after the tradition of men, after the rudiments of the world, and not after Christ. For in him dwelleth all the fulness of the Godhead bodily. (Col. 2:8–9)

And since at that time, You, Light of my heart, know, apostolic Scripture was not known to me, I was delighted with that exhortation, only insofar as I was thereby strongly roused and kindled and inflamed to love and seek and obtain and hold and embrace not this or that sect, but wisdom itself, whatever it was. The only thing that checked my zeal was that the name of Christ was not in it. This name, according to Your mercy, Lord, this name of my Savior, Your Son, my young heart had, even as a child, devoutly drunk in and deeply treasured, and whatever was without that name, though ever so learned, polished, or true, did not take entire hold of me.

I resolved then to apply my mind to the Holy Scriptures, that I might see what they were. But behold, I observed something not understood by the proud nor revealed to children, something humble when accessing it, but exalted in its depths and veiled with mysteries, and I was not such as could enter into it or stoop my neck to follow its steps. For when I turned to those Scriptures, I did not feel as I do now, but they seemed to me unworthy to be compared to the stateliness of Tully. For my swelling pride shrank from their lowliness, and my sharp wit could not pierce their interior. Yet they were such that they would mature someone who was humble of heart. But I disdained to humble myself as a child and, swollen with pride, took myself to be a great one.

Therefore, I fell among foolishly proud men, exceedingly carnal and boasting, in whose mouths were the snares of the Devil, entangled with the mixture of the syllables of Your name and of our Lord Jesus Christ and of the Holy Ghost, the Paraclete, our Comforter. These names did not depart out of their mouths, but they were only sounds and the noises of the tongue, for their hearts were void of truth. They cried out "Truth, Truth" and spoke much of it to me, yet it was not in them. (See 1 John 2:4.) They spoke falsehood, not of You only, who truly are Truth, but even of those elements of this world, Your creatures. I indeed ought to have passed by even philosophers who spoke truth concerning them, out of love for You, my Father, who are supremely good, Beauty of all things beautiful. Oh, Truth, Truth, how inwardly did even then the marrow of my soul pant after You when they often and diversely, and in many and huge books, echoed of You to me, though it was but an echo? I hungered after You, yet these were the dishes in which they, instead of You, served to me the sun and moon, beautiful works of Yours, but yet Your works, not Yourself, no, nor Your first works. For Your spiritual works are before these bodily works, celestial though they may be, and shining.

But I hungered and thirsted not even after those first works of Yours but after You Yourself, the Truth, in "whom is no variableness, neither shadow of turning" (James 1:17). Yet they still set before me in those dishes glittering fantasies. It was much better to love this very sun, which is real to our sight at least, than those fantasies which through our eyes deceive our mind. Yet because I thought they were You, I fed on them, not eagerly, for in them You did not taste to me as You are. For You were not these emptinesses, nor was I nourished by them; rather, I was exhausted by them. Food that we dream about looks very much like real food, yet those who are asleep are not nourished by it, for they are asleep. But those fantasies were not similar to You in any way, as You have now revealed Yourself to me. For those were physical fantasies, false bodies. True bodies, celestial or terrestrial, which we see with our own eyes, are far more certain. The beasts and birds discern these things as well as we, and they are more certain than when we imagine them. And again, we do with more certainty imagine that which is real, than by our fantasizing conjecture about other vaster and infinite bodies which have no being. Such empty husks I was then fed on, and still I was not fed.

But You, my soul's love—for whom I am weak that I may become strong—are neither those bodies which we see in heaven nor those which we do not see there, for You have created them and do not consider them among the best of Your works. How far then are You from those fantasies of mine, fantasies of bodies which altogether do not exist, than from the images of those bodies that do exist and are far more certain. More certain still are the bodies themselves. But You are not the body or the soul, which is the life of the body. So then, better and more certain is the life of the bodies than the bodies. But You are the life of souls, the life of lives, having life in Yourself, and You do not change, life of my soul.

Where were You then in relation to me, and how far were You from me? Far truly was I straying from You, prevented from eating even the husks with which I fed the swine. (See Luke 15:16.) How much better are the fables of poets and grammarians than these snares? For verses, poems, and "Medea flying," are more profitable truly than these men's five elements, variously disguised, answering to five dens of darkness which have no being yet slay the believer. Verses and poems I can benefit from. Though I did celebrate "Medea flying" in song, I did not defend it; though I heard it sung, I did not believe it. Those fantasies, though, I did believe. Woe, woe by what steps I was brought down to the depths of hell, toiling and turmoiling through a lack of truth, because—to You I confess it, who had mercy on me, even though I did not yet believe—I sought after You, my God, not according to the understanding of my mind, in which You willed that I should excel above the beasts, but according to a fleshly understanding. But You were more inward than my most inward part and higher than my highest.

I lighted upon that brazen woman, simple and knowing nothing, shadowed out in Solomon, sitting at the door and saying, "Eat bread of secrecies willingly, and drink stolen waters which are sweet." (See Proverbs. 9:13–17.) She seduced me because she found that my soul had strayed into the thoughts of my flesh and was ruminating on carnal food.

For I did not know the truth, and I was persuaded through what I thought was sharpness of wit to assent to foolish deceivers when they asked me: "Where does evil come from?" "Is God bounded by a bodily shape, and does He have hair and nails?" "Are they who had many wives at the same time and who killed men and sacrificed living creatures to be esteemed righteous?" At which I, in my ignorance, was much troubled, and I departed from the truth, even though it seemed to me that I was moving towards it. This was because, as yet, I did not know that evil was nothing but the absence of good, until at last a thing ceases to exist altogether. How could I see the truth when I could only see things that were tangible or imagine things that were fantasies? I did not know that God is Spirit, not one who has parts extended in length and breadth or whose being is mass. Every mass is less in its part than in its whole, and if it is infinite, it must be less in such a part as is defined by a certain space than in its infinitude. So it is not wholly everywhere, as a spirit is, as God is. I was altogether ignorant that we also have spirits by which we are like to God, and might in Scripture be rightly said to be after the image of God (Gen. 1:27).

And I did not know that true inward righteousness which does not judge according to man's custom but out of the most rightful law of God Almighty, to which the ways of people of certain places and times were adapted according to those times and places. The law itself, meantime, is the same always and everywhere. According to this law, Abraham and Isaac and Jacob and Moses and David and all those commended by the mouth of God were righteous but were judged unrighteous by silly men, who judged out "of man's judgment" (1 Cor. 4:3), and measured by their own petty habits the moral habits of the whole human race.

It is like someone who is ignorant of armor, which has different pieces that are adapted to certain parts of the body, trying to cover his head with greaves or seeking to be shod with a helmet and complaining that they did not fit! Or it is as if on a day when business is publicly stopped in the afternoon, one were angered at not being allowed to keep open shop because he had been open in the morning. Or it is like one who observes in one house some lesser servant take a thing in his hand which the butler is not allowed to meddle with. Or like something permitted out-of-doors which is forbidden in the dining room, and one being angry, that in one house and one family the same thing is not allotted everywhere and to all.

These are the type of people who are agitated to hear that something that was lawful for righteous men in the past is now not permitted, or that God, for certain temporal respects, commanded them one thing and these another, even though both obey the same righteousness. However, they see that in one man and one day and one house, different things are appropriate for different members, and a thing that was lawful in the past is not permitted. They see something permitted or commanded in one situation, but in another rightly forbidden and punished.

Is justice therefore various or changeable? No, but the times, over which it presides, do not flow evenly because they are temporal. But men whose days are few upon the earth cannot, through their own understanding, reconcile the reasons for doing things in former ages and in other nations with which they have no familiarity, with those with which they do have experience. Although, when considering the same body, day, or family, they easily see what is fitting for each member and season, part and person. They object to the former and consent to the latter.

In those days, I did not know or observe these things; they pierced my sight on all sides, but I did not see them. For example, I wrote poems in which I could place each foot throughout, but differently in different meters and not even in any one meter the same foot in all places. Yet the art itself, by which I inscribed, did not have different laws for these different cases but was always the same. Still I did not see how that righteousness, which good and holy men obeyed, did far more excellently and sublimely contain in one all those things which God commanded and in no part varied; although, in varying times it did not prescribe everything at once but assigned and commanded what was fit for each. And I, in my blindness, criticized the holy fathers, not only when they made use of things present as God commanded and inspired them, but also when they were foretelling things to come, as God was revealing in them.

Can it at any time or place be unjust for a person to love God with all his heart, with all his soul, and with all his mind and his neighbor as himself? (Matt. 22:37, 39). Therefore those foul offenses which are against nature are everywhere and at all times detested and punished, such as were those of the men of Sodom. Should all nations commit these offenses, they should all stand guilty of the same crime by the law of God which has not so made men that they should so abuse one another. Even that intercourse, which should be between God and us, is violated when that same nature, of which He is author, is polluted by perversity of lust. But those actions which are offenses against the customs of men are to be avoided according to the customs individually prevailing, so that a thing agreed upon and confirmed by custom of law of any city or nation may not be violated at the lawless pleasure of any, whether native of foreigner. Any part which harmonizes not with its whole is offensive. But when God commands a thing to be done, against the customs or compact of any people, though it was never done by them previously, it is to be done. If it was suspended, it is to be restored, and if never ordained, it is now to be ordained.

If it is lawful for a king in the state which he reigns over to command that which no one before him, nor he himself previously, had commanded (and to obey him cannot be against the common principles of the state; rather, it would against them if he were not obeyed, for to obey princes is a general compact of human society) how much more unhesitatingly ought we to obey God, in all which He commands, the Ruler of all His creatures! For as among the governments of men, the greater authority is obeyed in preference to the lesser, so God must be obeyed above all.

The same is true in acts of violence where there is a wish to hurt, whether by reproach or by injury. Either of these can be done for revenge, as one enemy against another; or to gain what belongs to another, as the robber to the traveler; or to avoid some evil, as towards one who is feared; or through envy, as one less fortunate to one more so; or one prospering in anything to one whom he fears being on an equal par with; or for the mere pleasure at another's pain, as spectators of gladiators, or deriders and mockers of others. These are the heads of iniquity which spring from "the lust of the flesh, [or] the lust of the eyes" (1 John 2:16), or the lust of power—from one or two or all three combined. In this way men live evil lives against the three and seven, that "psaltery...of ten strings" (Ps. 144:9), the Ten Commandments, Your Commandments, God, most high, and most sweet.

But what foul offenses can there be against You, who cannot be defiled? Or what acts of violence can there be against You, who cannot be harmed? But You avenge what men commit against themselves, seeing that when they sin against You they do so wickedly against their own souls. Iniquity deceives itself, so to speak, by corrupting and perverting men's own nature, which You have created and ordained, by an immoderate use of things allowed or by lusting for things not allowed to "that which is against nature" (Rom. 1:26). Or, when they are found guilty by raging with heart and speech against You, kicking "against the pricks" (Acts 9:5). Or, when bursting the boundaries of human society, they boldly delight in headstrong conspiracies or fraternities, depending on whether they have something to gain or something to protest. These things are done by those who forsake You, Fountain of Life, You who are the only and true Creator and Governor of the universe, and when, by a self-willed pride, any one false thing is selected from there and loved.

So then, by a humble devoutness we return to You. You cleanse us from our evil habits and are merciful to those who confess their sins. You "hear the groaning of the prisoner" (Ps. 102:20) and loose us from the chains which we have made for ourselves, if we do not lift up against You the horns of an unreal liberty, suffering the loss of all through coveting more by loving our own private good more than You, the Good of all.

Amidst these offenses of foulness and violence and so many iniquities, are sins of men who are on the whole making progress. Those sins are rightly disapproved of by those who judge according to the perfect law, yet the people are commended in the hope that they will bear fruit in the future, as in the green blade of growing corn. And there are those which seem like foul or violent offenses which are not sins because they offend neither You, our Lord God, nor human society. Such offenses are when, for example, things appropriate for a given period are obtained for everyday life, and we do not know whether or not this was done out of covetousness. Or when the legal authorities punish for the sake of correction, and we do not know whether or not they do so out of a desire to harm.

Many an action, then, which in men's sight is disapproved, is approved by Your testimony. Conversely, many actions which are praised by men are—You being witness—condemned because the appearance of the action, the mind of the doer, and the unknown demands of the period vary respectively. But when You, all of a sudden, command us to do an unaccustomed and unthought of thing, although You have at one time forbidden it and still for the time hide the reason of Your command, and it is against the ordinance of some society of men, who could doubt that it is to be done, seeing that the society of men who serve You is just? But blessed are they who know Your commands! For all things were done by Your servants, either to show forth something needful for the present or to foreshadow things to come.

Being ignorant of these things, I scoffed at Your holy servants and prophets. And what did I gain by scoffing at them, but to be scoffed at by You, being insensibly and step-by-step drawn on to those follies, as to believe that a fig wept when it was plucked and that the tree, its mother, shed milky tears? And that if some (Manichean) saint had eaten it—plucked by some other's, not his own, guilty hand—and mingled it with his intestines, that he would be able to breath out angels. Furthermore, that particle of divinity would burst forth at every moan or groan in his prayer, particles of which the most high and true God would have remained bound in, in that fig, unless they had been set at liberty by the teeth or belly of some elect saint! And I, miserable, believed that more mercy was to be shown to the fruits of the earth than to men for whom they were created. For if anyone who was not a Manichean hungered and should ask for fruit, it would seem as if that morsel were condemned to capital punishment.

But You sent "thine hand from above" (Ps. 144:7) and drew my soul out of that profound darkness because my mother, Your faithful one, wept over me to You, more than mothers weep when their children die. She, by that faith and spirit which she had from You, discerned the death in which I lay, and You heard her, Lord. You heard her and did not despise her tears when, streaming down, they watered the ground under her eyes in every place where she prayed. You heard her; for from where else did that dream come by which You comforted her, so that she allowed me to live with her and to eat at the same table with her, which she had begun to shrink from, abhorring and detesting the blasphemies of my error?

She saw herself standing on a certain wooden ruler and a shining youth coming towards her, cheerful and smiling upon her, herself grieving and overwhelmed with grief. But he having inquired of her—in order to instruct, as is the custom, not to be instructed—the causes of her grief and daily tears, and she answering that she was bewailing my perdition, he implored her to rest contented and told her to look and observe, "That where she was, there was I also." And when she looked, she saw me standing by her in the same rule. From which source was this, but that Your ears were towards her heart? Good Omnipotent, who cares for every one of us, as if You cared for him alone; and so You regard everyone, as if they each were but the only one!

From what source was this also, that when she had told me this vision and I wanted gladly to bend it to mean, "That she rather should not despair of my being what I already was," she immediately, without any hesitation, replied, "No; for it was not told me that, 'where he is, there you are also,' but 'where you are, there he is also.'" I confess to You, Lord, that to the best of my remembrance (and I have often spoken of this) Your answer through my watchful mother, that she was not perplexed by the plausibility of my false interpretation and so quickly saw what was to be seen and which I certainly had not perceived before she spoke, even then moved me more than the dream itself. This dream, which was a joy to this holy woman, which was predicted so long before, and which would be fulfilled so long after, was for the purpose of comforting her in her present anguish.

Almost nine years passed in which I wallowed in the mire of that deep pit and the darkness of falsehood, often attempting to rise, but then dashed down the more grievously. All of this time that chaste, godly, and sober widow, such as You love, was now more comforted with hope. Yet she did not slacken her weeping and mourning one bit; she did not cease praying for hours, bewailing my case to You. Her prayers entered into Your presence, and yet You allowed me to be yet involved and re-involved in that darkness.

You gave her, in the meantime, another answer which I call to mind; for I pass by, hastening to those things which I am more compelled to confess to You, and there is much I do not remember. You gave her then another answer by a priest of Yours, a certain bishop brought up in Your church and well studied in Your books. When my mother had entreated him to agree to talk with me, to refute my errors, to unteach me evil things, and to teach me good things, for this he was accustomed to do when he found people ready to receive it, he refused, wisely, as I afterwards perceived. He answered that

I was yet unteachable, being puffed up with the novelty of that heresy, and that I had already perplexed many unskilled people with captious questions, as she had told him. "But let him alone a while," said he, "only pray to God for him; by reading, he will discover for himself what his error is and how ungodly it is."

At the same time he told her how he, when he was a boy, had been given over to the Manichees by his deceived mother, and how he had not only read but frequently copied out almost all their books and had, without any argument or proof from any one, seen how much that sect was to be avoided and had avoided it. When he had said these things and she still was not satisfied but urged him even more with pleas and many tears that he would see me and reason with me, he, a little displeased at her persistent urging, said, "Go your ways, and God bless you, for it is not possible that the son of these tears should perish." She took this answer, as she often mentioned in her conversations with me, as if it had sounded from heaven.

Book Four

*Augustine's life from age nineteen to twenty-eight.
Himself a Manichean, misleading others in the
same heresy. Partial obedience amid vanity and
sin, consulting astrologers, only partially shaken
in this. Loss of an early friend, who is converted by
being baptized when unconscious. Reflections on
grief, on real and unreal friendship, and love of
fame. Writes on "the fair and fit," yet cannot
rightly do so, though God had given him great talents, since he entertained wrong notions of God,
and so even his knowledge he applied ill.*

For this space of nine years then, from my
nineteenth year to my twenty-eighth, we
lived seduced and seducing, deceived and deceiving, in diverse lusts, openly by education which
they call liberal, and secretly with a false-named
religion: in the first we were proud, in the second
we were superstitious, and in all things we were
vain! Through education, we hunted after the
emptiness of popular praise, even down to theatrical applause, poetic prizes, strivings for grassy
garlands, the follies of shows, and the overindul-
gence of desires. There, through a false religion,
we desired to be cleansed from these defilements
by carrying food to those who were called "elect"
and "holy," out of which, in the workhouse of their

stomachs, they should forge for us angels and gods by whom we might be cleansed. These things I followed and practiced with my friends, who were deceived by me and with me.

Even though the arrogant may mock me, those who have not been, for the good of their souls, stricken and cast down by You, my God, I will still confess to You my own shame in Your praise. Allow me, I beseech You, my God, and give me grace to recall the wanderings of my past and to offer "to thee the sacrifice of thanksgiving" (Ps. 116:17). What am I to myself without You but a guide to my own downfall, or what am I even at my best but an infant sucking the milk You give and feeding upon You, the food that does not perish? (See John 6:27.) But what sort of man is any man, seeing he is but a man? Let now the strong and the mighty laugh at us, but let us, the poor and needy, confess to You.

In those years I taught rhetoric and, overcome by greed, profited financially by getting the better of people through my speaking ability. Yet, Lord, You know that I preferred those who are considered honest scholars, and to these I, without deception, taught deception, not to be practiced against the life of the innocent, though sometimes for the life of the guilty. And You, God, from afar perceived me stumbling in that slippery course, and, amid much smoke, sending out some sparks of faithfulness which I showed by guiding my companions, who loved vanity and sought after leasing (Ps. 4:2).

In those years I had a woman, not as my lawful wife, but one whom I had taken in a wayward passion, without understanding. Yet I remained faithful to her. Through this, for my own part, I experienced the difference between the self-restraint of the marriage covenant, made for the sake of children, and the bargain of a lustful love, where children are born against their parents' will; although, once born, they compel them to love.

I remember also, that when I had decided to enter the contest for a theatrical prize, some fortune-teller asked me what I would give him to win. I, detesting and abhorring such foul mysteries, answered, "Though the garland were made of imperishable gold, I would not allow a fly to be killed in order to gain it." For he intended to kill some living creatures in his sacrifices and by that homage to invite the devils to favor me. But this ill I also rejected, not out of a pure love for You, God of my heart, for I did not know how to love You. I did not know how to conceive of anything beyond a material splendor. And does not a soul, which pines after such falsehoods, commit fornication against You by trusting in illusory things and feeding the wind (Hos. 12:1)? Still, I would certainly not have sacrifices offered to devils for me, yet I was sacrificing myself to these devils by that superstition. For what else is it to feed the wind, but to feed the devils, that is, by going astray to become their pleasure and derision?

I consulted those impostors then, who are called astrologers, without scruple, because they did not seem to use sacrifices or to pray to any spirit in their divination. However, Christian and true piety consistently rejects and condemns these things. It is a good thing to confess to You and to say, "Be merciful unto me: heal my soul; for I have sinned against thee" (Ps. 41:4). It is also good not to abuse Your mercy as a license to sin, but to remember the Lord's words, "Behold, thou art made whole: sin no more, lest a worse thing come unto thee" (John 5:14). The astrologers work hard to destroy all this wholesome advice, saying, "The cause of your sin is inevitably determined in heaven" and "Venus or Saturn or Mars did this," so that man, indeed, flesh and blood, and proud corruption might think he is blameless, while the Creator and Ordainer of heaven and the stars is to bear the blame. And who is He but our God? He is very sweetness and the wellspring of righteousness, who rewards every man according to his works (Rom. 2:6; Matt. 16:27), and "a broken and a contrite heart...thou wilt not despise" (Ps. 51:17).

There was in those days a wise man, very skillful and renowned in the field of medicine. He had, with his own proconsular hand, placed the garland I had won in a contest upon my immoral head. But he did not do this as a physician, for only You can cure this disease, You, who "resisteth the proud, and giveth grace to the humble" (1 Pet. 5:5; James 4:6). But did You fail me through that old man or refuse to heal my soul?

For I became more acquainted with him and hung earnestly and intently on his words, and though he spoke in simple terms, his speech was serious-minded. When he had discerned through my discourse that I was inclined to study the books of astrologers, he advised me in a kindly and fatherly way to cast them away and not fruitlessly give these vanities my attention and diligence, which are necessary for useful things. He did this saying that he had in his earliest years studied astrology, in order to make it the profession with which he should earn his living, and that, understanding Hippocrates, he could soon have understood such a study as this. Yet he had given it over and taken to medicine for the single reason that he found it utterly false, and he, an influential man, would not get his living by deluding people. "But you," said he, "have rhetoric with which to support yourself, so that you follow this out of free choice, not out of necessity. How much more, then, should you believe me concerning this, since I worked so hard to master it to perfection in order to obtain my support from it alone."

I then demanded that he tell me how many true things could be foretold by it, and he answered me, as much as he could, "that the force of chance, diffused throughout the whole order of things, brought this about. It is like when a man, while thinking of something entirely different, randomly opens the pages of some poet who composed, and verses repeatedly jump out that are amazingly applicable to his present situation. It is not to be wondered at, if out of the soul of a man, unconscious of his own thoughts, he gives an answer by some higher instinct, that—by chance, not by art—corresponds to the business and actions of the inquirer."

And this much, either from or through him, You conveyed to me and recorded in my memory that I might hereafter examine for myself. But at that time neither he, nor my dear friend Nebridius, a singularly good youth who had a holy fear and who scoffed at the whole body of divination, could persuade me to cast it aside because the authority of the authors I was reading swayed me even more. As yet I had found no certain proof, such as I sought, by which it might without all doubt appear that what had been truly foretold by those consulted was the result of chance and not from the art of the stargazers.

In those years when I first began to teach rhetoric in my native town, I had made a friend my own age, and who like myself was in the first opening flower of youth. This friend was dear to me because we had many of the same interests. He had grown up with me, and we had been both schoolfellows and playfellows. But at that time he was not the friend that he later came to be. Nor even then did our friendship come to be a true friendship, for it cannot be true unless You cement together those who are devoted to You, by that love which is "shed abroad in our hearts by the Holy Ghost which is given unto us" (Rom. 5:5). Yet our friendship was too sweet, over-ripened by our enthusiasm for similar interests. When he was a youth, he had not soundly and thoroughly absorbed the true faith, and I had corrupted him by those superstitious and pernicious falsehoods for which my mother bewailed me. With me he now strayed in his beliefs, and my soul could not be without him. But behold, You were close on the steps of Your fugitives. You were at the same time a God of vengeance (Ps. 94:1) and a Fountain of mercies, turning us to Yourself by amazing means. You took him out of this life when he had hardly filled up one whole year of my friendship—a friendship sweeter to me than all the sweetness of my life.

Who can recount all Your praises (Ps. 106:2), which only he has known? What did You do then, my God, and how unsearchable is the depth of Your judgments? My friend was on his sickbed for a long time, extremely ill from a fever, delirious in a death sweat, and he was baptized while unconscious because his recovery was despaired of. I, meanwhile, had little regard for the baptism and presumed that his soul would retain instead what it had received from me, not what was wrought on his unconscious body.

But it proved to be far different, for he was revived and restored. Without delay, as soon as I could speak with him—and I could, as soon as he was able, for I never left him, and we depended too much upon each other—I tried to jest with him as though he would jest with me about that baptism which he had received when utterly absent in mind and feeling, but which he had now knew that he had received. But he shrank from me as from an enemy, and with an amazing and sudden frankness implored me, if I wanted to continue to be his friend, to refrain from using such language with him. I, all astonished and amazed, suppressed all my emotions until he should grow well and his health be strong enough for me to deal with him, as I would. But he was taken away from my rage, that with You he might be preserved for my comfort. A few days later, in my absence, he was attacked again by the fever, and died.

At this grief my heart was utterly darkened, and everything I saw was death to me. My native country was a torment to me, and my father's house had a strange unhappiness. Whatever I had shared with him became a distracting torture without him. My eyes sought him everywhere, but they were not permitted to see him. I hated to go anywhere because he was not there, nor could anyone tell me, "he is coming," as when he was alive and absent. I became a great puzzle to myself, and I asked my soul why it was so sad, and why it painfully disturbed me (Ps. 42:5). But it did not know what to answer. And if I said, "trust in God," it very rightly did not obey me because that most dear friend, whom it had lost, was, being a man, both more true and more good than that illusion in which it was told to trust. Only tears were sweet to me, for they replaced my friend in the dearest of my affections.

And now, Lord, these things are in the past, and time has healed my wound. May I learn from You who are truth and bend the ear of my heart to Your mouth, that You may tell me why weeping is sweet to the miserable? Have You, although present everywhere, cast our misery far away from You? You abide in Yourself, but we are tossed about in various trials. And yet, unless we are able to mourn in Your ears, we would have no hope left. From where, then, is sweet fruit gathered from the bitterness of life, from groaning, tears, sighs, and complaints? Does this sweeten it, that we hope You hear? This is true of prayer, for in that practice there is a longing to approach You. But is it also in grief for a thing lost and in the sorrow with which I was then overwhelmed? I neither hoped he should return to life, nor did I desire this with my tears. I only wept and grieved. I was miserable and had lost my joy. Or is weeping in reality a bitter thing? Does it please us to recoil from the things which we enjoyed earlier and actually to loathe them?

Why do I speak of these things? Now is no time to question, but to confess to You. Wretched I was, and wretched is every soul bound by the friendship of perishable things. He is torn apart when he loses them, and then he feels the wretchedness which he had before he lost them. So it was then with me; I wept most bitterly and found my rest in bitterness. Thus was I wretched, and I held that wretched life dearer than my friend. Though I would willingly have changed it, I was more unwilling to part with it than with him. I do not know whether I would have parted with it even for him, as is told, if not imagined, of Pylades and Orestes, that they would gladly have died for each other or together, for not to live together was to them worse than death. Some unexplained feeling had arisen in me which was too contrary to this, for at the same time, I hated exceedingly to live and was afraid to die. I suppose, the more I loved him, the more I hated and feared—as a most cruel enemy—death which had deprived me of him. I imagined that death would quickly make an end of all men, since it had power over him. This is how it was with me, I remember.

Behold my heart, my God, behold and see into me, for I remember it well, my Hope who cleanses me from the impurity of such perspectives, directing my eyes towards You and plucking my feet out of the snare (Ps. 25:15). I marveled that others, subject to death, were alive, since he whom I loved, as if he should never die, was dead. I marveled even more that I, who was to him a second self, could be alive while he was dead. One of his friends said it very well: "You are half of my soul." For I felt that my soul and his soul were one soul in two bodies and therefore my life was a horror to me because I did not want to live as half a person. And therefore, perhaps I was afraid to die for fear that he whom I had loved so would die completely.

Oh, madness, which does not know how to love men like men should be loved! Oh, foolish man that I then was, enduring impatiently the lot of man! At that time I fretted, sighed, wept, was distracted, and had neither rest nor purpose. I bore about a shattered and bleeding soul, tired of being borne by me, yet I did not find anywhere to lay it to rest. Not in calm groves, nor in games and music, nor in fragrant spots, nor in elegant feasts, nor in the pleasures of the bed and the couch, nor, finally, in books or poetry, did my soul find rest. All things looked ghastly, even light itself. Whatever was not what he was, was revolting and hateful, except groaning and tears. For in those alone I found a little refreshment. But when I was not engaged in them, a huge load of misery weighed me down.

To You, Lord, my soul ought to have been raised, so that You could lighten it. I knew it, but I neither could nor would, even more, since, when I thought of You, You were not to me any solid or substantial thing. For You were not Yourself, but a mere phantom, and my delusion was my god. If I had pleaded to discharge my load on that, that it might rest, it would have glided through the void and come rushing down again on me, and I would have remained in a doomed spot where I could neither be, nor be away from. For where could my heart flee to away from my heart? Where could I flee from myself? Where could I go and not follow myself? And yet I fled out of my country, for in this way I would have less of an inclination to look for him where I was not accustomed to seeing him. And so from Thagaste I came to Carthage.

Time loses no time, nor does it roll idly by. Through our senses it works strange effects on our minds. Behold, it came and went, day by day, and, by coming and going, introduced into my mind other thoughts and other memories. Little by little my old familiar delights, which my sorrow had replaced, patched me up again. And yet there followed, not really other griefs, but the causes of other griefs. For from what place had that former grief so easily reached my very inmost soul, so that I had poured out my soul upon the dust, in loving one that must die, as if he would never die?

What restored and refreshed me chiefly was the solaces of other friends with whom I shared a love for falsehood instead of for You: a great fable and protracted lie by whose adulterous stimulus our souls, which lay itching in our ears, were being defiled. (See 2 Timothy 4:3.) But that fable would not die to me, as when any of my friends died. There were other things which occupied my mind through their friendship: talking and joking together; taking turns doing kind things for one another; reading good books together; clowning around or being serious together; engaging in good-natured debates, as a man might with his own self, and having the rarity of these disagreements temper our more frequent consentings; sometimes teaching and sometimes learning; longing impatiently for friends who are absent, and joyfully welcoming those who arrive. These and similar gestures of friendship, proceeding out of the hearts of we who loved and were loved again, through our conduct, our speech, our expressions, and a thousand pleasing gestures, were fuel that melted our souls together and out of many made but one.

This is what we love about friends, and when one is loved in this way, his conscience condemns him if he does not love the one who loves him in return, or does not love in return the one who loves him, looking for nothing from the other person but indications of his love. Out of this unity comes that mourning, if a friend should die, and gloomy sorrows, that steeping of the heart in tears, all sweetness turned to bitterness, and upon the loss of life of the dying, the death of the living.

Blessed is the one who loves You and loves his friend in You and his enemy for You. For he alone loses none dear to him, if all are dear in Him who cannot be lost. And who is this but our God, the God that "made the earth and the heavens" (Gen. 2:4) and filled them (Jer. 23:24) because by filling them He created them? You lose none but the one who leaves You. And if one should leave You, where can he go or where can he flee except from You being well-pleased to You being displeased? Where does he not find Your law fulfilled in his own punishment? And "thy law is the truth" (Ps. 119:142), and You are truth (John 14:6).

"Turn us again, O LORD God of hosts, cause thy face to shine; and we shall be saved" (Ps. 80:19). For wherever the soul of man turns itself, unless towards You, it is riveted upon sorrows even though it is riveted on things beautiful. And yet they, outside of You and outside of the soul, would not be beautiful unless they came from You. They rise and set, and by rising, they begin, as it were, to be. They grow that they may be perfected, and perfected, they grow old and wither. All do not grow old, but all wither. So then when they rise and cultivate themselves, so that they may more quickly grow to perfection, they only hasten their own demise. This is the law they are operating under. You have allotted them this much because they are only portions of things which do not exist simultaneously, but as they pass away and others take their place, they together complete that universe of which they are portions.

In a similar process, we speak by uttering words. But, this also is not accomplished unless one word passes away when it has sounded its part so that another may follow it. Out of all these things let my soul praise You, God, Creator of all, yet do not let my soul be riveted to these things with the glue of love through the senses of the body. They go where they were meant to go, so that they might not be. Yet they rend the soul with pestilent longings because while it longs to be perfected, it loves to repose in the things it loves. But in these things there is no place of repose; they do not abide, they flee, and who can follow them with the senses of the flesh? Who can grasp them even when they are close by? The sense of the flesh is slow because it is the sense of the flesh, and thereby is it limited. It serves the purpose for which it was made, but it does not serve to keep things running their course from their appointed starting place to the appointed end. For in Your Word, by which they are created, they hear their decree, "from here to there."

Do not be foolish, my soul, nor become deaf in the ear of your heart through the clamor of your foolishness. Hear this also: the Word itself calls you to return, and there is a place of serene rest, where love is not forsaken, if it does not forsake that place. Behold, these earthly things pass away so that others may replace them, and so this lower universe is completed by all its parts. "But do I depart anywhere?" asks the Word of God. It is there you should fix your dwelling; there you should entrust whatever you have from now on, my soul. At least now you are tired of vanities. Entrust to the truth whatever you have from the truth, and you will lose nothing; your decay will bloom again, and all your diseases will be healed

(Ps. 103:3). Your mortal parts will be reformed and renewed and made secure around you. They will not drag you down where they themselves descend, but they will stand fast with you and abide forever before God, who abides and stands fast forever.

Why then be perverted and follow your flesh? Let it be converted and follow you. Whatever you understand by the flesh, you have in part. The whole, of which these are parts, you do not know, and yet they delight you. But, if your fleshly understanding had a capacity for comprehending the whole, and had not been justly restricted to a part of the whole because of your punishment, you would desire that whatever presently exists should pass away so that the whole might please you better. By the same fleshly understanding, you hear what we speak also, yet you do not want the syllables to stay but to fly away so that others may come. Then you hear the whole. And so, when any one thing is made up of many, all of which do not exist together, all of them collectively, perceived collectively, would please more than they do individually. But far better than these is He who made all, and He is our God. He does not pass away, and nothing succeeds Him.

If bodies please you, praise God for them and turn back your love upon their Maker, so that in these things which please you, you will not displease Him. If souls please you, let them be loved in God. They too are changeable, but in Him they are firmly established, or else they would change and pass away. Let them be loved in Him, then;

and carry to Him along with you what souls you can, and say to them:

"Let us love Him; let us love Him. He made us, and He is not far off. For He did not make all things and then depart, but they are of Him and in Him. See, there He is, where truth is loved. He is within the very heart, yet the heart has strayed from Him. Go back into your heart, you transgressors, and cleave fast to Him who made you. Stand with Him, and you will stand fast. Rest in Him, and you will be at rest. Why do you travel along rough paths? Where are you going? The good that you love is from Him. But, it is good and pleasant only in reference to Him. Anything that we love which comes from God becomes unrighteous to us if He is forsaken for it, and it is right that it should become bitter to us. For what reason then do you continue to walk these difficult and toilsome ways? There is no rest where you seek it. Seek what you are looking for, but it is not where you are looking. You seek a blessed life in the land of death; it is not there. For how can there be a blessed life where life itself does not exist?

"But our true Life came down to this place and bore our death and slew it out of the abundance of His own life. He thundered, calling aloud to us to return to Him into that secret place where He came forth to us. First, He came into the Virgin's womb, in which He embraced the human creation, our mortal flesh, that it might not be mortal forever. Then, He came like 'a bridegroom coming out of his chamber, and [rejoicing] as a strong man to run a race' (Ps. 19:5). For He did not linger, but ran, calling aloud by his words and deeds, his death and life, his descent and ascension, crying aloud to us to return to Him. And He departed from our eyes so that we might return into our hearts and find Him there. He departed, and behold, He is here. He was not with us very long, yet He did not leave us. For He departed from here, from where He never really parted because 'the world was made by him' (John 1:10). And He was in this world, and into this world He 'came...to save sinners' (1 Tim. 1:15). To Him my soul confesses. He healed it, for it has sinned against Him (Ps. 41:4). You sons of men, how long will you be so slow of heart? Even now, after the descent of Life to you, will you not ascend and live? But how can you ascend when you have set yourself on high and 'set [your] mouth against the heavens' (Ps. 73:9)? Descend, that you may ascend, and ascend to God. For you have fallen by ascending against Him."

Tell them this, that they may weep in the valley of tears. (See Psalm 84:6.) Carry them up with you to God because it is through His Spirit that you speak to them in this matter, if you speak burning with the fire of love.

These things I did not know at that time. I loved these lower beauties and was sinking to the very depths, and to my friends I said: "Do we love anything except the beautiful? What then is the beautiful? And what is beauty? What is it that attracts and wins us to the things we love? Unless there were a grace and beauty in them, we would not be drawn to them." And I took note and perceived that in bodies themselves there was a beauty from their forming a sort of whole and another from mutual suitability, as of a part of the body to its whole, or as a shoe to a foot, and the like. And this consideration sprang up in my mind, out of my inmost heart, and I wrote two or three books "on the fair and fit," I think. You know, Lord, for it is gone from me. I do not have them. I lost them, but I do not know how.

But what moved me, Lord my God, to dedicate these books to Hierius, an orator of Rome, whom I did not know by face but loved because he was famous for his knowledge in which he had distinguished himself, and because of some statements of his that I had heard which pleased me? But he pleased me even more because he pleased others who highly praised him, who were amazed that a Syrian, first instructed in Greek eloquence, should afterwards become a wonderful Latin orator and one most learned in things pertaining to philosophy. One is commended, and, unseen, he is loved. Does this love enter the heart of the hearer from the mouth of the commender? Not so. But one love kindles another. Therefore, the one who is commended is loved when the commender is believed to praise him with a sincere heart, that is, when one who loves him praises him.

I also used to love men in that way, upon the judgment of other men, not upon Yours, my God, in whom no man is deceived. Yet why did I not feel the same way about other qualities, like those of a famous charioteer or a fighter of beasts in the theater, known far and wide by common people? But I felt differently, and eagerly, about how I would want to be commended myself. I did not want to be commended or loved as actors are, though I myself did commend and love them, but I would rather be unknown than famous as an actor. I would even rather be hated! Where now are the motives for such various and diverse kinds of loves laid up in one soul? Why, since we are equally men, do I love in another what, if I did not hate, I would not spurn and cast from myself? For it does not follow that as a man who loves a good horse would not want to be that horse, even if he could, that the same may be said regarding an actor who shares our nature. Do I then love in a man what I would hate to be because I am a man? Man himself is a great mystery, whose very hairs You numbered (Matt. 10:30) Lord, and they "shall not fall on the ground without [You]" (Matt. 10:29). And yet the hairs of his head are more easily numbered than his feelings and the beatings of his heart.

But that orator was the kind of person whom I loved, and that I wished to be myself, and I erred through a swelling pride and was tossed "about with every wind" (Eph. 4:14). Yet I was steered by You, though very secretly. And how do I know, and how do I confidently confess to You, that I loved him more for the love of those who praised him, than for the very things for which he was praised? Because, had he not been praised, and these same men had criticized him and with criticism and contempt said the very same things about him, I would never have been so stimulated and excited to love him. And yet the things would not have been different, nor would he himself have been different; only the feelings of the relaters would have been different. See where the powerless soul droops along, one that is not yet supported by the solidity of truth! Just as stormy speeches blow from the breast of the opinionated, so is it carried this way and that, driven forward and backward. The light, then, is blocked by clouds, and the truth unseen. And yet, it is before us. And it meant a great deal to me that my treatise and work should be known to that man. If he should approve of them, I would be more impassioned, but if he disapproved, my empty heart, void of Your solidity, would have been wounded. And yet the "fair and fit," on which I wrote to him, I dwelled on with pleasure and reviewed and admired, though no one else joined with me.

But I did not yet see on what this weighty matter turned in Your wisdom, You, Omnipotent, who alone does wonders. My mind categorized bodily forms; I defined and distinguished the qualities of "fair" and also "fit," whose beauty is in correspondence to some other thing, and this I supported with material examples. And I turned to the nature of the mind, but the false notion which I had of spiritual things did not let me see the truth. Yet the force of truth flashed into my eyes on its own, and I turned my hungering soul away from metaphysical things to physical features and colors and large dimensions. And not being able to see these in the mind, I thought I could not see my mind.

Although in virtue I loved peace, and in depravity I hated discord, in the first I observed a unity, but in the other a sort of division. And that unity, I conceived, consisted of the rational soul and the nature of truth and the chief good. But in this division I miserably imagined there to be some unknown substance of irrational life and the nature of the chief evil, which was not only substance but real life also; yet it was not derived from You, my God, of whom all things are derived. And yet the first I called a Monad, as if it were a soul without sex. The latter I called a Dyad: like anger, in deeds of violence, and like lust, in depravity. I did not know what I was talking about. For I had not known or learned that evil is not a substance, and our soul is not that chief and unchangeable good.

Deeds of violence arise if that emotion of the soul from which vehement action springs is corrupted, stirring itself insolently and waywardly; and lusts arise when that passion of the soul is undisciplined, and carnal pleasures are indulged in. In the same way, errors and false opinions defile the conversation, if the rational mind itself is corrupted, as it was then in me, who did not know that it must be enlightened by another light, that it may be a partaker of truth, since the rational mind itself is not the nature of truth. "For thou wilt light my candle: the LORD my God will enlighten my darkness" (Ps. 18:28). "And of [Your] fullness have all we received" (John 1:16), for You are "the true Light, which lighteth every man that cometh into the world" (John 1:9). In You there "is no variableness, neither shadow of turning" (James 1:17).

But I pressed towards You and was driven from You that I might taste death (see John 8:52), for You "resisteth the proud" (James 4:6; 1 Pet. 5:5). For what can be prouder than for me, with a strange madness, to maintain myself to be that which by nature You are? Although I was subject to change, so that much being clear to me through my very desire to become wise, my wish was to progress from worse to better, yet I chose rather to imagine that You are subject to change than to think that I am not what You are. Therefore, I was repelled by You, and You resisted my vain stiff-neckedness.

I imagined bodily forms, and, though I myself am flesh, I accused flesh. As "a wind that passeth away" (Ps. 78:39), I did not return to You, but I passed on and on to things which have no being, neither in You nor in me nor in the body. And they were not created for me by Your truth; rather, my vanity contrived them out of bodily things. And I used to ask Your faithful little ones, my fellow-citizens, from whom, unknown to myself, I stood exiled, I pratingly and foolishly used to ask them, "Why then does the soul which God created err?" But I did not want to be asked, "Why then does God err?" And I maintained that Your unchangeable substance did err when forced to, rather than confess that my changeable substance had gone astray voluntarily and now, in punishment, lay in error.

I was then twenty-six or twenty-seven years old when I wrote those volumes, material fantasies swirling within me, buzzing in the ears of my heart, which I turned, sweet Truth, to Your inward melody, meditating on the "fair and fit," and longing to stand and listen to You and to rejoice "greatly because of the bridegroom's voice" (John 3:29). But, I could not, for by the voices of my own errors I was hurried beyond, and through the weight of my own pride, I was sinking into the lowest pit. For You did not "make me to hear joy and gladness," nor did my bones which were not yet humbled rejoice (Ps. 51:8).

And what did it profit me that when I was scarcely twenty years old, a book of Aristotle, which they call *The Ten Predicaments* (categories),[1] fell into my hands, and that I was able to read and understand it unaided? I hung on this very name as on something great and divine, since my rhetoric master of Carthage, and others thought of as learned, so often spoke it with cheeks bursting with pride. And when I conferred with others, who said that they scarcely understood it with very able tutors, and who not only orally explained it but illustrated many things in the sand, they could tell me no more of it than I had learned by reading it on my own. And the book appeared to me to speak very clearly of substances such as man, of his qualities, such as: man's physique, of what sort it is, and his stature, how many feet high; his relationship,

---

[1] The interrelationships of things were comprised by Aristotle under nine classes of properties: quantity, quality, relation, action, passion, time, place, situation, and clothing (in the sense of a uniform). These, along with that in which they might be found, or "substance," make up the ten categories or predicaments.

whose brother he is; where placed; when born; whether he stands or sits; whether he is equipped with shoes or armed; whether he does or suffers anything; and all the innumerable things which might be placed under these nine predicaments, of which I just have given some examples, or under that chief predicament of substance.

What did I gain from all this, seeing that it hindered me? I believed that whatever existed was understood under those ten predicaments. I endeavored in this way to understand, my God, Your wonderful and unchangeable unity also, as if You had been subjected to Your own greatness or beauty, so that, as in bodies, they should exist in You, as if You were their subject. But, You Yourself are Your greatness and beauty. A body is not great or fair simply because it is a body, since even though it would become less great or fair, it would not cease to be a body. But my conception of You was based on falsehood, not truth, on illusions of my misery, not the realities of Your blessedness. For You had commanded, and it was done in me, that the earth should bring forth briars and thorns to me, and that in the sweat of my brow I should eat my bread (Gen. 3:18).

And what did it profit me, that all the books I could obtain of the so-called liberal arts, I, the vile slave of vile affections, read by myself and understood? And I delighted in them, but I did not know where all that was true or certain within them came from. I had my back to the light and my face to things enlightened, yet my face, with which I discerned the things enlightened, was not enlightened

94

by them. Whatever was written, either on rhetoric or logic, geometry, music, or arithmetic, I understood by myself without much difficulty or any instructor. You know this, Lord my God, because both quickness of understanding and acuteness in discerning are Your gifts, yet I did not then sacrifice them to You. So then they were not used to my good, but rather to my destruction, since I attempted to get this good portion of my substance into my own keeping, and I did not keep my strength for You but wandered from You into a far country to spend it upon prostitution. (See Luke 15:13.) What profit did I receive from good abilities that were not employed to good use? I did not know that those arts were attained with great difficulty, even by the studious and talented, until I attempted to explain them to such and discovered that the one who excelled most in them, was the one who followed me the least slowly.

But how did this help me, to imagine that You, Lord God, the Truth, were a vast and bright body and I a fragment of that body? Perverseness too great! But this is what I was. Nor am I embarrassed, my God, to confess to You Your mercies towards me and to call upon You, I, who did not blush then to profess to men my blasphemies and to bark against You. How did my nimble wit profit me in those sciences and all those most knotty volumes, which I unraveled without aid from human instruction, seeing that I erred so disgracefully, and with such sacrilegious shamefulness, in the doctrine of godliness? Or what hindrance was a far lesser intelligence to Your little ones, since they did not depart far from You, so that in the nest of Your church they might securely be reared and nourish the wings of love by the food of a sound faith? Oh, Lord our God, "under the shadow of thy wings" (Ps. 17:8) let us hope; protect us, and carry us. You will carry us when we are little, and You will carry us even to our old age (Isa. 46:4). Our firmness, when it is You, is firmness, but when it is our own, it is infirmity. Our good ever lives with You, from which, when we turn away, we are turned aside. Let us now, Lord, return, that we may not be overturned. With You our good lives without any decay; You are our good. We do not need to fear that there is no place to return to after our fall. For in our absence, our mansion, Your eternity, did not fall.

Book Five

Augustine's twenty-ninth year. Faustus, a snare of Satan to many, is made an instrument of deliverance to Augustine by showing the ignorance of the Manichees on those things in which they professed to have divine knowledge. Augustine gives up all thought of going further among the Manichees. Is guided to Rome and Milan, where he hears St. Ambrose, leaves the Manichees, and becomes again a catechumen in the church.

Accept the sacrifice of my confessions from the ministry of my tongue, which You have formed and stirred up to confess to Your name. Heal all my bones, and let them say, "LORD, who is like unto thee?" (Ps. 35:10). For he who confesses to You does not teach You what takes place within him, seeing that a closed heart does not close out Your eye. Nor can man's hardheartedness thrust back Your hand, for according to Your will You dissolve it in pity or in vengeance, and nothing can hide itself from Your heat (Ps. 19:6). But let my soul praise You so that it may love You, and let it confess Your own mercies to You so that it may praise You. Your whole creation does not cease, nor is it silent in Your praises. Neither does the spirit of man cease Your praises through words directed to You. Creation, animate or inanimate, also praises You through the language of those who meditate on it, who look to those things which You have created, and who move on from them to You who made them wonderfully, so that out of our weariness our souls may arise towards You. In these things there is refreshment and true strength.

Even though the restless, the godless, may depart and flee from You, You still see them and divide the darkness. Behold, the universe is pure, even though they who are in it are foul. In what way have they injured You? How have they disgraced Your reign, which, from heaven to this lowest earth, is just and perfect? Where did they flee when they fled from Your presence? Or where do You not find them? But they fled so that they might not see You seeing them, and, blinded, they might stumble against You—because You forsake nothing You have made—that the unjust, I say, might stumble upon You and justly be hurt because they withdrew themselves from Your gentleness and stumbled at Your uprightness and fell upon their own ruggedness. They are indeed ignorant that You are everywhere, that nothing can hem you in. They do not know that You alone are near, even to those who remove themselves far from You. Let them then repent and seek You because You have not forsaken Your creation as they have forsaken their Creator. Let them repent and seek You, and behold, You are there in their heart, in the heart of those that confess to You and cast themselves upon You and weep in Your bosom, after all their rebellious ways. Then You gently wipe away their tears, and they weep even more for joy because You, Lord, not man of flesh and blood, but You, Lord, who made them, renew and comfort them. But where was I when I was seeking You? You were before me, even though I had gone away from You, and I did not find myself, much less You!

I will now lay open before my God that twenty-ninth year of my life. At that time a certain bishop of the Manichees, Faustus by name, a great "snare of the devil" (1 Tim. 3:7) had come to Carthage, and many were entrapped by him through the lure of his smooth language. Though I did praise his elocution, I was able to separate it from the truth of the things which I was zealous to learn. I did not regard the style of oratory as much as the knowledge which this Faustus, so praised among them, set before me to feed upon. His fame had preceded him, and he was spoken of as being most knowledgeable in all valuable learning and exquisitely skilled in the liberal arts. And since I had read and remembered much of the philosophers, I compared some things of theirs with those long fables of the Manichees. I found the former to be more probable, even though they could only succeed in making conclusions about this lower world; the Lord of it they could by no means find out. For You are great, Lord, and have "respect unto the lowly: but the proud [You] knoweth afar off" (Ps. 138:6). You do not draw near, except to the contrite in heart (Ps. 34:18), nor are You found by the proud, no, not even if by unusual skill they could number the stars and the sand, measure the starry heavens, and track the courses of the planets.

Through their understanding and knowledge, which You gave them, they sought out these things, and they have discovered much. They foretold, many years before, eclipses of those luminaries, the sun and moon—what day and hour, and the quantity of the eclipse—and their calculations did not fail. It came to pass as they foretold, and they wrote down the principles they had discovered. These are read to this day, and from them others foretell in what year and month of the year, and what day of the month, and what hour of the day, and what part of the sun's or moon's light is to be eclipsed. And it will occur just as they predict.

Men who do not know this science are amazed and astonished at these things, and those who do know it brag and are conceited. Departing from You with an ungodly pride and failing to see Your light, they foresee a failure of the sun's light in the future, but they do not see their own present failure. They do not reverently seek to discover where their intelligence comes from, through which they are able to decipher this. Upon finding that You made them, they do not give themselves up to You to preserve what You have made, nor do they sacrifice to You what they have made themselves. They do not slay their own soaring imaginations, as fowls of the air, nor their own sinking curiosities, with which, like the fishes of the sea, they wander over the unknown paths of the abyss, nor their own indulgence, as beasts of the field (see Psalm 8:7–8), that You, Lord, "a consuming fire"

(Deut. 4:24), may burn up their dead cares and recreate them in immortality.

But the philosophers did not know the way, Your Word, by whom You made these things which they number (You also made and numbered them) the discernment by which they perceive what they number, and the understanding out of which they number. Of Your wisdom there is no number. (See Psalm 147:5.) But, the Only Begotten is Himself "made unto us wisdom, and righteousness, and sanctification" (1 Cor. 1:30) and was numbered among us and paid tribute "unto Caesar" (Matt. 22:21).

They did not know the way by which to descend to Him from themselves, and by Him to ascend to Him. They did not know this way and considered themselves shining and exalted among the stars. Behold, they fell upon the earth, and "their foolish heart was darkened" (Rom. 1:21). They converse correctly on many things concerning the creature, but they do not piously seek Truth, the Artisan of creation, and therefore do not find Him. Or, if they find Him, knowing Him to be God, they do not glorify him as God, neither are they thankful, but they become vain in their imaginations, professing themselves to be wise (see Romans 1:21–22), attributing to themselves what is Yours. Thereby with most perverse blindness, they diligently study to attribute to You what is their own, forging lies of You who are the Truth, and changing "the glory of the uncorruptible God into an image made like to corruptible man, and to birds, and fourfooted beasts, and creeping things"

(Rom. 1:23). They change Your truth into a lie, and worship and serve the creature more than the Creator (Rom. 1:25).

Yet I retained many truths concerning Your creation from these men and understood the order of creation from their calculations, the succession of the seasons, and the visible testimonies of the stars. I compared them with the saying of Manicheus, since he had written widely on these subjects in his delirium, but discovered no account of the solstices, equinoxes, the eclipses of the greater lights, nor anything else of this sort that I had learned in the books of secular philosophy. I was commanded to believe it, and yet it did not agree with what had been established by scientific calculations and by my own observation. Rather, it was quite contrary.

Lord God of Truth, does the person who knows these things therefore please You? Surely he who knows all these things but does not know You is unhappy, but happy is he who knows You even though he does not know these. And whoever knows both You and them is not happier because of them, but only because of You, if, knowing You, he glorifies You as God and is thankful and does not become vain in his imaginations (Rom. 1:21). He who knows how to possess a tree and return thanks to You for the use of it, although he does not know how many cubits high it is or how wide it spreads, is better off than he who can measure it and count all its boughs, but neither owns it nor knows or loves its Creator. It is the same with a believer, to whom all this world of wealth belongs, who has nothing and yet possesses all things (2 Cor. 6:10) by cleaving to You, whom all things serve. Though he does not know even the circles of the Great Bear, it is folly to doubt that he is in a better state than one who can measure the heavens, number the stars, and weigh the elements, yet neglect You who have made all things in number, weight, and measure.

Who urged Manicheus to write on these things also, this knowledge in which there was no element of piety? You have said to man, "Behold, the fear of the Lord, that is wisdom" (Job 28:28). Manicheus might be ignorant of this, though he claimed to have perfect knowledge of other things. Since, even though he did not know these things, he most impudently dared to teach them, he plainly could have no knowledge of piety. It is vanity to make a profession of these worldly things even when you thoroughly know them, but to make confession to You is piety. Because of this, this wanderer spoke much of these things, so that when exposed by those who had truly learned them, it might be apparent what kind of understanding he had in the other more difficult things. He would not have himself thought of as inferior, but he went about to persuade men that the Holy Spirit, the Comforter and Enricher of Your faithful ones, personally resided within him with complete authority. Then when he was found to have taught falsely about the heaven and stars and of the motions of the sun and moon, although these things do not pertain to the doctrine of religion, his sacrilegious presumption would become evident enough.

He spoke about things which he not only did not know, but which were falsified with so mad a vanity of pride that he sought to attribute them to himself as to a divine person.

When I encounter any Christian brother who is ignorant of astronomy and mistaken about it, I can bear patiently with such a man's opinions. I do not see that any ignorance regarding the position or character of the physical world can injure him, as long as he does not believe anything unworthy of You, Lord, the Creator of all. But it does injure him if he believes that it is the equivalent of Christian doctrine and stubbornly asserts what he is ignorant of. Yet such a fault is, in the infancy of faith, carried by our mother love until the newborn may grow up "unto a perfect man," so as not to be "carried about with every wind of doctrine" (Eph. 4:13–14). But in the case of Manicheus— who in these ways presumed to be the teacher, source, guide, and chief of all whom he could so persuade, that whoever followed him thought that he did not follow a mere man but Your Holy Spirit—who would not agree, when once he had been exposed as having taught false things, that so great a folly should be detested and utterly rejected? But I had not yet clearly determined whether or not the changes of longer and shorter days and nights, and of day and night itself, with the eclipses of the greater lights, and whatever else of the kind I had read of in other books, might be explained consistently with his sayings. If they by any means might, it should remain a question to me whether what he said was true or not; I might still, on the basis of his alleged sanctity, rest my belief upon his authority.

And for almost all the nine years in which with unsettled mind I had been the disciple of the Manicheans, I had longed but too intensely for the coming of Faustus. The rest of the sect, whom by chance I had come upon, when unable to solve my objections about these things, still held out to me the coming of this Faustus. By meeting with him, they said, these and greater difficulties would be cleared up quickly. When he finally came, I found him to be a man of pleasing discourse who could speak fluently, using better language, yet he still said the same things which they had been saying. What good was the utmost neatness of the cup-bearer when I was thirsting for a more precious drink? My ears were already numbed with that talk, and they did not seem to me any better because they were better stated, nor more true because more eloquently said, nor the soul more wise because the face was handsome and the language graceful. But they who held him out to me were not good judges of such things; therefore, to them he appeared understanding and wise because his talk was pleasing. I had perceived, however, that another type of people was suspicious even of truth and refused to assent to it, if delivered with smooth and plentiful words.

You, my God, had already taught me by wonderful and secret ways. I believe that it was You who taught me because I learned the truth. And besides You there is no other teacher of truth, where or whenever it may shine upon us. From

You I had now learned that nothing should be accepted as true simply because it is spoken eloquently, nor false merely because it is spoken badly. Also, neither should anything be considered true because it is unskillfully spoken, nor false because the language is rich. I learned that wisdom and folly are like wholesome and unwholesome food, and that adorned or unadorned phrases are like courtly or country vessels; either kind of meat may be served up in either kind of dish.

That greedy anticipation then, in which I had for so long expected that man, was truly delighted with his demeanor and emotion when debating, and with his choice and readiness of words to clothe his ideas. I was then delighted, and, along with many others—and even more than they—I praised and extolled him. It troubled me, however, that in the assembly of his hearers, I was not allowed to participate and ask those questions that had troubled me when I had engaged in informal discussions with him. When my friends and I began to get his attention at those times when it was appropriate for him to enter into a discussion with me, I found him at first utterly ignorant of the liberal arts, except grammar, and of that he had but an ordinary knowledge. But because he had read some of Cicero's Orations, a very few books of Seneca, some things of the poets, and such few volumes of his own sect as were written in Latin and well-composed, and had practiced speaking daily, he had acquired a certain eloquence which proved even more pleasing and seductive because it was under the guidance of a good intellect and had a kind of natural gracefulness. Is it not so, as I recall it, Lord my God, Judge of my conscience? Before You are my heart and my memory, You, who at that time directed me by the hidden mystery of Your providence and set those shameful errors of mine before my face that I might see and hate them.

After it was clear that he was ignorant of those arts in which I thought he excelled, I began to despair that he would explain and solve the difficulties which perplexed me. However ignorant he might have been of them, he might have held the truths of piety, had he not been a Manichee. Their books are filled with verbose fables of the heavens, the stars, sun, and moon, and I now no longer thought him able to resolve satisfactorily what I very much wanted to know: whether, when comparing these things with the computations I had read elsewhere, the account given in the books of Manicheus was preferable, or at least as good. When I proposed that these things be considered and discussed, he modestly declined the challenge. For he knew that he did not know these things and was not ashamed to confess it. He was not one of those loose-tongued people, many of whom I had endured, who undertook to teach me these things but said nothing. This man had a heart, though not one that was right towards You. Yet neither was his heart altogether treacherous to himself. He was not altogether ignorant of his own ignorance, and he would not rashly be entangled in a dispute from which he could neither retreat nor completely disentangle himself. For this I liked him even better because the modesty of a candid mind is more honorable than the knowledge of those things which I desired. I found him to be the same way in all the more difficult and subtle questions.

My zeal for the writings of Manicheus was therefore blunted, and I despaired even more of learning anything from their other teachers, seeing that, in the various things which had perplexed me, he who was so renowned among them had turned out this way. However, I began to embark with him on the study of that literature on which he also was much set, and which as rhetoric-reader I was at that time teaching young students in Carthage. I read with him, either what he himself desired to hear, or that which I thought appropriate for his ability. But all my efforts, by which I had purposed to advance in that sect, came completely to an end after getting to know that man. Not that I detached myself from them altogether, but at the time I had not found anything better, and I had decided in the meantime to be content with what I had in whatever way fallen into, unless by chance something more preferable should dawn upon me. In this way, Faustus, who was to so many a snare of death, had now, neither willingly nor knowingly, begun to loosen that in which I was deceived. For Your hands, my God, in the secret purpose of Your providence, did not forsake my soul, and out of my mother's heart's blood, through her tears which were poured out night and day, a sacrifice was offered for me to You. You dealt with me through wondrous ways (Joel 2:26).

You did it, my God, for "the steps of a good man are ordered by the LORD: and he delighteth in his way" (Ps. 37:23). How will we obtain salvation except by Your hand, which remakes what it has made?

You dealt with me so that I would be persuaded to go to Rome and teach there what I had been teaching at Carthage. And how I was persuaded to do this, I will not neglect to confess to You, because in this also the deepest recesses of Your wisdom and Your most present mercy to us must be considered and confessed. I did not wish to go to Rome because my friends who persuaded me to do this told me I would receive higher earnings and higher honors, though even these things had an influence on me at that time. Rather, the chief and almost sole reason was that I heard that young men there studied more peacefully and were kept quiet under the restraint of more regular discipline, so that they did not, at will, petulantly rush into a teacher's school when they were not even his students, nor were they even allowed in without his permission. Whereas at Carthage there reigns among the students a most disgraceful and unruly license. They burst in recklessly and, with almost frantic gestures, disturb all order which anyone has established for the good of his students. They commit diverse outrages with an amazing indifference, things that would be punishable by law if custom did not uphold them; that very custom revealing them to be even more contemptible, in that they now do things as lawful that by Your eternal law will never be lawful. They think they do it unpunished, whereas they are punished with the very blindness with which they do it and suffer incomparably worse than what they do.

The behavior that I would never have engaged in when I was a student, I was made to endure in others as a teacher, and so I was very happy to go where everyone who was familiar with it assured me similar things were not done. But that I might change my earthly dwelling for the salvation of my soul, You, "my refuge and my portion in the land of the living" (Ps. 142:5), pushed me at Carthage so that I might thereby be torn from it, and You offered me allurements in Rome, so that I might be drawn there. You did this through men in love with a dying life, the one doing frantic, the other promising vain things, and, to correct my steps, You secretly used their and my own perverseness. Those who stirred me up were blinded with a disgraceful frenzy, and those who invited me elsewhere smacked of earthly things. And I, who in Carthage detested real unhappiness, was in Rome seeking unreal happiness.

You knew, God, why I went away and went to that place, yet You neither showed it to me nor to my mother, who grievously bewailed my journey and followed me as far as the sea. But I deceived her while she was holding me by force either to keep me back or to go with me. I pretended that I had a friend whom I could not leave until he had a fair wind to sail. I lied to my mother, to such a godly mother, and escaped. For this also You have mercifully forgiven me even though I was full of detestable defilements, preserving me from the waters of the sea, for the water of Your Grace. Whereby when I was cleansed, the streams of my mother's eyes should be dried from the tears which for me she daily watered the ground under her face. Still refusing to return without me, I scarcely persuaded her to stay that night in a place nearby our ship where there was an oratory in memory of the blessed Cyprian. That night I secretly departed, but she did not, remaining behind in weeping and prayer.

What, Lord, was she with so many tears asking of You but that You would not allow me to sail? But You, in the depth of Your counsels and hearing the main point of her prayer did not answer what she asked at that time, that You might make me what she always asked. The wind blew and filled our sails, and the shore withdrew from our sight. The next day she was there, frantic with sorrow, and she filled Your ears with complaints and groans, You who at that time disregarded them, while through my desires, You were hurrying me to put an end to all my lusts. The earthly part of her affection for me was disciplined through the scourge of sorrows which she was allotted. She loved my being with her, as mothers do, but she much more than many, and she did not know how great a joy You were about to work for her out of my absence. She did not know; therefore, she wept and wailed, and through this agony the inheritance of Eve was manifest in her, with sorrow seeking what in sorrow she had brought forth. (See Genesis 3:16.) And yet, after blaming me for my treachery and hard-heartedness, she again took it upon herself to intercede to You for me. She went home, and I went to Rome.

And behold, in Rome I was afflicted with bodily sickness, and I was going down to hell, carrying all the many and grievous sins which I had committed against You, myself, and others, over and above that bond of original sin through which we all die in Adam (1 Cor. 15:22). You had not forgiven me any of these things in Christ, nor had He abolished by His cross the enmity which by my sins I had incurred with You. (See Ephesians 2:16.) How could He abolish this enmity by the crucifixion of an illusion, which I believed Him to be? The death of my soul was as true as His flesh seemed false to me, and the death of His body was as true as the falseness of the life of my soul, which did not believe it.

The fever heightened; I was parting and departing forever. Had I then parted from this world, where would I have departed to, but into fire and torments such as my misdeeds deserved in light of the truth of Your decree? My mother did not know this, yet in my absence she prayed for me. But You, who are present everywhere, heard her where she was and had compassion upon me where I was, so that I should recover the health of my body, though I was still delirious in my sacrilegious heart. For in all that danger I did not desire Your baptism, and I was better as a boy when I begged it of my mother's love, as I have before related and confessed. But to my own shame I had grown up, and I rashly scoffed at the prescriptions of Your medicine, You who would not allow me, in my shame, to die a double death. Had my mother's heart been pierced with this wound, it could never have been healed. I cannot describe the love she showed me and with how much more vehement anguish she was now in labor of me in the spirit, than when she was in labor at my birth. (See Galatians 4:19.)

I do not know how she could have been healed had such a death of mine pierced her heart. And what effect would her strong and unceasing prayers have made, if they had simply made it to Your throne? But would You, God of mercies, despise the contrite and humbled heart (Ps. 51:17) of that chaste and sober widow? She was so frequent in almsgiving, so full of duty and service to Your saints, never missing a day of offering at Your altar: twice a day, morning and evening, without any interruption, coming to Your church, not for idle stories and old wives' fables, but that she might hear You in Your sermons and You might hear her in her prayers. Could You despise and reject from Your aid the tears of such a one, with which she did not beg You for gold or silver, nor any changeable or short-lived good, but for the salvation of her son's soul? You, by whose gift she was this way? Never, Lord. You were at hand and were hearing and doing things in the true order in which You had determined before that they should be done. Far be it that You should deceive her in Your visions and answers, some of which I have mentioned, some I have not mentioned, which she laid up in her faithful heart, and, always praying, urged upon You as if written in Your own hand-writing. Since Your "mercy endureth for ever" (Ps. 118:1), You grant to those to whom You forgive all their debts that You also become a debtor by Your promises.

You healed me then of that sickness. You healed the son of Your handmaid, for the time being, in body, that he might live for You to bestow upon him a better and more abiding health. And even then, in Rome, I joined myself to those deceiving and deceived "holy ones." I did not join only with their disciples, among whom was the man in whose house I had fallen sick and recovered, but also with those whom they call "the elect."

I still thought that it was not we who sin, but that some other nature sinned in us. It delighted my pride to be free from blame, and, when I had done any evil, not to confess I had committed any that You might "heal my soul; for I have sinned against thee" (Ps. 41:4). But, I loved to excuse it and to accuse some other thing which was within me but which I was not. But in reality it was entirely me, and my ungodliness had divided me against myself. (See Matthew 12:26.) That sin was the more incurable by which I did not judge myself to be a sinner. What an abominable iniquity it was, that I would rather have You, You, God Almighty, to be defeated within me to my destruction, than myself overcome by You for my salvation. You had not yet set a watch before my mouth and a door of safekeeping around my lips that my heart might not turn aside to wicked speeches, to make excuses for sins with men who work iniquity. (See Psalm

141:3–4.) Therefore, I was still connected to their elect.

But now, despairing to become proficient in that false doctrine, I was now more lax and careless regarding those things with which, if I should find nothing better, I had resolved to rest contented. For I half thought that those philosophers, whom they call Academics, were wiser than the rest because they held that men ought to doubt everything and claimed that no truth can be comprehended by man. Even though at that time I did not even understand their message, I was clearly convinced that they believed these things as they are commonly reported to believe. I freely and openly discouraged my host from that overconfidence which I perceived him to have in those fables of which the books of Manicheus are full.

Yet I lived in closer friendship with them than with others who were not of this heresy. I did not sustain it with my former eagerness; still, my intimacy with that sect (Rome secretly harbored many of them) made me less apt to seek any other way. This was especially true since I despaired of finding the truth, from which they had turned me aside, in Your church, Lord of heaven and earth, Creator of all things visible and invisible, because it seemed to me indecent to believe that You have the form of human flesh and are limited by the confines of our bodies. And because, when I wished to think on my God, I did not know what to think of but a bodily mass, for anything other than that did not seem to me to be anything. This was the greatest and almost sole cause of my inevitable error.

Consequently, I believed evil also to be some such kind of substance and to have its own foul and hideous mass, whether gross, which the Manicheans called earth, or thin and subtle, like the body of the air, which they imagine to be some malignant mind, creeping through the earth. And because a piety, such as it was, constrained me to believe that a good God never created any evil nature, I conceived two masses contrary to one another, both limited, but the evil narrower and the good more expansive. And from this harmful beginning, other sacrilegious conceits followed me.

When my mind endeavored to return to the Christian faith, I was driven back since I did not think it was the true Christian faith. And I thought it would be more reverential to believe that You, my God, to whom Your mercies confess out of my mouth, were limitless, at least on other sides; although, on that side where the mass of evil was opposed to You, I was forced to confess that You were limited. I thought it more reverential to believe that than to imagine that you were limited on all sides by the form of a human body. It seemed to me better to believe that You created no evil—which in my ignorance seemed to be not only some kind of substance, but a bodily substance, because I could not conceive of the mind unless as a subtle body spread out into limited spaces—than to believe that the nature of evil, such as I conceived it, could come from You.

I believed our Savior Himself, Your Only Begotten, as having been reached forth, as it were, for our salvation out of the mass of Your most glorious substance, so that I believed nothing about Him except what I could imagine in my vanity. His nature then, being such, I thought could not be born of the Virgin Mary without being mingled with the flesh. In my particular conception of our Savior, I did not see how He could be mingled and not defiled. I was afraid, therefore, to believe He was born in the flesh, for fear that I should be forced to believe He was defiled by the flesh. Now let Your spiritual ones gently and lovingly smile upon me if they read these confessions of mine. Yet such was I.

Furthermore, what the Manichees had criticized in Your Scriptures, I thought could not be defended; yet at times I truly wished to discuss these points with someone who was well versed in those books, and to find out what he thought of them. The words of one Elpidius, as he spoke and disputed face to face against the aforementioned Manichees, had begun to stir me even at Carthage because he had produced things out of the Scriptures that could not easily be opposed. The Manichees' answer to these things seemed weak to me. And they did not like to answer them publicly but only to us in private. Their answer was that the Scriptures of the New Testament had been corrupted by some unknown person who wished to join the law of the Jews to the Christian faith. Yet they themselves produced no uncorrupted copies of the Scriptures. But because I could only conceive of things in bodily form, I was, for the most part, held back, strongly oppressed as if suffocated by those masses I believed in. I panted under them

117

after the pure and untainted breath of Your truth, but I could not breathe it in.

I then diligently began to practice that for which I came to Rome: to teach rhetoric. First, I gathered some to my house, to whom and through whom I had begun to be known. But then I learned about other offenses that were committed in Rome to which I was not exposed in Africa. True, those subversions by unprincipled young men were not practiced here, as was told me. But, I was informed that, to avoid paying their teacher's salary, a number of youths would suddenly plot together and go to another teacher, breakers of faith, who for love of money hold justice cheap. My heart hated them, though not with a "perfect hatred" (Ps. 139:22), for perhaps I hated them more because I was to suffer by them than because they did things utterly unlawful.

In truth, such are vile people, and they "go a whoring from thee" (Ps. 73:27), loving these fleeting mockeries of temporal things and filthy lucre which fouls the hand that grasps it, hugging the fleeting world and despising You, who endure forever and call back and forgive the adulterous soul of man when it returns to You. And now I hate such depraved and crooked people, though I love them if they are set right so that instead of money, they prefer the learning which they acquire and learning of You, O God, the truth and fullness of assured good and most pure peace. But at that time I would rather, for my own sake, have disliked them for being evil than to have liked and wished them good for You.

Then, the people of Milan sent a message to the prefect of Rome, asking him to furnish them with a rhetoric reader for their city and to send him at the public expense. I applied for this position through those very people, intoxicated with Manichean vanities, from whom I was leaving Rome to be freed. Neither I nor they, however, knew it at the time. Symmachus, who was then prefect of the city, tested me by setting before me some subject, and then he sent me.

To Milan I came, to Ambrose the Bishop, known to the whole world as among the best of men, Your devout servant, whose eloquent discourse plentifully dispensed to Your people "the finest of the wheat" (Ps. 81:16; 147:14), the gladness of Your oil (Ps. 45:7), and the sober inebriation of Your wine (Ps. 104:15). To him I was unknowingly led by You so that by him I might knowingly be led to You. That man of God received me as a father and showed me a priestly kindness on my coming.

Thereafter I began to love him, at first indeed not as a teacher of the truth, which I utterly despaired of finding in Your church, but as a person who was kind to me. And I listened diligently to him preaching to the people, not with the intent that I ought, but, as it were, testing his eloquence, whether it lived up to its fame or was better or worse than was reported. I hung on his words attentively, but regarding the subject matter, I was as a careless and scornful onlooker. I was delighted with the agreeableness of his discourse, which was more profound, yet in method less winning and pleasing than that of Faustus. Of the subject matter, however, there was no comparison, for the one was wandering amid Manichean delusions, the other was teaching salvation most soundly. But "salvation is far from [sinners]" (Ps. 119:155), and that is what I then was. I was unconsciously drawing nearer, little by little.

Though I took no pains to learn about what he spoke but only to hear how he spoke, for that empty concern was the only thing left for me since I despaired of ever finding a way open for man to come to You, still the things which I rejected came into my mind at the same time as the pleasing words, for I could not separate them. And while I opened my heart to admit the eloquence with which he spoke, the truth that he spoke also entered in, but this occurred by degrees. For first, the things of which he spoke had also now begun to appear to me to be capable of defense. The faith with which I had thought nothing could be said against the Manichees' objections, I now thought might be held without shame, especially after I had heard him explain one or two places in the Old Testament which he often interpreted figuratively, passages through which when I had taken them literally, I had been slain spiritually. (See 2 Corinthians 3:6.) A great many places, then, of those books having been explained, I now blamed my own despair for believing that no answer could be given to those who hated and scoffed at the law and the prophets. Yet I did not then see that the Christian way was to be held, even though it also could find learned maintainers who could at large and with some show of reason answer objections. Nor did I see that what I held was therefore to be condemned because both sides could be maintained. Even though the Christian cause no longer seemed to me to be defeated, it still did not yet seem victorious.

Immediately after this I earnestly bent my mind to see if there was any way in which I could by any certain proof convict the Manichees of falsehood. If only I could have conceived a spiritual substance, all their strongholds would have been beaten down and cast utterly out of my mind. But I could not. Notwithstanding, concerning the structure of this world and the whole of nature which the senses of the flesh can grasp, as I considered and compared things more and more, I judged the tenets of most of the philosophers to have been much more probable. So then, after the manner of the so-called "Academics" who doubted everything and wavered between all, I settled this much: that the Manichees were to be abandoned. I determined that, with my doubts, I should not continue in that sect when I already preferred some philosophers over it. Even so, I refused to commit the cure of my sick soul to these philosophers because they were without the saving name of Christ. I determined therefore to be a catechumen in the Church, to which I had been commended by my parents, until something certain should dawn upon me where I might steer my course.

Book Six

Arrival of Monnica at Milan. Her obedience to St. Ambrose, and his esteem for her. St. Ambrose's habits. Augustine's gradual abandonment of error. Finds that he has blamed the church wrongly. Desire for absolute certainty, but struck with the contrary analogy of God's natural providence. How shaken he is in his worldly pursuits. God's guidance of his friend Alypius. Augustine debates with himself and his friends about their mode of life. His habitual sins, and dread of judgment.

Oh, You, my hope from my youth (Ps. 71:5), where were You in relation to me, and where had You gone? Had You not created me and separated me from the beasts of the field and the fowls of the air? You had made me wiser; yet I walked in darkness and in slippery places, and I sought You outside of myself and did not find the God of my heart. I had come into the depths of the sea and doubted and despaired that I would ever find truth.

My mother had now come to me, resolute in her piety, following me over sea and land, in all perils trusting in You. In dangerous seas she comforted the very mariners, by whom passengers unacquainted with the deep are accustomed rather to be comforted when troubled, assuring them of a safe arrival because You had assured her of it by a vision. She found me in grievous danger through my despair of ever finding truth. But when I told her that I was now no longer a Manichean, though I was not yet a Christian, she was not overjoyed as at something unexpected; although, she was now assured concerning that part of my wretchedness in which she bewailed me as one dead, though I would be reawakened by You. She carried me forth upon the bier of her thoughts that You might say to the son of the widow, "Young man, I say unto thee, Arise" (Luke 7:14), and that he should revive and begin to speak, and that You should deliver him to his mother (Luke 7:15).

Her heart, then, was not shaken with any tumultuous exultation when she heard that what she daily pleaded of You with tears was already in so great part realized. Though I had not yet attained the truth, I was rescued from falsehood. She was assured that You who had promised the whole, would one day give the rest. Most calmly and with a heart full of confidence, she replied to me that she believed in Christ that before she departed this life, she would see me become a believer. This much she said to me. But to You, Fountain of Mercies, she poured forth many more prayers and tears, that You would bring Your help quickly and "enlighten my darkness" (Ps. 18:28), and she hurried even more eagerly to the church and hung upon the words of Ambrose, praying for the fountain of that water which springs up to life everlasting (John 4:14). She loved that man as an angel of God because she knew that by him I had been brought for the time being to that doubtful state of faith I now was in, through which she anticipated most confidently that I would pass from sickness to health, after the return, so to speak, of a more severe convulsion, which physicians call "the crisis."

Once when my mother had, as she was accustomed in Africa, brought to the churches built in memory of the saints certain cakes and bread and wine, she was forbidden to do so by the doorkeeper. As soon as she knew that the bishop had forbidden this, she so piously and obediently embraced his wishes that I myself was amazed at how readily she censured her own practice rather than discuss his prohibition. For wine drinking did not threaten her spirit, nor did love of wine provoke her to a hatred of the truth as it does to many, both men and women, who rebel at a lesson of sobriety as men well-drunk revolt at a drink mingled with water. But she, when she had brought her basket with the accustomed festival food which was only to be tasted by herself and then given away, never included more than one small cup of wine, diluted according to her own sober habits, which for courtesy she would taste. If there were many churches of the departed saints that were to be honored in that manner, she still carried round that same cup to be used everywhere. This, though not only made very watery but unpleasantly warm from being carried about, she would distribute to those about her in small sips, for she sought their devotion, not pleasure.

As soon, then, as she found that this custom was forbidden by that famous preacher and most pious prelate—even to those that would use it soberly, for fear that drunks might use it as an excuse for indulgence and that these, as it were, anniversary funeral solemnities very much resembled the superstition of the Gentiles—she most willingly abstained from it. Instead of a basket filled with fruits of the earth, she had learned to bring to the churches of the martyrs a heart filled with more purified petitions and to give what she could to the poor, so that the communion of the Lord's Body might be acceptably celebrated there, where, after the example of His Passion, the martyrs had been sacrificed and crowned.

Yet it seems to me, Lord my God, and so my heart thinks of it in Your sight, that perhaps she would not so readily have yielded to the cutting off of this custom had it been forbidden by someone whom she did not love as much as Ambrose. Because of my salvation, she loved him most entirely, and he loved her for her most godly example by which, so "fervent in spirit" (Rom. 12:11), she was constantly at church doing good works. So, when he saw me, he often broke out in praise of her, congratulating me that I had such a mother, not knowing what a son she had in me, who doubted of these things and imagined that the way to life could not be found out.

Nor did I yet groan in my prayers for You to help me; rather, my spirit was wholly intent on learning and restless to dispute. I considered Ambrose himself a happy man, as the world measures happiness, because such renowned people held him in such honor; only his celibacy seemed to me to be difficult duty. But what hope he bore within him, what struggles he had against the temptations which attacked his most excellent character, or what comfort in adversities and what sweet joys Your bread had for the hidden mouth of his spirit, when meditating on Your Word, I could neither imagine nor had experienced. And he did not know the tides of my feeling or the abyss of my danger. I could not ask him what I wanted when I wanted because I was shut out both from his listening ear and his counsel by multitudes of busy people whose weaknesses he served. When he was not involved with them, which was not often, he was either refreshing his body with absolutely necessary nourishment or his mind with reading.

When he was reading, his eye glided over the pages, and his heart searched out the meaning; however, his voice and tongue were at rest. Often when we had come to see him, for no man was forbidden to enter, nor was it his custom that any who came should be announced to him, we saw him reading to himself in this way, and never otherwise. Seeing that he sat silently for so long—for who dares to intrude on one so intent?—we were inclined to depart. We surmised that in the small amount of time which he found free from the din of others' business to refresh his mind, he was reluctant to be interrupted. Perhaps he was afraid that if the author of the book he was reading should present something in an unclear way, that some attentive or perplexed hearer would want him to expound on it or to discuss some of the harder questions, so that if his time was taken up in this way, he could not go through as many volumes as he wanted to. However, the preservation of his voice, which only a little bit of speaking would weaken, might be the real reason that he read to himself. But for whatever reason he did it, certainly in such a man, it was good.

I, however, certainly had no opportunity to inquire what I wanted to from that so holy oracle of Yours—Ambrose's heart—unless the thing might be answered briefly. Those currents within me, if they were to be poured out to him, would require his full attention, but I never found it. I heard him indeed every Lord's day, correctly expounding the Word of Truth (2 Tim. 2:15) among the people, and I was more and more convinced that all the knotty difficulties of those crafty false charges, which our deceivers had knit against the Scriptures, could be unraveled. But when I comprehended, moreover, that Your spiritual sons—whom You have born again through grace—did not conceive of man, created by You after Your own image, as though they believed and conceived of You as limited by human form, although, I had not even a faint or shadowy notion of what a spiritual substance should be, I blushed with joy that I had for so many years barked not against faith but against the fictions of carnal imaginations. So rash and irreverent had I been, that I had judged, condemning, what I ought to have learned through honest inquiry. For You, most high and most near, most secret and most present, who do not have some larger and some smaller limbs but are wholly everywhere and are never confined in space, do not exist in such a bodily shape. Yet You have made man after Your own image, and behold, from head to foot he is contained in space.

Therefore, in my ignorance of how Your image should subsist, I should have knocked and proposed the doubt, "How is this to be believed," not insultingly opposed it, as if I solidly believed something else. Doubt, then, as to what to believe for certain gnawed at my heart even more sharply, and I was even more ashamed that, so long deluded and deceived by the promise of certainties, I had with childish error and vehemence babbled of so many uncertainties. That they were falsehoods became clear to me later. However, I was certain that they were uncertain and that I had formerly considered them certain, when with a blind contentiousness I accused Your church, which I now discovered, not to the extent that I believed it taught the truth, that at least it did not teach that for which I had grievously judged her. So I was put to shame and changed my outlook, and I rejoiced, my God, that the one and only church, the body of Your only Son, in which the name of Christ had been put upon me as an infant, had no taste for infantile conceits, nor in its sound doctrine maintained any tenet which should confine You, the Creator of all, in space, that however great and large you might be, that you were still confined everywhere by the limits of a human form.

I rejoiced also that the old Scriptures of the law and the prophets were laid before me, not to be perused with that eye to which they had earlier seemed absurd when I reviled Your holy ones for thinking of them in that way, since indeed they did not think so. With joy I often heard Ambrose in his sermons to the people, very diligently recommend this text as a standard for living, "The letter killeth, but the spirit giveth life" (2 Cor. 3:6). He drew aside the mysterious veil, laying open spiritually what according to a literal reading seemed to be unsound teaching. Nothing in his teaching offended me, though he taught things that I did not yet know to be true. I kept my heart from assenting to anything, afraid to fall headlong, but by hanging in suspense, I was killed in a worse manner.

I wished to be as assured of the things I did not see as I was that seven and three are ten. I was not so mad as to think that even this could not be comprehended, but I desired to have other things as clear as this, whether bodily things, which were not present to my senses, or spiritual things which I did not know how to conceive, except bodily. If I had believed, I might have been cured, in that the eyesight of my soul, being cleared, might have in some way been directed to Your truth, which always abides and in no way fails. But like someone who has tried a bad physician is afraid to trust himself with a good one, so it was with the health of my soul, which could not be healed except by believing. For fear that it would believe falsehoods, it refused to be cured, resisting Your hands—You, who have prepared the medicines of faith and have applied them to the diseases of the whole world, and who have given to them great authority to heal.

Being led, however, from my former beliefs to prefer Christian doctrine, I felt that its way was more unassuming and honest in that it required belief in things which could not be demonstrated, whether it was that they themselves could be demonstrated, but not to certain people, or that they could not be demonstrated at all. Whereas among the Manichees our willingness to believe was mocked by a promise of certain knowledge, when we were told to believe so many extremely false and absurd things because they could not be demonstrated. Then You, Lord, persuaded me little by little with Your most tender and merciful hand, as you moved and formed my heart.

I considered what innumerable things I believed in, which I did not see or for which I was not present when they were done: many things in secular history, many reports of places and of cities which I had not seen, many reports of friends, many reports of physicians, constant reports from other men. Unless we believe these things, we would do nothing at all in this life. Lastly, I considered with how unshaken an assurance I believed what parents I had been born to, which I could not know unless I had not believed what others had told me. Considering all this, You persuaded me that it was not they who believed Your Scriptures, which You have established with such great authority among almost all nations, but they who did not believe them, who were to be faulted, and that those who might say to me, "How do you know those Scriptures to have been imparted unto mankind by the Spirit of the one true and most true God?" were not to be listened to. This last thing was to be believed most of all, since no perverse and blasphemous questionings, of all that multitude which I had read in the self-contradicting philosophers, could wring this belief from me: that You exist, whatever Your nature is—what, I did not know—and that the government of human things belongs to You.

This I believed, sometimes more strongly and sometimes more weakly. Yet, I always believed that You exist and that you care for us, though I was ignorant about what to believe about Your nature and what was the true way that led up or led back to You. Since, then, we were too weak to discover truth through abstract reasoning, we needed the authority of Holy Writ. I had now begun to believe that You would never have given such perfect authority to that Scripture in every land had You not purposed to be believed in it and sought through it. Now those things that sounded strange in the Scripture used to offend me, but having heard many of them satisfactorily explained, I attributed this to the depth of their mysteries. Its authority appeared to me all the more honorable and more worthy of reverential belief in that, while it was accessible for all to read, it retained the majesty of its mysteries within its more profound meanings, stooping to all in the great plainness of its words and lowliness of its style, yet calling forth the most intense study from those who are not light of heart. It does this so it might receive all in its open heart and, through difficult passages, waft over towards You a few more, yet many more than if it did not stand alone on such a height of authority, or if it did not draw multitudes within its heart by its holy lowliness. I pondered these things, and You were with me. I sighed, and You heard me. I wavered, and You guided me. I wandered through the broad way of the world (see Matthew 7:13), and You did not forsake me.

I longed for honors, wealth, and marriage, and You mocked me. In these desires I underwent very bitter trials, and You were the more gracious, the less You allowed anything to grow sweet to me which was not You. Behold my heart, Lord, whose will it is that I should remember all this and confess to You. Let my soul cling to You now that You have freed it from that fast-holding birdlime of death. How wretched it was! And You irritated its painful wound, so that forsaking all else, it might be converted to You, who are above all and without whom all things would be nothing, so that it might be converted and be healed.

How miserable I was then, and how You dealt with me to make me feel my misery on that day when I was preparing to recite an elaborate praise of the Emperor. In this tribute I was to speak many lies and, lying, was to be applauded by those who knew I lied, and my heart was racing with these anxieties and boiling with the feverishness of consuming thoughts. As I was going along one of the streets of Milan, I observed a poor beggar who was, I suppose, drunk, joking and happy. I sighed and spoke to the friends around me of the many sorrows of our frenzies. That for all our efforts, such as those in which I then toiled, being dragged along under the impulse of desire, the burden of my own wretchedness, and, by being dragged, compounding it, we still aimed to arrive at that same happiness at which that beggar-man had arrived before us, we who would perhaps never attain it. What he had obtained by means of a few pennies he had begged, the joy of a temporary happiness, was the same thing I was plotting by much toilsome turning and winding. For he did not have the true joy; yet I, with my ambitious designs, was seeking one much less true. He was happy, I was anxious; he was carefree, I was full of fears. But if anyone should any ask me if I would rather be lighthearted or fearful, I would answer, lighthearted. Again, if anyone should ask if I would rather be as the beggar was or what I then was, I would choose to be myself, though worn with cares and fears. But I would answer out of wrong judgment, for was it the truth? I ought not to prefer myself to him because I was more learned than he, since I had no joy in it but only sought to please men by it, not in order to instruct them but simply to please them. Therefore, You broke my bones with the staff of Your correction.

Get away from my soul, you who say to it, "It makes a difference, where a man's joy comes from. That beggar-man delighted in drunkenness; you desired to delight in glory." What glory, Lord? That which is not in You. For even as his was not true delight, that was not true glory, and it conquered my soul even more. He that very night would get over his drunkenness. But I had slept and risen again with mine and was to sleep again, and would arise again with it, how many days, only You, God, know. But it does make a difference where a man's joy comes from. I know it, and the joy of a faithful hope lies incomparably beyond such vanity. So at that point, he was then beyond me because he truly was the happier one, not only because he was thoroughly drenched in merriment, while I was disemboweled with cares, but because he, by good wishes, had gotten wine, while I, by lying, was seeking empty, swelling praise. Many things like this I said then to my friends at that time, and I often noted in them how it fared with me. I found it went badly with me, which grieved and doubled that very sickness. If any prosperity smiled on me, I was afraid to catch at it, for almost before I could grasp it, it flew away.

These things we, who were living as friends together, bemoaned together, but chiefly and most ultimately I spoke about them with Alypius and Nebridius. Alypius was born in the same town that I was, of people of prominence, but he was younger than I. He had studied under me, both when I first lectured in our town and afterwards at Carthage, and he greatly loved me because I seemed to him to be kind and learned. And I loved him because of his great tendency towards virtue which was notable enough in one of his young age. Yet the whirlpool of Carthaginian habits, among which those idle spectacles are hotly followed, had drawn him into the madness of the circus. But while he was miserably tossed in that, I had a public school and taught rhetoric there. Up until then, he had not known of my teaching because of some unpleasantness that had risen between his father and me. At that time, I had found out how dearly he adored the circus and was deeply grieved that he seemed likely to throw, or had thrown away, such great promise. Yet I had no means of advising or, with a sort of restraint, reclaiming him, either by the kindness of a friend or the authority of a master. I had supposed that he thought of me as his father did, but that was not the case. He put aside his father's opinion in that matter, and he began to greet me. Sometimes he would come into my lecture room, listen a little, and be gone.

I, however, had forgotten to deal with him, so that he should not, through a blind and headlong desire of vain pastimes, ruin so good a mind. But You, Lord, who guide the course of all You have created, had not forgotten him who was one day to be among Your children as a priest. Therefore, the amendment of his ways may clearly be attributed to Yourself; You effected it through me, though I did not know it. One day, as I sat in my accustomed place with my scholars before me, he entered, greeted me, sat down, and applied his mind to what I was then expounding upon. I had by chance a certain passage in hand, and while I was explaining it, an analogy from the circus races occurred to me, which I thought was likely to make what I would convey more pleasant and clear, seasoned with biting mockery of those whom that madness had enslaved. God, You know at that time I did not think of curing Alypius of that infection. But he took it wholly to himself and thought that I had said it simply for his sake. And while another would have taken offense with me over it, that right-minded youth took it as the basis for being offended at himself and for loving me more fervently.

You had said it long ago and put it into Your Book, "Rebuke a wise man, and he will love thee" (Prov. 9:8). I had not rebuked him, but You, who employ all, whether they know it or not, in that order which You Yourself know—and that order is just—did of my heart and tongue make burning coals by which to set on fire the hopeful mind, thus languishing, and so cure it. Let him be silent in Your praises, who does not consider Your mercies, which confess to You out of my inmost soul.

When he heard that speech, he burst out of that deep pit, in which he was willfully plunged, and was blinded with its wretched pastimes. He shook his mind with a strong self-discipline, at which all the filth of the circus pastimes flew off of him, nor did he return there again. With this, he prevailed upon his unwilling father that he might be my student. His father, then, gave way and gave in. And Alypius, beginning to study with me again, became involved in the same superstition with me, loving in the Manichees that show of self-restraint which he supposed to be true and genuine. On the contrary, it was a senseless and seducing self-restraint, ensnaring precious souls who are yet unable to reach the depths of virtue, yet it readily deceived them with the surface of what was but a shadowy and counterfeit virtue.

He, not forsaking that secular course which his parents had insisted he pursue, had gone ahead of me to Rome to study law, and there he was unbelievably carried away with an incredible eagerness for the gladiator shows. At first utterly averse to and detesting such spectacles, he was met one day by chance by some of his acquaintances and fellow students coming from dinner, and they with a friendly violence hauled him, vehemently refusing and resisting, into the amphitheater for these cruel and deadly shows. He protested: "Though you haul my body to that place, and set me there, can you also force me to turn my mind or my eyes to those shows? I shall then be absent while present, and so shall overcome both you and them." Hearing this, they led him on nevertheless, desirous perhaps to try that very thing, to see whether or not he could do as he said.

After they had arrived and found seats where they could, the whole place caught fire with that savage pastime. But he, by closing his eyes, did not allow his mind to run after such evils. If only he could have stopped his ears also! For whenever a gladiator fell during the fight, the whole audience let out a mighty cry; this had a strong impact on him, and he was overcome by curiosity. He opened his eyes, prepared to despise and be superior to it, whatever it was, even while seeing it, and he was stricken with a deeper wound in his soul than the gladiator, whom he wanted to see, had experienced in his body. He fell more miserably than the one whose fall caused that mighty outcry. The noise entered through his ears and unlocked his eyes to make way for the striking and beating down of a soul that was bold rather than resolute, and the weaker because it had presumed on itself when it ought to have relied on You.

At the moment he saw that blood, he drank down savageness and did not turn away from it. He was riveted to it, drinking in frenzy unawares, and was delighted with that wicked fight and intoxicated with the bloody pastime. Nor was he now the same man that he was when he had first come; he had become one of the crowd, a true associate of the acquaintances who had brought him to that place. Why say more? He saw, shouted, and was inflamed, and he carried away with him the madness which would drive him to return, not only with those who first drew him there, but also before them, and to draw in others as well. Yet You plucked him out of this with a most strong and merciful hand, and You taught him to have confidence not in himself, but in You. But this was after.

This was already being stored up in his memory to act as a cure later on. So also was what happened to him when he was still studying under me at Carthage. One midday in the marketplace when he was thinking over what he was to recite from memory, as students do, You allowed him to be arrested as a thief by the officers of the marketplace. I suspect that you, our God, allowed this for no other reason but that he, who was later to prove so great a man, would already begin to learn that in judging cases, a man should not readily be condemned by another man out of a rash credulity.

He had been walking up and down by himself in front of the court with his notebook and pen, when a young man, a lawyer, the real thief who had secretly brought a hatchet, got in, unknown to Alypius, as far as the leaden gratings which fence in the silversmiths' shops, and began to cut away the lead. The noise of the hatchet being heard, the silversmiths beneath began to make a stir and sent some to apprehend whomever they should find. Hearing their voices, the thief ran away, leaving his hatchet, because he was afraid to be seized. Now, Alypius, who had not seen him enter, noticed him leaving and saw the speed with which he made away. Curious about it, he entered the place, found the hatchet, and stood there, wondering and thinking about it. Then, those who had been sent found him alone with the hatchet in his hand, the noise of which had startled and brought them there. They seized him and hauled him away, and, gathering the inhabitants of the marketplace together, boasted of having caught a notorious thief. So he was being led away to be taken before the judge.

But Alypius was to be instructed only this far. For without delay, Lord, You proved his innocence, of which You alone were witness. As he was being led either to prison or to punishment, a certain architect met them, who had chief responsibility for the public buildings. They were especially glad to meet this man, who often suspected them of stealing the goods lost out of the marketplace, as though to show him at last by whom these thefts were being committed. He, however, had seen Alypius several times at the house of a certain senator, to whom he often went to pay his respects. Recognizing him immediately, he took him

139

aside by the hand, and asking him how such a misfortune had happened, he listened to the whole story. He then directed everyone, amid much uproar and threats, to go with him. So they came to the house of the young man who had done the deed. There, in front of the door, was a boy so young as to be likely, not anticipating any harm to his master, to disclose the whole thing. For he had gone with his master to the marketplace. As soon as Alypius remembered this, he told the architect, who showed the hatchet to the boy and asked him, "Whose is this?" "Ours," said the boy immediately, and upon further questioning, he revealed everything. Thus the crime was transferred to that house, and the multitude which had begun to triumph over Alypius was ashamed. Alypius, who was to administer Your Word and to try many cases in Your Church, went away better experienced and instructed.

Alypius, then, I had found at Rome. He bound himself to me with a very strong tie and went with me to Milan, so that he would not have to leave me and so that he might practice something of the law he had studied, more to please his parents than himself. He had sat three times as an assessor, showing an honesty that very much amazed people; he, on his part, was more amazed at others who could prefer gold to honesty. Moreover, his character was tried, not only with the bait of covetousness but with the incentive of fear. At Rome he was Assessor to the Count of the Italian Treasury. There was at that time a very powerful senator, to whose favors many stood indebted, and whom many feared. Because of his power, he naturally wanted to be granted something which was not lawfully allowed. Alypius resisted it, and a bribe was offered him. With all his heart, he scorned it. Threats were held out, but he trampled upon them. Everyone was amazed at such an unusual spirit, which neither desired the friendship nor feared the enmity of one so great and so mightily renowned for his great capacity for doing good or evil. And the very judge, whose counselor Alypius was, although he also did not approve of the special privilege, did not openly refuse it. Instead, he put the matter off upon Alypius, alleging that Alypius would not allow him to do it; for had the judge allowed it, Alypius would certainly have gone against him.

Yet, he was very nearly seduced because of one thing in regard to his academic pursuits. He wanted books copied for him at Praetorian (discount) prices, but consulting justice, he changed his decision for the better, considering justice by which he was hindered to be of more value than the power which he was allowed. These are just small things, but "he that is faithful in that which is least is faithful also in much" (Luke 16:10). And that which proceeds out of the mouth of Your Truth cannot be empty:

If therefore ye have not been faithful in the unrighteous mammon, who will commit to your trust the true riches? And if ye have not been faithful in that which is another man's, who shall give you that which is your own?
(Luke 16:11–12)

This is what he was like, and he clung to me at that time. He also wavered with me in purpose regarding what we should take in life.

Nebridius also, who having left his native country near Carthage, and Carthage itself where he had lived for so long, leaving behind his excellent family estate and house and a mother who was not to follow him, had come to Milan for no other reason, except that he might live with me in a most ardent search after truth and wisdom. Like me he sighed, like me he wavered, an ardent searcher after true life and a most acute examiner of the most difficult questions. Therefore, there existed the mouths of three impoverished people, sighing out their needs to one another and waiting upon You that You would "givest them their meat in due season" (Ps. 145:15). In all the bitterness, which by Your mercy followed our worldly affairs, as we looked for its purpose and asked why we should suffer all this, darkness met us, and we turned away groaning and saying, "How long shall these things be?" We often said this, but in saying so we did not forsake our worldly affairs, for nothing certain had yet dawned upon us which we might embrace in order to forsake them.

And I, viewing and reviewing these things, was extremely amazed at the length of time that had passed since my nineteenth year in which I had begun to be inflamed with the desire for wisdom and had settled that, when I had found it, I would abandon all the empty hopes and lying frenzies of vain desires. And here I was now in my thirtieth year, sticking in the same mire, greedy to enjoy temporal things which passed away and wasted my soul, while I said to myself, "Tomorrow I shall find it; it will clearly appear, and I shall grasp it. Faustus will come and clear everything! Oh, you great men, you academicians, it is true then, that the meaning of life cannot be found with any certainty! No, let us search more diligently and not despair. Look, things in the ecclesiastical books which sometimes seemed absurd are not absurd to us now and may be understood in a different light.

"I will take my stand, where, as a child, my parents placed me, until the clear truth is found out. Where will it be sought or when? Ambrose has no leisure; we have no leisure to read; where will we even find the books? Where or when can they be obtained? From whom could I borrow them? Let set times be appointed and certain hours be ordered for the health of our soul. Great hope has dawned; the church does not teach what we thought and what we foolishly accused it of. Her knowledgeable members consider it irreverent to believe God to be bounded by the figure of a human body. Do we doubt to 'knock,' that the rest 'shall be opened' (Matt. 7:7)? The mornings our students take up; what do we do during the rest? Why not this? But when then can we pay court to our great friends, whose favor we need? When can we write treatises that we may sell to students? When can we refresh ourselves, resting our minds from the intensity of these cares?

"Perish everything; let us dismiss these empty vanities and apply ourselves to the one search for truth! Life is vain, death uncertain; if it steals upon us all of a sudden, in what state will we depart from here? And where will we learn what we have neglected to learn here? And will we not rather suffer the punishment of this negligence? What if death itself should cut off and end all care and feeling? This must then be determined. But God forbid this! It is no vain and empty thing that the incomparable dignity of the authority of the Christian faith has spread over the whole world. Never would such and so many great things be created by God on our behalf, if, with the death of the body, the life of the soul also came to an end. Why delay then to abandon worldly hopes and give ourselves wholly to seeking after God and the blessed life? But wait! Even those things are pleasant; they give a great deal of enjoyment. We must not easily abandon them, for it would be a shame to return again to them. See, it would not be very hard now to obtain some position, and then what should we wish for? We have a storehouse of powerful friends. If nothing else is offered to us and we are in a hurry, at least a presidentship may be given to us, and a wife with some money, so that she does not increase our expenses, and this will be the limit of my desire. Many great men, who are very worthy of imitation, have given themselves to the study of wisdom as married men."

While I thought over these things, and these winds of confusion shifted and drove my heart this way and that, time went by, but I delayed turning to the Lord. From day to day I continually put off living in You, and I daily postponed dying to myself. Desiring a happy life, I was afraid to look for it where it could truly be found and actually fled from it while seeking it. I thought I would be too miserable unless folded in female arms. Not having tried the medicine of Your mercy which would have cured that weakness, I did not think of looking to it. As for self-restraint, I supposed that it was in our power, though in myself I did not find that power. I foolishly did not know that no one can be abstinent unless You give him the ability and that You would give it, if I pounded Your ears with fervent prayer, and if with a steadfast faith I did cast my care on You.

In fact, Alypius kept me from marrying, insisting that it would be impossible for us to live together in the pursuit of wisdom in an undistracted way, as we had wanted for so long. He himself was at that time amazingly pure in this regard. It was even more amazing, considering the fact that at the beginning of his youth he had begun to be promiscuous but had not continued in it. Rather, he had felt remorse and revulsion in it, and had lived a chaste life from that time until now. But I countered him with examples of those who, as married men, had cherished wisdom and served God acceptably, and had retained their friends and loved them faithfully. I fell far short of their exceptional character and, bound with the disease of the flesh and its deadly sweetness, drew along my chain, dreading freedom. As if my wound had been chafed, I shook off his good argument as if it were given by the hand of one that would unchain me. Moreover, the serpent spoke to Alypius through me. (See Genesis 3:1.) By my convoluted ideas, I lay in his path pleasurable snares in which his virtuous and free feet might be entangled.

He was amazed that I, whom he highly regarded, should stick so fast in the birdlime of that pleasure, as to protest, as often as we discussed it, that I could never lead a celibate life. When I saw his amazement I argued in my defense that there was a great difference between his momentary and scarcely-remembered knowledge of that life, which enabled him to easily reject it, and my continued experience of it. If the honorable name of marriage were then added to it, he should not wonder why I could not condemn sexual activity. Then he also began to desire to be married, not because he was overcome with passion for such pleasure, but out of curiosity. He said he would be happy to discover what it was in my life, which was pleasing to him, without which my existence would seem to me to be a punishment instead of a life. His mind, free from that chain, was amazed at my bondage, and through that amazement he moved forward into a desire to try it. From there he might have experimented with it himself and then perhaps sunk into that bondage at which he had been amazed. He was willing to make "a covenant with death" (Isa. 28:15), for he who loves danger, will fall into it. Whatever honor there is in a well-ordered marriage and family life interested us only slightly. For the most part, the habit of satisfying an insatiable appetite tormented me and held me captive, and an admiring amazement was leading him captive. This is the state we were in until You, Most High, not forsaking us in the weakness of our flesh and pitying our wretchedness, came to our help in marvelous and unseen ways.

Continual effort was made to have me married. I wooed, and I was accepted, chiefly through my mother's efforts, in order that once married, the health-giving baptism might cleanse me. She rejoiced that I was daily being conformed to this, and she observed that her prayers and Your promises were being fulfilled in my faith. In fact, at this time, both at my request and because of her own longing, she daily begged You with heartfelt pleas to show her something concerning my future marriage. You never would. She did perceive certain false and imaginary things that the mind dreams up when it is contemplating such things. She told me about these, but not with the confidence she was accustomed to having when You showed her anything. Rather, she downplayed them. She could, she said, through a certain feeling, which she could not express in words, discern between Your revelations and dreams that came our of her own soul. Yet the matter was pressed, and a maiden was asked in marriage. She was two years under the suitable age, and, because she was pleasing, I waited for her.

Many of us friends, conferring about and detesting the turbulent turmoil of human life, had debated and had now almost decided to live apart from the concerns and the bustle of men. We were going to arrange it this way: each of us was to bring whatever we might acquire on our own and combine everything into one household. This would be done so that through the integrity of our friendship nothing would belong exclusively to any particular person; rather, everything collected from everybody, would belong to each and to all of us. We thought there might be about ten people in this community, some of whom were very rich, especially Romanianus our townsman, who had been a special friend of mine since childhood. The burdensome entanglements of his business affairs had brought him up to court, and he was the one most eager for this project. His voice had great weight because his ample estate far exceeded any of the rest of us. We had also decided that two officers appointed each year would provide for everything we needed; the rest of the money would be left undisturbed. But when we began to consider whether the wives, which some of us already had and others hoped to have, would allow this, our great plan, which was taking shape so well, fell to pieces in our hands, was completely destroyed, and cast aside. From that time on we took to sighing and groaning, and our steps followed the broad and beaten paths of the world. (See Matthew 7:13.) Many thoughts were in our hearts, but "the counsel of the LORD standeth for ever" (Ps. 33:11). In the wisdom of Your counsel You scoffed at our thoughts and prepared Your own, purposing to give us "meat in due season" and to open Your hand and to fill our souls with blessing (Ps. 145:15–16).

Meanwhile my sins were being multiplied, and my mistress was torn from my side as a hindrance to my marriage. My heart, which clung to her, was torn and wounded and bleeding. She returned to Africa, vowing to You never to know any other man, leaving our son with me. But I, who could not imitate a woman, was miserable and impatient since it would be two years before I was to be married. I was not so much a lover of marriage as I was a slave to lust, and so I procured another woman, although not as a wife, so that by slavish dependence to a lasting habit, the disease of my soul might be maintained, its strength sustained or even increased, into the estate of marriage. The wound which had been made by being cut off from my mistress had not been healed. But after becoming inflamed and causing very sharp pain, it turned gangrenous, and my pains became less piercing but more desperate.

Praise and glory to You, Fountain of Mercies. I was becoming more miserable, and You were drawing nearer. Your right hand was continually ready to pluck me out of the mire and to wash me thoroughly, but I did not know it. Nor did anything call me back from a yet deeper gulf of carnal pleasures but the fear of death and of Your judgment to come, which never left me in the midst of all my searching. And in my debates with my friends Alypius and Nebridius on the nature of good and evil, I would have held to the teachings of Epicurus if I had not believed that after death there remained a life for the soul and places of reward or punishment, according to what men deserve, which Epicurus would not believe. And I asked, "If we were immortal and lived in perpetual bodily pleasure without fear of losing it, why should we not be happy, or what else should we seek?" I did not know that great misery was involved in this very question. Having deteriorated and been blinded in this way, I could not discern that light of excellence and beauty which was to be embraced for its own sake, which the eye of flesh cannot see, and which is only seen by the inner man. Nor did I, being miserable, consider the evil source which influenced me to take pleasure in discussing these foul things with my friends. In addition, I could not, even according to the ideas I then had of happiness, be happy without friends no matter how many carnal pleasures I indulged in. And yet I loved these friends for their own sake, and I felt that I was also loved by them for my own sake.

Oh crooked paths! Woe to my audacious soul (Isa. 3:9), which hoped, by forsaking You, to gain something better! It has turned, and turned again, upon its back, sides, and belly, yet all was painful, and You alone are rest. And yet, You are at hand, and You deliver us from our wretched wanderings and place us in Your path. You comfort us and say, "Run; I will carry you; I will bring you through; there also will I carry you." (See Isaiah 46:4.)

Book Seven

Augustine's thirty-first year. Gradually extricated from his errors, but still having material conception of God. Much aided by an argument of Nebridius. Sees that the cause of sin lies in free will. Rejects the Manichean heresy, but cannot altogether embrace the doctrine of the church. Recovered from the belief in astrology, but miserably perplexed about the origin of evil. Is led to find in the Platonists the seeds of the doctrine of the divinity of the Word, but not of his humiliation; hence he obtains clearer notions of God's majesty, but, not knowing Christ to be the mediator, remains estranged from Him. All his doubts removed by the study of Holy Scripture, especially the apostle Paul.

My evil and abominable youth was now past, and I was moving into early manhood. I became more defiled by vain things as I grew in years. I could not imagine anything except what I was accustomed to seeing with my own eyes. I did not think of You, God, as having the form of a human body. From the time I began to learn anything about wisdom, I had always avoided this and rejoiced that I had found the same in the faith of the church. But how else was I to conceive of You, the sovereign, only true God! In my inmost soul, I believed that You are not corruptible, injurable, nor changeable because—I am not certain from where or how I knew this—I still clearly saw and was convinced that that which can be corrupted must be inferior to that which cannot be corrupted. What could not be injured I preferred unhesitatingly to what could receive injury, the unchangeable to things subject to change. My heart passionately cried out against all the phantoms of my imagination, and with this one blow I sought to beat away from the eye of my mind that whole unclean swarm which buzzed around it. But, they were hardly put off, when, in the twinkling of an eye, they again gathered thick about me, flew against my face, and clouded it, so that though I did not think of you as having the form of the human body, I was constrained to conceive of You—that incorruptible, uninjurable, and unchangeable One which I preferred more than the corruptible, injurable, changeable—as being in space, whether infused into the world or diffused infinitely outside it. Because whatever I conceived, outside of space, seemed to me to be nothing, altogether nothing, not even a void, as if an entry were taken out of its place, and the place remained empty of any body at all, of earth, water, air, or heaven, yet it still remained a void place, a spacious nothing.

I, then, being dense-hearted, and not even making sense to myself, believed that whatever was not extended over certain spaces, nor diffused nor condensed nor contracted, or which did not or could not receive some of these dimensions, was altogether nothing. For my heart only imagined the kinds of things my eyes were accustomed to seeing. And I did not yet understand that the conception of the mind, by which I formed those very images, was not like that either, and yet it could not have imagined them had itself not been some great thing. I also tried to imagine You, Life of my life, in this way, as vast, penetrating in all directions through infinite spaces the whole mass of the universe and beyond, through unmeasurable limitless spaces. Then the earth should have You, the heaven have You, all things have You, and they would be limited by You but You would not be limited anywhere. The body of air which is above the earth does not hinder the light of the sun from passing through it. The light penetrates it, not by bursting or by cutting it but by filling it entirely. Because of this I thought that not only was the body of heaven, air, and sea penetrable by You, but also the earth, so that in all its parts, the greatest as well as the smallest, it admitted Your presence through a secret inspiration, inside and outside, directing all things which You have created.

So I guessed, only because I was unable to conceive of anything else, but it was false. In this conception, a greater part of the earth would contain a greater portion of You, and a lesser part, a lesser portion of You. All things would in some way be full of You; the body of an elephant would contain more of You than would a sparrow because it is much larger and takes up more room. In this way, You would make the various portions of Yourself present to the various portions of the world in fragments: large amounts to the large, small amounts to the small. This is not Your nature, but You had not yet enlightened my darkness (Ps. 18:28).

It was enough for me, Lord, to oppose those men who were themselves deceived while they were deceiving others; they were mute even as they talked since they did not proclaim Your word. It was enough to answer them in the same way in which Nebridius used to address the question while we were still in Carthage and which dumfounded all of us who heard it: "Regarding that supposed nation of darkness, which the Manichees like to set as an opposing entity against You, what could it have done to You had You refused to fight with it? For, if they answered, 'it would have done You some harm,' then You would be subject to injury and decay. But if 'it could do You no harm,' then there would be no reason for You to fight with it, fighting in such a way that a certain portion or member of You, or offspring of Your very being, would be mingled with opposing powers and natures not created by You, and would be so corrupted and changed for the worse that it would be turned from happiness into misery and need assistance, by which it might be freed and purified. In the case where this offspring of Your being is the human soul, and it is enslaved, defiled, and corrupted, Your Word, which is free, pure, and whole, would have the ability to relieve it. Yet, on the other hand, Your Word itself would also be corruptible because it would exist as one and the same substance. So then, if they should affirm that You, whatever You are, that is, Your nature by which You exist, are incorruptible, then all these sayings are false and detestable. But if they should say You are corruptible, this very line of reasoning shows this also to be false and revolting." This argument then of Nebridius sufficed against those who completely deserved to be vomited out of an overstuffed stomach. For they had no escape, without horrible blasphemy of heart and tongue, for thinking and speaking of You in this way.

Although I believed and was firmly persuaded that You, our Lord, the true God, did not only make our souls but also our bodies, and not only our souls and bodies, but all beings and all things that are not able to be defiled and altered and are in no way changeable, I still did not yet understand, clearly and without difficulty, the cause of evil. I perceived that whatever it was, it was to be sought out in such a way that would not constrain me to believe that the unchangeable God could be changeable, for fear that I would become the evil which I was seeking out. Therefore, I sought it out, so far free from anxiety, certain of the untruth of what these men (the Manicheans) held, from whom I shrank with my whole heart. I saw that through inquiring about the origin of evil, they were filled with evil, in that they preferred to think that Your being is subject to evil, rather than that they could ever commit it.

And I strained to understand what I was hearing now, that free will was the means of our doing evil and that Your just judgment was the reason we suffer from evil. But I was not able to discern it clearly. So then, in endeavoring to draw my soul's vision out of that deep pit, I was again plunged into it; and as often as I endeavored, I was plunged back again. But this did lift me a little into Your light. I knew that I had a will as surely as I knew I lived. Therefore, when I willed or refused to will something, I was most sure that it was none other than I who was doing the willing or refusing to will, and I all but saw that there was the cause of my sin. But I believed that I suffered rather than was responsible for the things I did against my will. I considered this to be my punishment rather than my fault. However, I believed that You are just and quickly acknowledged to myself that I was not unjustly punished.

I also asked myself, "Who made me? Did not my God, who is not only good, but goodness itself? Then how did I come to want to do evil and not good so that I am therefore punished justly? Who set this in me and engrafted into me this 'root of bitterness' (Heb. 12:15), seeing that I was wholly formed by my most sweet God? If the Devil were the author of my sin, where does that same devil come from? And if he, who was once a good angel, became a devil through his own perverse will, where did his evil will come from, seeing the perfect nature of angels was made by that most good Creator?" By these thoughts I was again sunk down and choked. Yet I was not brought down to that hell of error, where no man acknowledges You, but would rather think that You suffer evil, than that man commits it.

I was in this way striving to find out the rest, as one who had already discovered that the incorruptible is better than the corruptible; and You, therefore, whatever You are, I confessed to be incorruptible. Never was there a soul, nor will there be, who is able to conceive of anything which is better than You, who are the sovereign and the best good. But since, most truly and certainly, the incorruptible is preferable to the corruptible, as I did now prefer it, if You were not incorruptible, I could have imagined something better than my God. Since I perceived that the incorruptible is preferable to the corruptible, I should have sought You and from Your vantage point observed where evil itself comes from. That is where corruption comes from, by which Your substance can by no means be tarnished. There is no way in which corruption can tarnish our God—by no one's will, by no necessity, by no un-looked-for chance—because He is God, and what He wills is good, and He Himself is that good. But to be corrupted is not good. Nor are You forced to do anything against Your will since Your will is not greater than Your power. But it would be greater, if You were greater than Yourself. For the will and power of God is God Himself. And what can take you by surprise, since You know all things? Nor is there any nature in things unless You know it. So why should we ask again and again, "Why can that substance, which God is, not be corruptible" seeing that if it were so, it would not be God?

I sought to know, "Where does evil come from?" I sought it in an evil way and did not see the evil inherent in my very search. I now placed the whole creation before the eyes of my spirit, whatever we can see in it: sea, earth, air, stars, trees, mortal creatures. I also placed before these eyes whatever we do not see in creation: the firmament of heaven, also all angels, and all the spiritual inhabitants of heaven. But my imagination arranged these same beings in order, as though they were bodies, and I made one great mass of Your creation, distinguished according to types of bodies: some real bodies, some that I myself had imagined as spirits. In my mind I created a huge mass, not as it was, which I could not know, but what I thought was agreeable, yet finite in every way. But I imagined that You, Lord, were surrounding and penetrating it on every part, though in every way infinite.

It was as if there were a sea, everywhere and on every side, through unmeasured space, only one boundless sea, and that it contained within it some sponge, huge, but limited. That sponge would need, in all its parts, to be filled from that unmeasurable sea. This is how I conceived Your creation, itself finite, yet full of You, the Infinite. And I said, "Behold God, and behold what God has created. God is good. He is most mightily and incomparably better than all of His creation, yet He, the Good, created them good. See how He surrounds and fills them. Where is evil then? Where does it come from, and how did it creep in here? What is its root, and what is its seed? Or does it have no being? Why then do we fear and avoid what does not exist? Or if we fear it in vain, then that very fear is evil, by which the soul is prodded and tormented for no reason. Yes it is evil, and it is an even greater evil, since we fear when we have nothing to fear. Therefore, either there is the evil which we fear, or else it is evil that we fear.

"Where does evil come from then, seeing that God, who is good, has created all these things good. Indeed, He, the greater and chiefest Good, has created these lesser goods; still, both Creator and created are good. Where does evil come from? Or, was there some evil matter out of which He created. Did He form and order this matter, yet leave something in it which He did not convert into good? Why would he do this? Did He not have a right to reverse and change the whole thing so that no evil would remain in it, seeing that He is almighty? Finally, why would He make anything at all out of it and not rather by the same almightiness cause it not to exist at all? Or, could it then live against His will? Or if it were from eternity, why did He allow it to exist for infinite spaces of times past, and then after a long time want to create something out of it? Or if He now suddenly wanted to create something, the Almighty should have arranged it so that the evil matter would not exist, but He alone would exist, the whole, true, sovereign, and infinite Good. Or if it were not good that He who is good should not also fashion and create something that is good, then, if that evil matter were taken away and brought to nothing, He could form good matter of which to create all things. For He would not be almighty if He could not create something good without the aid of that matter which He Himself had not created."

I brooded over these thoughts in my wretched heart and was overwhelmed with very gnawing cares, for fear that I would die before I had found the truth. Yet the faith of Your Christ, our Lord and Savior, professed in the church, was firmly fixed in my being, though it was in many ways still unformed and fluctuating from orthodox doctrine. Yet my mind did not utterly leave it; rather it daily took in more and more of it.

By this time I also had rejected the lying divinations and ungodly counsel of the astrologers. Let Your own mercies, out of my very inmost soul, confess to You for this also, my God. You, You only—for who else calls us back from the death of all errors, except the Life which cannot die and the Wisdom which, needing no light, enlightens the minds that need it, and by which the universe is directed, down to the whirling leaves of trees?— You made allowance for my obstinacy, with which I struggled against Vindicianus, a sharp-witted old man, and Nebridius, a young man of admirable talents. The first vehemently affirmed, and the latter often, though with some doubtfulness said, "There is no art with which we can foresee things to come; rather, men's conjectures are a sort of lottery. Out of many things which they said would come to pass, some actually did, unbeknownst to them who spoke it, who happened to stumble upon it through their speaking."

You then provided me with a friend who often consulted astrologers. He was not yet well-skilled in those arts, but, as I said, curiously consulted with them, yet he knew something, which he said he had heard from his father. He did not know how influential that was in overthrowing my regard for that art. This man then, Firminus by name, having had a liberal education and well taught in rhetoric, consulted me, as one very dear to him, about what, according to his so-called constellations, I thought regarding certain affairs of his in which his worldly hopes had risen. I, who had now begun to lean towards Nebridius's opinion about this, did not altogether refuse to speculate and tell him what came into my undecided mind. But I added that I was now almost persuaded that these were only empty and ridiculous absurdities.

He then told me that his father had poured over such books and had a friend who was as serious about them as he himself was. Through joint study and discussion, they fanned the flame of their desires for these trifles, so that they would observe the exact moments at which even the dumb animals, which bred about their houses, gave birth, and then observed the relative position of the heavens. In this way, they made new experiments in this so-called art. He then said that he had heard from his father that when his mother was about to give birth to him, Firminus, a woman-servant of that friend of his father's was also with child, a fact which did not escape her master. The master then took great pains to know the time of birth of even his puppies! And it happened that, the one for his wife and the other for his servant, in computing days, hours, even the lesser divisions of the hours with the most careful observation, both babies were delivered at the same instant. Both were then obliged to have the same horoscopes, even to the minutest points, the one for his son, the other for his newborn slave. As soon as the women began to be in labor, each man gave notice to the other what was happening in their houses. They had messengers ready to send to one another as soon as they had notice of the actual birth, which each easily provided for in his own province, in order to give instant news. Firminus declared that the messengers of the respective parties met at such an equal distance from either house that neither of them could make out any difference in the position of the stars or any other minute points. Yet, Firminus, born in a high estate in his parents' house, ran his course through the gilded paths of life, increased in riches, and was raised to honors, whereas that slave continued to serve his masters, without any relaxation of his yoke, as Firminus, who knew him, told me.

Upon hearing and believing these things, which were related by one of such credibility, all my resistance gave way. I first endeavored to reclaim Firminus himself from that curiosity by telling him that, upon inspecting his constellations, I ought, if I were to predict accurately, to have seen in them parents eminent among their neighbors, a noble family in its own city, high birth, good education, liberal learning. But if that servant had consulted me upon the same constellations, since they were his also, I ought again, to give him an accurate prediction as well, to see in them a very servile lineage, a slavish condition, and everything else utterly the opposite of the former. If I spoke the truth, I should, from the same constellations, make opposite predictions, or if I spoke the same ones I would have to speak falsely. It clearly follows, then, that whatever happened to come true after consulting the constellations, would not have been spoken out of art but out of coincidence, and whatever did not come true would not be due to ignorance of the "art" but rather to the failure of chance.

An opening thus made, I mused on similar things, so that none of those feeble-minded men, who lived by this "profession" and whom I longed to attack and with derision to disprove, could argue against me that Firminus had misinformed me, or that his father had misinformed him. Therefore, I directed my thoughts to those who are born twins. Twins for the most part come out of the womb so near to one another that the small interval of time in between their births, no matter how much importance people place on it, cannot be noted by human observation or be at all expressed in those figures which the astrologer is supposed to examine in order to make a true prediction. However, they cannot be true, for looking into the same figures, he would have had to have made the same prediction for Esau and Jacob; yet the same things did not happen to them. Therefore, he either must speak falsely, or if he does not speak the truth, then, in looking into the same figures, he cannot give the same answer. Not by art, then, but by chance, would he be able to predict accurately. For even though consulters and consulted do not know it, You Lord, most righteous Ruler of the Universe, work it so that by Your hidden inspiration, the consulter will hear what, according to the hidden merits of his soul, he ought to hear out of the unsearchable depth of Your just judgment. Let no man ask You, "What is this? Why is that?" Let him not ask this, for he is only a man.

Now then, my Helper, You had loosed me from those chains, and I sought an answer to the question, "Where does evil come from?" and did not find it. But you did not allow me by any fluctuations of thought to be carried away from the faith in which I believed that You exist and that Your nature is unchangeable, and that You are concerned about men and will judge them, and that in Christ, Your Son, our Lord, and through the Holy Scriptures, which the authority of Your church urged upon me, You have set the way of man's salvation to that life which is to be after this death.

These things being intact and immovably resolved in my mind, I anxiously sought the answer to the question, "Where does evil come from?" How great were the pangs of my overflowing heart, what inward groans I had, my God! Yet even then Your ears were open to me, though I did not know it. When in silence I vehemently sought an answer, those silent sorrows of my soul were strong cries to Your mercy. You knew what I suffered, though no man knew it. For, how much of this was distilled through my tongue into the ears of my closest friends? Did the whole tumult of my soul, which neither time nor speaking could suffice to express, reach them? Yet it all went up to Your hearing, all that I roared out from the groaning of my heart, and my desire was before You, and the light of my eyes was not with me (Ps. 38:9–10), for that was within, I was outside. Not that that was confined to any place, but I was intent on things contained in place, though I found I no resting place there. And they did not so receive me, that I could say, "It is enough; it is well." Nor did they yet allow me to turn back where it might be well enough with me. To these things I was superior, though inferior to You. When I am subject to You, You are my true joy, and You have made what You created below me, subject to me.

This was the true temperament and middle region of my safety, to remain in Your image, and by serving You, to rule the body. But when I rose proudly against You and ran against You, Lord, with my neck, with "the thick bosses of [my] buckler" (Job 15:26), even these inferior things were set above me and pressed me down, and nowhere was there respite or space for breathing. I saw them surround me on all sides in throngs and multitudes. Images of them presented themselves to my mind unsought, when I would return to You, as if they would say to me, "Where are you going, you who are unworthy and defiled?" And these things had grown out of my wound, for You humbled the proud like one who is wounded. Through my own swelling I was separated from You; my pride-swollen face closed up my eyes.

But You, Lord, abide forever, yet You are not angry with us forever because You pity our dust and ashes. It was pleasing in Your sight to correct my deformities, and with inward prods You roused me so that I would be ill at ease until You were revealed to my inward sight. Therefore, by Your secret healing hand my swelling went down, and by the painful anointing of healthful sorrows, the troubled and dimmed eyesight of my mind was being healed daily.

And You, who were first willing to show me how You "resisteth the proud, but giveth grace unto the humble" (James 4:6; 1 Pet. 5:5), and by how great an act of Your mercy You had mapped out for men the way of humility, in that Your "Word was made flesh, and dwelt among [men]" (John 1:14), You obtained for me certain books of the Platonists, translated from Greek into Latin through one who was puffed up with most unnatural pride. In them I read, not in the exact words, but in words to the same effect, supported by many different proofs, that,

> *In the beginning was the Word, and the Word was with God, and the Word was God. The same was in the beginning with God. All things were made by him; and without him was not any thing made.* [That which was made by him is life], *and the life was the light of men. And the light shineth in darkness; and the darkness comprehended it not.* (John 1:1–5)

I also read that the soul of man, though it bears witness to the light, is not itself that light (John 1:8), but the Word of God, being God, is that "true Light, which lighteth every man that cometh into the world" (John 1:9). And that "He was in the

world, and the world was made by him, and the
world knew him not" (John 1:10). But I did not
read there that,

> He came unto his own, and his own received
> him not. But as many as received him, to
> them gave he power to become the sons of
> God, even to them that believe on his name.
> *(John 1:11–12)*

Again I read there that God the Word was
"born, not of blood, nor of the will of the flesh, nor
of the will of man, but of God" (John 1:13). But I
did not read there that "the Word was made flesh,
and dwelt among us" (John 1:14). I traced in those
books that, though it was said in many different
ways, the Son was in the form of the Father and
"thought it not robbery to be equal with God"
(Phil. 2:6), for, naturally, He is the same substance. But those books do not have in them that,

> [He emptied himself], *and took upon him
> the form of a servant, and was made in the
> likeness of men: and being found in fashion
> as a man, he humbled himself, and became
> obedient unto death, even the death of the
> cross. Wherefore God also hath highly ex-
> alted him, and given him a name which is
> above every name: that at the name of Jesus
> every knee should bow, of things in heaven,
> and things in earth, and things under the
> earth; and that every tongue should confess
> that* [the Lord Jesus Christ is in the glory of
> God the Father]. *(Phil. 2:7–11)*

These books also contain the truth that, before all times and above all times, Your only begotten Son remains unchangeable, coeternal with You, and that "of his fulness have [souls] received" (John 1:16) that they may be blessed; and that by having wisdom abiding in them, they are renewed, in order to be wise. But the truth that "in due time Christ died for the ungodly" (Rom. 5:6), and that You "spared not [Your] own Son, but delivered him up for us all" (Rom. 8:32), is not there. For "thou hast hid these things from the wise and prudent, and hast revealed them unto babes" (Matt. 11:25), that they "that labour and are heavy laden" (Matt. 11:28) might come to Him and be refreshed by Him. He is "meek and lowly in heart" (Matt. 11:29), and He guides the meek in judgment, and He teaches the gentle His ways (Ps. 25:9), seeing our loneliness and trouble and forgiving all our sins (Ps. 25:18). But those who are lifted up in the lofty walk of some so-called superior learning do not hear Him saying, "Learn of me; for I am meek and lowly in heart: and ye shall find rest unto your souls" (Matt. 11:29). Although,

> They knew God, they glorified him not as God, neither were thankful; but became vain in their imaginations, and their foolish heart was darkened. Professing themselves to be wise, they became fools. (Rom. 1:21–22)

Therefore I also read there that they had changed the glory of Your incorruptible nature into idols and diverse shapes, "into an image made like to corruptible man, and to birds, and four-footed beasts, and creeping things" (Rom. 1:23), namely, into that Egyptian food for which Esau lost his birthright. (See Genesis 25:33–34.) For this Your firstborn people worshipped the head of a four-footed beast instead of You, turning back towards Egypt in their hearts (Acts 7:39) and bowing Your image, their own soul, before the image of a calf that eats hay (Ps. 106:20). I read about these things here, but I did not feed on them.

It pleased You, Lord, to take away the reproach of diminution from Jacob, that "the elder shall serve the younger" (Gen. 25:23; Rom. 9:12), and You called the Gentiles "into thine inheritance" (Ps. 79:1). I had come to You from among the Gentiles, and I set my mind upon the gold which You willed Your people to take from Egypt, since it belonged to You, wherever it was. (See Exodus 3:22; 11:2.) And to the Athenians You said by Your apostle that in You "we live, and move, and have our being" (Acts 17:28), as one of their own poets had said. Truly, these were Gentile books. But I did not set my mind on the idols of Egypt which they served with Your gold, they "who changed the truth of God into a lie, and worshipped and served the creature more than the Creator" (Rom. 1:25).

Having been warned, therefore, to return to myself, I entered even into my inward self, You being my Guide and my Helper. I entered and saw with the eye of my soul, such as it was, above the same eye of my soul and above my mind, the Light Unchangeable. Not an ordinary light, which everyone can see, nor even a greater light of the same kind, as though the brightness of that light should be made brighter and with its greatness take up all space. The Light was not like this. It was different, far different from all these. And It was not above my soul as oil is above water, as heaven is above earth, but It was above my soul because It made me. And I am below It because I was made by It. He who knows the Truth, knows what that Light is, and he who knows It, knows eternity. Love knows it, O Truth who is Eternity, Love who is Truth, and Eternity who is Love! You are my God; to You do I sigh night and day.

When I first knew You, You lifted me up, that I might see that there was something I have the ability to see and that I was not yet able to see. And You overcame the weakness of my sight, streaming forth Your beams of light upon me very strongly, and I trembled with love and awe. I perceived myself to be far off from You, in a place very unlike You, as if I heard Your voice from on high: "I am the food of grown men. Grow, and you will feed upon Me. You will not change Me into you, like food which you digest, but you will be transformed into Me." And I learned that You "correct man for iniquity" and that You made my soul "to consume away like a [moth]" (Ps. 39:11). And I said, "Is truth therefore nothing because it is not diffused through space, finite or infinite?" You cried to me from afar: "I AM THAT I AM" (Exod. 3:14). I heard, as the heart hears, and I did not have room to doubt; and I would sooner doubt that I live than that truth is not that which is "clearly seen, being understood by things that are made" (Rom. 1:20).

And I observed the other things that are below You, and I perceived that they are neither altogether existent nor altogether nonexistent. They have life, since they are from You, but they do not have life because they are not what You are. For only that which unchangeably remains truly exists. It is then "good for me to [hold fast] to God" (Ps. 73:28), for if I do not remain in Him, I cannot remain in myself. But He remains in Himself and renews all things. You are the Lord my God since You do not stand in need of my goodness. (See Psalm 16:2.)

And it was made manifest to me that those things which can be corrupted are still good. Unless they were good, they could not be corrupted. If they were sovereignly good, they would be incorruptible. If they were not good at all, there would be nothing in them to be corrupted. Corruption injures, but unless it diminished goodness, it could not injure. Then, either corruption does not injure, which cannot be, or all that is corrupted is deprived of good, which is most certain. But if things are deprived of all good, they will cease to be. If they exist and can now no longer be corrupted, they are better than before, because they will live incorruptibly. And what is more monstrous than to claim that things become better by losing all their good? Consequently, if they are deprived of all good, they will no longer exist. Therefore, as long as they exist, they are good. For that reason, whatever exists is good. That evil nature, then, which I sought, about which

I asked "Where does evil come from," is not any substance, for if it were a substance, it would be good. Either it would be an incorruptible substance, and therefore a chief good, or a corruptible substance, which could not be corrupted unless it were good. I perceived, therefore, and it was manifested to me that You made all things good, and there is no substance at all which You did not make. You did not make all things equal; therefore, all things exist because each is good, and altogether very good. This is so because our God made all things "very good" (Gen. 1:31).

To You nothing whatever is evil, and not only to You but also to Your creation as a whole, because there is nothing outside which may break in and corrupt the order which You have appointed to it. But in the various parts of creation, some things, because they are not harmonizing with other parts, are considered evil. Those very things harmonize with other things and are good, and they in themselves are good. All these things which do not completely harmonize, still harmonize with the lower part, which we call earth, which has its own cloudy and windy sky that harmonizes with it. Far be it then that I should say, "These things should not be." If I saw nothing but these, I would indeed long for the better; but still, even for these, I must praise You alone. That You are to be praised can be clearly seen from what you have created on the earth:

Dragons, and all deeps: fire, and hail; snow, and vapours; stormy wind fulfilling [Your]

word: mountains, and all hills; fruitful
trees, and all cedars: beasts, and all cattle;
creeping things, and flying fowl: kings of the
earth, and all people; princes, and all judges
of the earth: both young men, and maidens;
old men, and children: Let them praise
[Your name].   *(Ps. 148:7–13)*

From heaven, these praise You, praise You, our
God:

In the heights...all [Your] *angels...all*
[Your] *hosts...sun and moon...all ye stars of*
light...ye heavens of heavens, and ye waters
that be above the heavens. Let them praise
[Your name].   *(Ps. 148:1–5)*

I did not now long for better things because I
thought about them all. With a sounder judgment
I perceived that the things above are better than
these below, but all things put together are better
than those above by themselves.

There is no soundness in people who are displeased with anything in Your creation, just as
there was none in me when much of what You
have made displeased me. Because I did not dare
to be displeased with my God, I gladly did not
want to consider that anything of Yours displeased
me. That is why I had gone into the opinion of two
substances, and had no rest but talked foolishly.
Returning from there, I had fashioned for myself a
god who existed through infinite measures of all
space. I thought this god was You and placed it in
my heart. Again my soul had become the temple of

its own idol and was abominable to You. But after You had calmed my mind, unbeknownst to me, and closed my eyes so that they would not contemplate vanity (Ps. 119:37), I ceased a little from being my former self, and my frenzy was lulled to sleep. I awoke in You and saw that You are infinite, but in a different manner, and this insight did not come out of my flesh.

I looked back on other things, and I saw that they owed their being to You. They were all finite in You, but in a different way; they did not exist in space because You contain all things in Your hand by Your truth. All things are true insofar as they exist, and there is no falsehood unless that which does not exist is thought to be. I saw that all things did harmonize, not only with their appointed places but with their appointed times. And I saw that You, who alone are eternal, did not begin to work only after innumerable spaces of times spent, because all periods of time, both those which have passed and those which will pass, neither go nor come except through You, as You work and abide.

I perceived and did not find it strange that bread, which is pleasant to a healthy appetite is loathsome to one who is ill, and that light is offensive to sore eyes, while it is delightful to healthy ones. And Your righteousness displeases the wicked; the viper and reptiles, which You have created good, displease them even more. They fit in with the inferior portions of Your creation into which the wicked themselves also fit. The wicked conform more with lower things by how much they are unlike You; they conform to Your superior creatures as they become more like You. I inquired what iniquity was, and I found that it is not a substance, but the perversion of the will, turned aside from You, God, the Supreme, towards these lower things, disemboweling itself and puffing up outwardly.

I marveled that I now loved You, and not an illusion of You. Yet I did not press on to enjoy my God; I was carried up to You by Your beauty and was soon carried down from You by my own weight, sinking with sorrow into these inferior things. This weight was carnal custom. Yet a remembrance of You stayed with me. I did not in any way doubt that there was One to whom I might cleave, but I was not yet ready to cleave to You. For the body which is corrupted presses down the soul, and the earthly tabernacle weighs down the mind that muses upon many things. I was very certain that Your invisible works "from the creation of the world are clearly seen, being understood by the things that are made, even [Your] eternal power and Godhead" (Rom. 1:20). I examined why it was that I admired the beauty of celestial or terrestrial bodies and what assisted me in making sound judgments about things which were fleeting, saying, "This ought to be thus, this ought not to be." I examined, I say, why it was that I made these judgments, seeing that when I judge in this manner, it is because I have found the unchangeable and true eternal truth above my changeable mind.

In this way I moved by degrees from a consideration of the nature of bodies to the soul, which initially perceives through the bodily senses, and moves from there to its inward faculty, to which the bodily senses present external things—the animals have this ability—and from there to the reasoning faculty, to which what is received from the senses of the body is referred to be judged. This faculty, which is also a changeable thing in me, raised itself up to its own understanding and drew my thoughts away from the power of habit, withdrawing itself from those multitudes of contradictory illusions, so that it might in this way discover what that light was, by which it was revived, when, without any doubting, it cried out that the unchangeable was preferable over the changeable. From that time on it also knew that unchangeable, which, if it had not known in some way, it would have had no sure ground on which to prefer it to the changeable. Thus with the flash of one trembling glance it arrived at *that which is*. And then I saw Your invisible things "understood by the things that are made" (Rom. 1:20). But I could not fix my gaze on them, and when my weakness was struck back, I was thrown again on my accustomed habits, carrying along with me only a loving memory and a longing for what I had, as it were, perceived the aroma of but was not yet able to feed on.

Then I sought a way of obtaining strength, sufficient to enjoy You, and I did not find it until I embraced that "mediator between God and men, the man Christ Jesus" (1 Tim. 2:5), "who is over all, God blessed for ever" (Rom. 9:5), who called to me saying, "I am the way, the truth, and the life"

(John 14:6), and mingled with my flesh that food which I was unable to receive. For "the Word was made flesh" (John 1:14), so that Your wisdom, through which You created all things, might provide milk for our infant state. However, I did not hold to my Lord Jesus Christ—I, who was humbled to the Humble One—nor did I yet know where His weakness would lead. Your Word, the Eternal Truth, far above the higher parts of Your Creation, raises the yielded to Himself. In this lower world He built for Himself a lowly habitation out of our clay, in which those who are willing to be humbled could be abased and brought over to Himself. He relieves their swelling and stirs up their love so that they might go on no further in self-confidence, but rather consent to become weak, seeing before their feet the example of the Divinity who was made weak by taking our "coats of skin" (Gen. 3:21), and that wearied, they might cast themselves down upon Him, and He, rising, might lift them up.

I thought otherwise, conceiving of my Lord Christ as only a man of excellent wisdom to whom no one could be equal. Since he was amazingly born of a virgin, He especially seemed, in conformity with that, through the divine care for us, to have attained that great eminence of authority as a living example of one who despised temporal things for the sake of obtaining immortality. What mystery there lay in "The Word was made flesh" (John 1:14), I could not even imagine. From what we know about what is written about Him—that He ate and drank, slept, walked, rejoiced in spirit, was sorrowful, talked with others—I had learned only that flesh did not cling to Your Word by itself, but with the human soul and mind. All who know the unchangeableness of Your Word know this which I now knew, as far as I could, nor did I doubt it at all. To move the limbs of the body at will one moment and not the rest, to be moved by some emotion one moment and not the next, to deliver wise sayings through human language one moment and then to keep silence, belong to soul and mind, which are subject to change. Should these things be falsely written about Him, all the rest would also be in question, and there would not remain in Scripture any saving faith for mankind. Since they were written truthfully, I acknowledged a perfect man to be in Christ, not the body of a man only, nor, with the body, a sensitive soul without a rational mind, but very man himself. I thought of Him not only as being a form of truth, but because of a certain great excellence of human nature and a more perfect share of wisdom, I judged Him to be preferred before all others.

Alypius imagined that Christians believe that God was clothed with flesh to the extent that besides God and flesh, there was no soul at all in Christ, and he did not think that Christ had a human mind. Because he thoroughly believed Christ's recorded actions could only be performed by a living and rational creature, he moved more slowly towards the Christian faith. But when he understood that this false belief was an error of the Apollinarian heretics, he rejoiced in and was conformed to faith. But I confess that it was sometime later that I learned how in that saying, "the Word was made flesh" (John 1:14), the Christian truth is distinguished from the falsehood of Photinus. The rejection of heretics makes the tenets of Your church and sound doctrine stand out more clearly. "For there must be also heresies...that they which are approved may be made manifest among [the weak]" (1 Cor. 11:19).

Having then read those books of the Platonists and been taught to search for spiritual truth, I saw Your "invisible things...understood by the things that are made" (Rom. 1:20). Though thrown back, I perceived what it was that, through the darkness of my mind, I was hindered from contemplating. I was assured that You exist and are infinite, yet not diffused in space, finite or infinite; and that You truly are He who is the same forever, who in no way varies; and that all other things are from You, on this most sure ground alone: that they exist. Of these things I was assured, yet too unsure to enjoy You.

I babbled as one well skilled, but I had not sought Your way in Christ our Savior. I had proven to be killed, not skilled. Now I had begun to wish to seem wise, being filled with my own punishment. Yet I did not mourn over this, but rather I was one who scorned, puffed up with knowledge. Where was that love which builds upon the foundation of humility, which is Christ Jesus? When would these books ever teach it to me? I believe You therefore willed that I should come across these books before I studied Your Scriptures, so that it might be imprinted on my memory how I was affected by them. Then, afterwards, when my spirits were tamed through Your Books and my wounds touched by Your healing fingers, I could discern and distinguish between presumption and confession, between those who saw where they were to go yet did not see the way, and those who saw the way that leads not only to seeing the joyful country but to living in it. If I had first been shaped by Your Holy Scriptures and if You had grown sweet to me in the familiar use of them, and if I had then come across those other volumes, they might perhaps have pulled me away from the solid ground of piety. Or, had I continued in that healthful framework in which I would therefore have been immersed, I might have thought that I could have obtained it by the study of those books alone.

Most eagerly then did I seize the venerable writings of Your Spirit, and chiefly those of the apostle Paul. Consequently, those difficulties, in which he once seemed to contradict himself, and in which the text of his discourse seemed not to agree with the testimonies of the law and the prophets, vanished away. The face of that pure Word appeared to me one and the same, and I learned to "rejoice with trembling" (Ps. 2:11). So I began, and whatever truth I had read in those other books I found here amid the praise of Your grace, so that whoever sees may not glory, as if he had not received not only what he sees but also his ability to see. For what does he have which he has not received? (See 1 Corinthians 4:7.) It is also so that he may not only be admonished to look to You, who are always the same (Ps. 102:27), but also healed, in order to hold on to You. In this way, he who cannot see far away may still walk on that way by which he may arrive, see, and hold on to You.

For though a man is delighted with "the law of God after the inward man" (Rom. 7:22), what will he do with that other law in his members "warring against the law of [his] mind, and bringing [him] into captivity to the law of sin which is in [his] members (Rom. 7:23)? For, You are righteous, Lord, but "we have sinned, and have committed iniquity, and have done wickedly" (Dan. 9:5), and "Thy hand was heavy upon [us]" (Ps. 32:4), and we are justly delivered over to that ancient sinner, the king of death, because he persuaded our will to be like his will, through which he "abode not in [Your] truth" (John 8:44). What will wretched man do? "Who shall deliver [him] from the body of this death" (Rom. 7:24), but only Your grace, through Jesus Christ our Lord, whom You have begotten coeternal and formed "in the beginning of [Your] way" (Prov. 8:22), in whom the prince of this world found "nothing worthy of death" (Luke 23:15), yet killed Him? And the handwriting, that testified against us, was blotted out (Col. 2:14).

Those writings of the Platonists do not contain this. Those pages do not present the image of this piety; the tears of confession; a troubled spirit, which is your sacrifice: "a broken and a contrite heart" (Ps. 51:17); the salvation of the people; the bridal city (see Revelation 21:2); "the earnest of the Spirit" (2 Cor. 1:22; 5:5); the cup of our redemption.

No man sings in those books: "Shall not my soul be submitted to God?" For "from him cometh my salvation. He only is my [God] and my salvation; he is my [guardian]; I shall not be greatly moved" (Ps. 62:1–2). No one in them hears Him call, "Come unto me, all ye that labour" (Matt. 11:28). They scorn learning of Him because He is "meek and lowly in heart" (Matt. 11:29), for these things You have "hid...from the wise and prudent, and hast revealed them unto babes" (Matt. 11:25).

It is one thing to see the land of peace from the mountain's shaggy top and to find no way to it and in vain to endeavor to get to it by unpassable ways, opposed and beset by fugitives and deserters, under their captain, the "lion and the dragon" (Ps. 91:13). It is another thing to keep on the way that leads to it, guarded by the host of the heavenly General, where there are none lying in wait who have deserted the heavenly army, for they avoid it as they would avoid torment itself. These things sank wonderfully into my innermost being when I read the writings of "the least of [Your] apostles" (1 Cor. 15:9) and had meditated upon Your works and trembled exceedingly.

Book Eight

Augustine's thirty-second year. Consults Simplicanus, and from him hears the history of the conversion of Victorinus, and longs to devote himself entirely to God, but is mastered by his old habits. Is still further roused by the history of St. Antony, and the conversion of two courtiers. During a severe struggle, hears a voice from heaven in a child's song, opens Scripture, and is converted with his friend Alypius. His mother's vision fulfilled.

Oh, my God, let me, with thanksgiving, remember and confess to You Your mercies toward me. Let my bones be renewed with Your love, and let them say to You, "Who is like unto thee?" (Ps. 35:10). You have broken "my bonds," and "I will offer to thee the sacrifice of thanksgiving" (Ps. 116:16–17). I will declare how You have broken them, and when they hear this, all who worship You will say, "Blessed be the Lord in heaven and in earth, great and wonderful is His name."

Your words had stuck fast in my heart, and You protected me on all sides. (See Job 1:10.) I was now certain of Your eternal life, though I saw it in a figure and as "through a glass, darkly" (1 Cor. 13:12). Yet I had ceased doubting that there was an incorruptible substance, out of which all other substances came. I did not now desire to be more certain of You, but more steadfast in You. But as for my temporal life, all was shaky, and my heart had to be purged from the "old leaven" (1 Cor. 5:7). The Way, the Savior Himself, pleased me very much, but I still shrank from going through its narrowness. You put it into my mind, and it seemed good in my eyes, to go to Simplicianus, who seemed to me a good servant of Yours, and Your grace shone in him. I had heard also that even from his youth he had lived very devoted to you. Now he had grown older, and because he had spent so many years zealously following Your ways, it seemed likely to me that he had gained much wisdom. So he had. Out of his storehouse of knowledge, I wished that he would tell me, as I set before him my anxieties, which was the best way for one in my situation to walk in Your paths.

I saw that the church was full of people, and one went this way and another that way. I was displeased that I was leading a secular life now that my desires no longer inflamed me as they used to, with hopes of honor and profit. It was a very grievous burden to undergo so heavy a bondage. In comparison with Your sweetness and the beauty of Your house which I loved, those things delighted me no longer; however, I was still enthralled with the love of women. Your apostle did not forbid me to marry, although he advised me to something better, chiefly wishing that all men were as he himself was (1 Cor. 7:8). But I, being weak, chose the more indulgent place, and because of this alone I was tossed up and down in every way. I was faint and consumed with withering cares because I would be hindered in other matters against my will if I were settled into a married life, to which I was already committed and enslaved. I had heard from the mouth of the Truth that there were some "eunuchs, which have made themselves eunuchs for the kingdom of heaven's sake." But, He also says, "He that is able to receive it, let him receive it" (Matt. 19:12). Surely all men who are ignorant of God, and who could not out of the good things which are seen discover Him who is good, are vain. I was no longer in that vanity. I had surmounted it, and by the combined witness of all Your creatures I had found You, our Creator, and Your Word, who is God with You, and who is together with You one God by whom You created all things.

There is yet another kind of ungodly man, who knowing God, "glorified him not as God, neither [was] thankful" (Rom. 1:21). Into this also I had fallen, but "thy right hand hath holden me up" (Ps. 18:35) and took me from there. You placed me where I might recover. For You have said to man, "Behold, the fear of the Lord, that is wisdom" (Job 28:28), and, "Be not wise in thine own eyes" (Prov. 3:7) because, "professing themselves to be wise, they became fools" (Rom. 1:22). But I now "had found one pearl of great price" (Matt. 13:46), which I ought to have bought, selling all that I had, but I hesitated.

To Simplicianus then I went, the spiritual father of Ambrose, who was a bishop now, in receiving Your grace, and one whom Ambrose truly loved as a father. To him I related the mazes of my wanderings. When I mentioned that I had read certain books of the Platonists translated into Latin by Victorinus, a former rhetoric professor of Rome who I had heard had died a Christian, he told me how happy he was that I had not come across the writings of other philosophers that were full of fallacies and deceits, "after the rudiments of the world" (Col. 2:8), since in many ways the Platonists led to the belief in God and His Word. Then, to exhort me to follow the humility of Christ, "hid...from the wise" and "revealed...unto babes" (Matt. 11:25), he spoke of Victorinus himself, whom he had known most intimately while in Rome. What he related to me of him I will not conceal. It contains great praise for Your grace (Eph. 1:6), to be confessed to You, how that aged man, most learned and skilled in the liberal arts, had read and weighed so many works of the philosophers and was the instructor of so many noble senators. He also, as a monument to his excellent service in his office, had both deserved and obtained a statue in the Roman Forum, which men of this world esteem a high honor. He was until old age a worshiper of idols and a partaker of the sacrilegious rites, which almost all the nobility of Rome embraced, and had inspired the people with the love of

> Anubis, barking deity, and all
> The monster gods of every kind, who fought
> 'Gainst Neptune, Venus, and Minerva.[1]

---

[1] From *The Aeneid*, xiii

These whom Rome once conquered and now adored, the aged Victorinus had, with thundering eloquence, so many years defended. Now he was not ashamed to be the child of Your Christ and the newborn babe of Your fountain, submitting his neck to the yoke of humility and subduing his forehead to the reproach of the Cross.

Oh, Lord, Lord, You who have bowed the heavens and come down, who have touched the mountains and made them smoke (Ps. 144:5), by what means did You convey Yourself into his heart? He used to read the Holy Scripture, as Simplicianus said, and he most studiously sought and searched into all the Christian writings. He said to Simplicianus, not openly, but privately and as a friend, "Understand that I am already a Christian." To which Simplicianus answered, "I will not believe it, nor will I rank you among Christians, unless I see you in the church of Christ." The other, in banter, replied, "Do walls, then, make Christians?" He often said that he was already a Christian. Simplicianus just as often made the same answer, while Victorinus always countered this with his conceit about "walls." He was afraid to offend his friends, proud demon-worshippers. He supposed that the weight of their hostility would fall on him from the height of their Babylonian dignity, as from "cedars of Lebanon," which the Lord had not yet broken down (Ps. 29:5).

After that, by reading and earnest thought, he had gathered his determination. He was afraid to be denied by Christ "before the angels of God" should he now be afraid to confess Him "before men" (Luke 12:9). He considered himself guilty of a heavy offense in being ashamed of the mysteries of the humility of Your Word and not being ashamed of the sacrilegious rites of those proud demons, whose pride he had imitated and whose rites he had adopted. He became bold against vanity and humble towards the truth, and suddenly and unexpectedly he said to Simplicianus, who related it to me, "Let us go to the church, I wish to become a Christian." Simplicianus, not being able to contain himself for joy, went with him. He received initial instruction, and not long after he gave in his name so that he might be regenerated by baptism. Rome wondered; the Church rejoiced. The proud saw, and were angry; they gnashed their teeth and melted away (Ps. 112:10). But the Lord God was the hope of Your servant, and He had no regard for "lying vanities" (Ps. 31:6).

When the hour had come for him to make his profession of faith, which, in Rome, those who are about to draw near to Your grace deliver from an elevated place in sight of all the faithful, in a set form of words committed to memory, the presbyters gave Victorinus permission to make his profession more privately, as was done for those who seemed likely to panic because of their extreme shyness. But he chose rather to profess his salvation in the presence of the holy multitude. He had not taught salvation when he had taught rhetoric, and yet he had taught it publicly. How much less then, ought he, when pronouncing Your word, to dread Your meek flock, considering that he, when delivering his own words, had not feared a mad multitude! When, then, he went up to make his profession, all who knew him whispered his name to each other with congratulations. And who there did not know him? A low murmur ran through the rejoicing multitude, "Victorinus! Victorinus!" When they saw him there was a sudden burst of enthusiasm, and then just as suddenly they were quiet so that they might hear him. He pronounced the true faith with a striking boldness, and everyone wished to draw him into their very heart. By their love and joy they drew him to themselves. Such were the hands with which they drew him.

Good God, what takes place in man that he rejoices more in the salvation of a soul who had been despaired of and who was then freed from greater peril, than if there had always been hope for him, or the danger had been less? You also, merciful Father, rejoice more over "one sinner that repenteth, more than over ninety and nine just persons, which need no repentance" (Luke 15:7). And we hear with great joy as often as we hear with what joy the sheep which had strayed is brought back upon the shepherd's shoulder (Luke 15:5–6), and that the piece of silver is restored to Your treasury, the neighbors rejoicing with the woman who found it (Luke 15:8–9). The joy of the solemn service of Your house forces us to tears when it is read in Your house of Your younger son who "was dead, and is alive again...was lost, and is found" (Luke 15:24). You rejoice in us and in Your holy angels, who are holy through holy love. For You are always the same, and all things which do not stay the same or which do not live forever, You know forever in the same way.

What then takes place in the soul when it is more delighted at finding or recovering the things it loves than if it had always had them? Other things bear witness to this, and all things are full of witnesses crying out, "This is so." The conquering commander triumphs, yet he would not have conquered unless he had fought. The more peril there was in the battle, the more joy there is in the triumph. The storm tosses the sailors and threatens shipwreck; all grow pale at approaching death. Sky and sea are then calmed, and they are as exceedingly joyful as they were exceedingly afraid. A friend is sick, and his weak pulse threatens danger; all who long for his recovery are sick in their minds in sympathy with him. He is restored, and though he does not yet walk with his former strength, there is more joy than there was earlier when he walked sound and strong. Men acquire the very pleasures of human life by difficulties, not only those which fall upon us unlooked for and against our wills, but those troubles which are self-chosen and pleasure-seeking. Eating and drinking give no pleasure unless they are preceded by the pinching of hunger and thirst. Men, given to drink, eat certain salty food to create an unpleasant dryness which the drink alleviates, causing pleasure. Also, according to custom, an engaged woman should not be given in marriage too soon, for fear that her husband will hold cheaply his bride whom he did not long for during their engagement.

This same law stands for foul and accursed joy; it stands for joys that are permitted and lawful; it stands for the very purest perfection of friendship; it stands for him who "was dead, and is alive again; [who] was lost, and is found" (Luke 15:24). Everywhere the greater joy is ushered in by the greater pain. What does this mean, Lord, my God, since You are everlasting joy to Yourself and some things around You forever rejoice in You? What does this mean, that this portion of Your creation ebbs and flows in this way, alternately displeased and reconciled? Is this their allotted measure? Is this all You have assigned to them, while from the highest heavens to the lowest earth, from the beginning of the world to the end of ages, from the angel to the worm, from the first motion to the last, You set each in its place and bring each into being in its season, everything good after its kind? Woe is me! How high are You in the highest and how deep in the deepest! You never depart from us, and we scarcely return to You.

Rise up, Lord, and act; stir us up, and call us back; kindle and draw us; inflame, grow sweet to us. Let us now love; let us "run after thee" (Song 1:4). Do not many return to You out of a deeper hell of blindness than Victorinus? As they approach, are they not enlightened? Do they not receive that Light and through it receive power from You to become Your sons? (See John 1:12.) But if they are less famous, even those who know them rejoice less for them. For when many rejoice together, each also has more exuberant joy because they are kindled and inflamed by one another. Again, those who are well-known influence more people towards salvation and pave the way for many more to follow. And, therefore, those who preceded them also rejoice greatly in them because they do not rejoice in them alone.

Far be it, that in Your tabernacle the rich should be accepted before the poor, or the noble before the lowly. (See James 2:1-4.) You have chosen rather,

> *The foolish things of the world to confound the wise; and...the weak things of the world to confound the things which are mighty... and things which are despised, hath* [You] *chosen, yea, and things which are not, to bring to nought things that are.*
>
> *(1 Cor. 1:27–28)*

Even that "least of the apostles" (1 Cor. 15:9) —by whose tongue You proclaimed these words, when Paulus the Proconsul, his pride conquered through his warfare, was made to pass under the easy yoke of Your Christ and became a peasant of the great King—was pleased to be called Paul instead of his former name, Saul, in testimony of so great a victory. Victory over the enemy is greater in one on whom he has more of a hold and through whom he has a hold on others. He has more of a hold on the proud through their overemphasis on social standing, and he has a hold on many more through their authority. The heart of Victorinus, which the devil had held as an unconquerable possession, was therefore received with much greater appreciation, as well as his tongue, with which as a sharp and mighty weapon he had slain many. How much more abundantly should Your sons rejoice because our King has bound "the strong man" (Matt. 12:29), and because they saw the enemy's vessels taken from him, "sanctified, and [made] meet for [Your] use, and prepared [for the Lord] unto every good work" (2 Tim. 2:21).

When Your servant, Simplicianus, related to me these facts about Victorinus, I was on fire to imitate him, and it was for this very reason that he had related it. Then he also added how in the days of the Emperor Julian a law was enacted which prohibited Christians from teaching literature and rhetoric, and how he, obeying this law, chose rather to give up the school for words than give up Your Word, by which You enable the mute to speak eloquently. He then seemed to me to be more blessed than determined in having found this opportunity to serve You only. This is what I was longing for, chained as I was, not with another's irons, but by my own iron will. The enemy held my will, and therefore had made a chain for me and bound me. For lust is made out of a disobedient will, and a lust that is indulged in becomes habit, and habit that is not resisted becomes necessity. By these links, as it were, joined together (that is why I called it a chain) a hard bondage held me enslaved. But that new will to serve You freely and to desire to enjoy You, the only sure happiness, which had begun in me, was not yet able to over-come my former willfulness which had been hardened over time. Therefore, my two wills, one new and the other old, one carnal, the other spiritual, struggled within me, and by their discord, they unraveled my soul.

Then I understood by my own experience what I had read, how "the flesh lusteth against the Spirit, and the Spirit against the flesh" (Gal. 5:17). I was certainly influenced by both sides, yet I was more myself in that which I approved in myself than in that which I disapproved. (See Romans 7:18.) For regarding the latter, it was now for the most part not myself because I endured much of it against my will rather than acted willingly. And yet it was through me that habit had obtained this power of warring against me because I had come willingly to the place where I no longer wanted to be. Who has any right to speak against it, if just punishment follows the sinner? I also no longer had my former excuse, that I still hesitated to be above the world and serve You because the truth was not completely certain to me. Now it was certain. But I, still under service to worldly things, refused to fight under Your banner and was as much afraid to be freed of all encumbrances, as we should fear to be encumbered with them.

Thus, with the baggage of this present world I was held down pleasantly, as in sleep. The thoughts with which I meditated on You were like the efforts of those who want to awake, but who are overcome with a heavy drowsiness and are again drenched in it. No one would sleep forever, and in all men's sober judgment waking is better. When a man feels a heavy lethargy in all his limbs, he, for the most part, delays shaking off sleep, and though half-annoyed, he yields to it with pleasure, even after it is time to rise. In this way, I was assured that it was much better for me to give myself up to Your love than to give myself over to my own lust. Though the first satisfied me and was gaining control over me, the other pleased me and held me under control. And I did not have anything to answer You when You were calling to me, "Awake thou that sleepest, and arise from the dead, and Christ shall give thee light" (Eph. 5:14). Everywhere I turned, You showed me that what You have said is true. But I, convicted by the truth, had nothing at all to answer but these dull and drowsy words, "Immediately, immediately," "presently," "leave me for just a little while." But "presently, presently," had no present, and my "little while" went on for a long while. In vain I delighted "in the law...after the inward man" (Rom. 7:22) when "another law in my members, [rebelled] against the law of my mind, and [led] me into captivity to the law of sin which [was] in my members" (Rom. 7:23). For the law of sin is the strength of habit, whereby the mind is drawn and held, even against its will, but deservedly, because it willingly fell into it. "O wretched man that I am! who [should] deliver me from the body of this death" (Rom. 7:24) but Your grace only, "through Jesus Christ our Lord" (Rom. 7:25)?

How You delivered me out of the chains of desire with which I was so tightly bound to carnal lust and out of the drudgery of worldly things, I will now declare and confess to Your name, "O LORD, my strength, and my redeemer" (Ps. 19:14).

Amid increasing anxiety, I was going about my usual business and daily sighing to You. I attended Your church, whenever free from the business under the burden of which I groaned. Alypius was with me, now that he had completed his third term as assessor and was released from his law responsibilities and was looking for those to whom to sell his counsel, as I sold the skill of speaking, if indeed teaching can impart it. Nebridius had now, in view of our friendship, agreed to teach under Verecundus, a citizen and a grammarian of Milan and a very close friend of all of us, who urgently desired, and by the right of friendship demanded from us the dependable help that he greatly needed. Nebridius, then, was not drawn to this by any desire to get ahead, for he might have made much more of his education if he had wanted to, but as a very kind and gentle friend, he would not slight our request. He was very discreet in this, avoiding becoming known to people considered great according to this world, avoiding the distraction of mind this would bring him. As a result, he wanted to keep his mind free and uninterrupted, as many hours as he could, in order to seek or read or hear something concerning wisdom.

One day then, when Nebridius was absent—I cannot remember why—Ponticianus, our countryman in that he was an African, who had a high office in the Emperor's court, came to see me and Alypius. I do not know what he wanted with us, but we sat down to converse. He happened to observe a book lying on a game table in front of us. He took it and opened it and, contrary to his expectation, found it was by the apostle Paul, for he had thought it was one of those books which I was wearing myself out by teaching. Then, smiling and looking at me, he expressed his joy and amazement that he had suddenly found this book and this book alone before my eyes. He was a baptized Christian and often bowed himself before You our God in the church in frequent and continued prayers.

When I then told him that I spent a great deal of time and study in those Scriptures, a conversation arose, prompted by his account of Antony the Egyptian monk, whose name was in high reputation among Your servants, though up to that time we had not heard of him. When he discovered this, he spent even more time on that subject, informing us and being amazed at our ignorance of one so eminent. We also stood amazed, hearing Your wonderful works so completely verified, in times so recent and almost in our own, which were done in the true faith and church. We all wondered: we, that they were so great, and he, that we had not heard about them.

From there his discourse turned to the flocks in the monasteries and their holy ways, a sweet-smelling savor to You, and the fruitful deserts of the wilderness, of which we knew nothing. There was a monastery at Milan outside of the city walls, full of good brothers and under the fostering care of Ambrose, and we did not know of it. He went on with his discourse, and we listened in intent silence. He then told us how one afternoon at Trier, when the Emperor was busy with the circus games, he and three others, his companions, went out to walk in gardens near the city walls. There they happened to walk in pairs. One went apart with him, and the other two wandered by themselves. These, in their wanderings, came upon a certain cottage inhabited by some of Your servants, "poor in spirit," of whom "is the kingdom of heaven" (Matt. 5:3), and there they found a little book containing the life of Antony.

One of them began to read, admire, and become inflamed by it, and as he read, he meditated on taking up such a life and giving over his secular service to serve You. These two were among those whom they call agents for the public affairs. Suddenly, filled with a holy love and a sober shame, and angry with himself, he looked over at his friend, saying, "Tell me, I ask you, what will we attain by all these affairs of ours? What do we aim for? For what purpose do we serve? Can our ambition in court rise higher than to be the Emperor's favorites? And in this, what is there that is not fragile and full of dangers? And by how many dangers will we arrive at a greater peril? When will we arrive there? But I can become a friend of God right now if I want to." This is what he said.

In the birth pangs of a new life, he returned to the book, read on, and was changed inwardly, where You saw it. His mind was stripped of the world, as was soon evident. As he read and rolled up and down the waves of his heart, he stormed at himself a while, then he understood and decided on a better course. Now belonging to You, he said to his friend, "Now I have broken loose from our ambition, and I am resolved to serve God, and from this hour, in this place, I will begin doing it. If you do not want to imitate me, do not oppose me." The other answered that he would join him to share in so glorious a reward, so glorious a service. They were both now Yours, and they were building the tower, counting the cost, forsaking all that they had, and following You. (See Luke 14:26–30.)

Then Ponticianus and the man who was with him, who had walked in other parts of the garden, came to the same cottage in search of them, and finding them, they reminded them to return, for it was getting late in the day. The men related their resolution and purpose and how that decision had begun and was settled in them, and they begged them, if they would not join, not to attack them with criticism. But Ponticianus and his companion, though they remained unchanged, did grieve over themselves, as he affirmed, and reverently congratulated them, commending themselves to their prayers. So, with hearts lingering on the earth, they went away to the palace. But the other two, fixing their hearts on heaven, remained in the cottage. Both had fiancées who, when they heard of this, also dedicated their virginity to God.

This was Ponticianus's story, but while he was speaking, You, Lord, turned me around towards myself, taking me from behind my back where I had placed myself, unwilling to observe myself. You set me before my face so that I might see how foul I was, how crooked and defiled, stained and ulcerous. And I saw and stood aghast, and I could not find anywhere to flee from myself. If I tried to turn my eye away from myself, he went on with his story, and You again set me over against myself and thrusted me before my eyes, that I might find out my iniquity and hate it. (See Psalm 36:2.) I had known it, but I had acted as though I did not see it. I winked at it and forgot it.

But now, the more fervently I loved those whose healthful affections I had heard of, that they had resigned themselves wholly to You to be healed, the more I abhorred myself when compared with them. Many years, some twelve, had now passed since my nineteenth year when, upon reading Cicero's *Hortensius*, I was stirred with an earnest love for wisdom. And still I held off rejecting mere earthly pleasure and giving myself to search out that wisdom. Not the discovery only, but the very search for wisdom, was preferable to the treasures and kingdoms of the world, though already found, and to the pleasures of the body, though spread around me at my will. But I, wretched, most wretched, in the very beginning of my early youth, had begged chastity of You and said, "Give me chastity and self-control, only not yet." For I feared that You would quickly hear me and cure me of the disease of lust which I wished to have satisfied rather than extinguished. I had wandered through crooked ways in a sacrilegious superstition, not assured of it, but preferring it to the others which I did not devoutly seek but rather maliciously opposed.

I had thought that I therefore delayed from day to day to reject the hopes of this world and follow You only because there did not appear anything certain in which to direct my course. And now the day had come in which I was to be laid bare to myself, and my conscience upbraided me. "Where are you now, my tongue? You said that for an uncertain truth, you did not like to cast off the baggage of vanity. Now, it is certain, and yet that burden still oppresses you while they who neither have worn themselves out with seeking it, nor for ten years or more have been thinking about it, have had their shoulders lightened and have received wings to fly away." My insides were being gnawed at, and I was greatly perplexed with a horrible shame while Ponticianus was speaking this. He, having finished his story and the business he came for, went his way, and I went into myself. What did I not say against myself? With what scourges of condemnation did I not lash my soul, that it might follow me, striving to go after You! Yet it drew back; it refused but did not excuse itself. All arguments were spent and disproved. There remained only a mute withdrawal, and my soul feared, as if of death, to be restrained from the current of that habit by which it was wasting to death.

Then, in this great inner conflict, which I had strongly raised against my soul in the chamber of my heart, and being troubled in mind and countenance, I turned upon Alypius. "What is the matter with us?" I exclaimed. "What is it? What did you hear? The unlearned jump up and take heaven by force (Matt. 11:12), and we who are learned but without heart, look where we wallow in flesh and blood! Are we ashamed to follow because others have gone before us? Why are we not ashamed that we are not following?" I said something to this extent, and my agonized mind tore me away from him, while he, gazing on me in astonishment, kept silent. I was not speaking in my usual way, and my forehead, cheeks, eyes, color, and tone of voice spoke my mind more than the words I uttered.

There was a little garden attached to our lodging, which we had the use of, just as we had the use of the whole house, for the master of the house, our host, was not living there. The tumult of my heart drove me there, where no man might hinder the hot conflict in which I was engaged with myself, until it should end in a way that You knew, but I did not know. But I was healthily deranged and dying to live, knowing what evil thing I was and not knowing what good thing I was shortly to become. I withdrew then into the garden, and Alypius followed on my steps. His presence did not lessen my privacy. How could he abandon me when I was so disturbed? We sat down as far away from the house as we could. I was troubled in spirit, most vehemently indignant that I did not enter into Your will and covenant (see Ezekiel 16:8), my God, which all my bones cried out to me to enter and praised to the skies. We do not enter into that place by ships or chariots or feet, nor do we need to move as far as I had come from the house to that place where we were sitting. The only way not to just go to, but to go in Your will, was to will to go, but to will resolutely and thoroughly, not tossing and turning this way and that, a maimed and half-divided will, struggling, with one part sinking as another rose.

Lastly, in the very fever of my indecision, I made many motions with my body that men sometimes want to, but cannot, because they do not have the limbs, or these limbs are bound with chains, weakened with infirmity, or hindered in any other way. Thus, if I tore my hair, beat my forehead, or locked my fingers and clasped my knees, I did it because I willed it. But I might have willed and not done it, if the power of motion in my limbs had not obeyed. I did so many things then, when to will was not in itself to be able. I did not do what I both longed incomparably more to do, and which soon after, when I did will, I was able to do, because soon after, when I did will it, I willed it thoroughly. In these things the ability was one with the will, and to will was to do. But as yet it was not done, and my body more easily obeyed the weakest desire of my soul, in moving its limbs at a nod of the head, than the soul obeyed itself in accomplishing in the will alone this its most crucial will.

Where does this monstrousness come from? And to what end? Let Your mercy shine forth that I may ask, so that the secret penalties of men, and those darkest pangs of the sons of Adam may perhaps answer me. Where does this monstrousness come from? And to what end? The mind commands the body, and it obeys instantly. The mind commands itself, and it is resisted. The mind commands the hand to move, and it does so with such immediacy; that command can hardly be distinguished from obedience. Yet the mind is mind, the hand is body. The mind commands the mind, its own self, to will, and yet it does not. Where does this monstrousness come from? And to what end? It commands itself, I say, to will and would not command unless it willed. What it commands is not done. It does not will completely; therefore, it does not command completely. For insofar as it commands, it wills, and in so far as the thing commanded is not done, it does not will. For the will commands that there be a will, not another, but its own. But it does not command entirely; therefore, what it commands does not exist. For if the will were entire, it would not even command it to be, because it would already be. It is therefore not a monstrous thing partly to will, partly not to will. But it is a disease of the mind that it does not wholly rise by truth but is brought down by habit. Therefore there are two wills because one of them is not entire, and what the one lacks, the other has.

Let them perish from Your presence, God (Ps. 68:2), as "vain talkers and deceivers" (Titus 1:10) of the soul perish, who, observing that in deliberating there were two wills, affirm that there are two kinds of minds in us: one good, the other evil. They themselves are truly evil when they believe these evil things. They will become good when they believe the truth and assent to the truth, that Your apostle may say to them, "Ye were sometimes darkness, but now are ye light in the Lord" (Eph. 5:8). But they, wishing to be light, not in the

Lord, but in themselves, imagining the nature of the soul to be that which God is, are transformed into more complete darkness through a dreadful arrogance. Because of that pride, they went back farther from You, the "true Light, which lighteth every man that cometh into the world" (John 1:9). Take heed what you say, and blush for shame. Draw near to Him and be enlightened, and your faces will not be ashamed (Ps. 34:5). As for me, when I was now deliberating about serving the Lord my God, as I had long purposed, it was I who willed and I who did not will—I, I myself. I neither willed entirely nor did I not will entirely. Therefore, I was at war with myself, and I was ripped apart by myself. This tearing happened to me against my will, and yet it did not indicate the presence of another mind, but rather the punishment of my own. Therefore, it was "no more I that [did] it, but sin that dwelleth in me" (Rom. 7:17), the punishment of a sin committed more freely in that I was a son of Adam.

If there are as many contrary natures as there are conflicting wills, there are not only two to consider but many. If a man deliberates whether he should go to the Manichees' meeting or to the theater, the Manichees cry out, "Behold, here are two natures: one is good which draws this way; another is bad which draws back that way. For where else does this hesitation between conflicting wills come from?" But I say that both are bad; that which draws to the Manichees is the same as that which draws back to the theater. But they do not believe that the will which draws to them is anything other than good. What would they say if one of us should deliberate and amid the strife of his two wills be in a dilemma whether he should go to the theater or to our church? Would not these Manichees also be in a dilemma as to what to answer? For either they must confess, which they would not gladly do, that the will which leads to our church is good, just as much as theirs who have received and are held by the mysteries of theirs, or they must suppose that two evil natures and two evil souls are battling within one man. It will not be true, what they say, that there is one good and another bad, or they must be converted to the truth and no longer deny that when one deliberates, one soul fluctuates between contrary wills.

When they perceive two conflicting wills in one man, let them no longer say, then, that the conflict is between two contrary souls of two contrary substances from two contrary principles, one good, and the other bad. For You, true God, refute, restrain, and convict them as if both wills are bad. For example, one may deliberate whether he should kill a man by poison or by the sword; whether he should seize this or that estate belonging to another when he take cannot both; whether he should purchase pleasure through indulgence or keep his money out of covetousness; whether he should go to the circus or the theater, if both are open the same day, or thirdly, to rob another's house, if he has the opportunity, or fourthly, to commit adultery if he has the means to do this also. All these may meet together in the same point in time, and all are equally desired but cannot be done at the same time. They tear the mind among four or more things, amid the vast variety of things desired: more conflicting wills. Yet the Manichees do not allege that there are so many diverse substances.

It is the same in regard to wills which are good. I ask them if is it good to take pleasure in reading the apostle, or if it is good to take pleasure in a sober Psalm, or if it is good to talk on the Gospel? They will answer to each, "It is good." What, then, if all give equal pleasure at the same time? Do not diverse wills distract the mind while it deliberates what it should choose? Yet they are all good and are in conflict until one is chosen, and the one entire will is made firm, which earlier was divided into many. Thus also, when eternity above delights us and the pleasure of temporal good holds us down below, it is the same soul which does not will this or that with an undivided will. Therefore, it is torn apart with grievous perplexities when the truth compels it to treasure the first, but out of habit it does not set the other aside.

Consequently, I was soul-sick and tormented, accusing myself much more severely than I normally did. I rolled and turned in my chain until it was completely broken, the chain by which I now was barely held, and yet was still held. And You, Lord, pressed upon me in my inward parts with a severe mercy, redoubling the lashes of fear and shame, for fear that I would give way again, and that small remaining link would not break, but would recover strength and bind me even more tightly. I said within myself, "Be it done now, be it done now," and as I spoke, I all but carried through with it. I all but did it, but I did not do it. Yet I did not sink back to my former state but stood fast and took a deep breath. And I tried again, and I got closer and closer to it, and all but touched and laid hold of it. Yet I did not come right up to it, touch it, or lay hold of it, hesitating to die to death and to live to life. The worse to which I was hardened had more power over me than the better with which I was not familiar. The very moment in which I was to become other than I was—the nearer it approached me—the greater horror it struck into me. Yet it did not strike me back, or turn me away, but it held me in suspense.

The very follies of follies and "vanity of vanities" (Eccl. 1:2), my ancient mistresses, still held me. They plucked my fleshly garment and whispered softly, "Do you cast us off?" and "From that moment shall we no longer be with you forever?" and "From that moment shall not this or that be lawful for you forever?" What was it they suggested when they said, "this or that"? What did they suggest, my God? Let Your mercy turn it away from the soul of Your servant. What defilements did they suggest! What shame! I much less than half heard them. Now they were not openly showing themselves and contradicting me but muttering as if they were behind my back and secretly pulling on me, as if I were departing, to look back on them. Yet they delayed me so that I hesitated to break away and shake myself free from them and to spring over to where I was called. A forceful habit was saying to me, "Think you can live without them?"

But now it spoke very faintly. For on that side to which I had set my face and where I trembled to go, there appeared to me the chaste dignity of continence, serene, yet not unseemly, joyful, honestly alluring me to come and not doubt. She stretched forth to receive and embrace me, her holy hands full of multitudes of good examples. There were so many young men and maidens here, a multitude of youths and people of every age, grave widows and aged virgins, and continence herself was in all, not barren, but a fruitful mother of children of joys (Ps. 113:9), by You her Husband, Lord. And she smiled on me with a persuasive mockery, as if she said, "Can you not do what these youths and these maidens can? Or can they do this in and of themselves and not rather in the Lord their God? The Lord their God gave me to them. Why do you stand on yourself and in this way not stand at all? Cast yourself upon Him; fear not, He will not withdraw Himself so that you will fall; cast yourself fearlessly upon Him. He will receive and will heal you."

I blushed profusely because I still heard the muttering of those follies and hung in suspense. And again, she seemed to say, "Stop your ears against those unclean members of the earth, that they may be put to death. They tell you of delights but not as does the law of the Lord your God." This controversy in my heart was self against self alone. But Alypius, sitting close by my side, waited in silence for the outcome of my unusual emotion.

But when my deep contemplation had drawn together all the misery from the secret bottom of my soul and heaped it up in the sight of my heart, a mighty storm arose, bringing a mighty shower of tears. I left Alypius so that I might pour it forth completely, without holding anything back. Solitude seemed better suited for the business of weeping, so I withdrew far enough that even his presence could not be a burden to me. That is the state I was in, and he perceived something of it, for when I stood up, I suppose I spoke something in which my voice appeared choked with weeping. He then remained where we were sitting, most extremely astonished. I threw myself down, I do not know how, under a certain fig tree, giving full vent to my tears. The floods of my eyes gushed out an acceptable sacrifice to You. And, not exactly in these words, but to this effect, I poured out my heart to You: "And You, Lord, how long? 'How long, LORD? wilt thou be angry for ever?' 'Remember not against us former iniquities'" (Ps. 79:5, 8). For I felt that I was held by them. I sent up these sorrowful words: "How long, how long, tomorrow, and tomorrow? Why not now? Why is there not in this hour an end to my uncleanness?"

I was speaking and weeping in this way, with the most bitter sorrow and repentance of heart, when, suddenly, I heard a voice from a neighboring house—I do not know if it was a boy or girl—chanting and continually repeating, "Take up and read. Take up and read." Instantly, my countenance changed. I began to consider very intently whether children usually sang such words in any of the games they play, and I could not remember ever hearing anything similar to this. So, holding back my torrent of tears, I got up, interpreting it to be none other than a command from God to open the book and read the first chapter I came to. For I had heard that Antony, coming in during the reading of the Gospel, had received an admonition as if what was being read was spoken directly to him: "Go and sell that thou hast, and give to the poor, and thou shalt have treasure in heaven: and come and follow me" (Matt. 19:21). By such a revelation he was immediately converted to You. I then eagerly returned to the place where Alypius was sitting, for that is where I had set down the volume of the apostle when I arose from there. I seized it and opened it, and in silence read that section on which my eyes first fell: "Not in rioting and drunkenness, not in chambering and wantonness, not in strife and envying; But put ye on the Lord Jesus Christ, and make not provision for the flesh, to fulfil the lusts thereof" (Rom. 13:13–14). No further would I read, nor did I need to, for instantly at the end of this sentence, by a light, as it were, of serenity infused into my heart, all the darkness of doubt vanished away.

Then, putting my finger or some other mark at that place in the book, I shut the volume, and with a now-peaceful countenance, I told Alypius what had happened. He then showed me what had happened in him, which I did not know. He asked to see what I had read. I showed him, and he went on even further than I had read. I did not know what came next. This is what followed: "Him that is weak in the faith receive" (Rom. 14:1). Alypius told me he believed that this applied to himself. He was strengthened by this admonition, and by a good resolution and purpose, in keeping with his character, in which he was always very different from me, to his credit, he joined me in faith without any agonized delay. Then we went in to my mother. We told her, and she rejoiced. We related in turn how it took place. She leaped for joy and triumph and blessed You, who are "able to do exceeding abundantly above all that we ask or think" (Eph. 3:20). She perceived that You had given her more, through me, than she used to beg for by her pitiful and most sorrowful groaning. For You converted me to Yourself so that I sought neither wife nor any hope belonging to this world. I stood in that rule of faith where You had shown me to her in a vision, so many years before. And You turned her mourning into a joy (Ps. 30:11) much more abundant than she had desired, and in a much more precious and purer way than she had formerly demanded in wanting grandchildren of my body.

Book Nine

Augustine determines to devote his life to God and to abandon his profession of rhetoric, quietly however. Retires to the country to prepare himself to receive the grace of baptism, and is baptized with Alypius and his son Adeodatus. At Ostia, on his way to Africa, his mother Monnica dies, in her fifty-sixth year, the thirty-third of Augustine. Her life and character.

O h, Lord, truly I am thy servant; I am thy servant, and the son of thine handmaid: thou hast loosed my bonds. I will offer to thee the sacrifice of thanksgiving" (Ps. 116:16–17). Let my heart and my tongue praise You; let "all my bones...say, LORD, who is like unto thee?" (Ps. 35:10). Let them say this, and may You answer me, and "say unto my soul, I am thy salvation" (Ps. 35:3).

Who am I, and what am I? What evil has not been in my deeds, or if not in my deeds, my words, or if not in my words, my will? But You, Lord, are good and merciful, and Your right hand has respected the depth of my death and, from the bottom of my heart, has emptied that abyss of corruption. And Your whole gift to me was not to will what I willed, and to will what You willed. But where was my free will through all those years, and out of what low and deep recess was my free will called forth in a moment so I could submit my neck to Your easy yoke (Matt. 11:30), and my shoulders to Your light burden, Christ Jesus, my Helper and my Redeemer? How sweet it suddenly became to me, to lack the "sweetness" of those follies, and what I was afraid to be separated from was now a joy to part with! You cast them forth from me, You who are the true and highest sweetness. You cast them forth and entered in their place Yourself, You who are sweeter than all pleasure, though not to flesh and blood, brighter than all light, but more hidden than all depths, higher than all honor, but not to the lofty in their own conceits. Now my soul was free from the biting cares of seeking and getting, weltering in filth, and scratching off the itch of lust. And my infant tongue spoke freely to You, my brightness and my riches and my health, Lord my God.

I resolved in Your sight not to break away suddenly but to quietly withdraw my rhetoric skills from the language marketplace. Then the young, not students of Your law nor of Your peace but of dosages of lies and legal skirmishes, would no longer buy ammunition for their madness out of my mouth. There were only a few days left until the vintage vacation. I decided to endure the students, then to take my leave in the regular way and, having been purchased by You, return for sale no more. Our purpose, then, was known to You, but not to anyone else except our own friends. We had agreed among ourselves not to make it widely known to anyone. To us, who were now ascending from the valley of tears and singing that "psalm of degrees," You had given sharp arrows and destroying coals to prevent us from having a deceitful tongue. This kind of tongue, seeming to advise us, would thwart us and would devour us out of love, as it does its meat.

You had pierced our hearts with Your love, and we carried Your words as if they were fixed in our inmost beings. The examples of Your servants, whom You had transformed from black into bright and from death to life, which were piled together in the receptacle of our thoughts, ignited and burned up our heavy apathy so that we should not sink down to the abyss. They vehemently inflamed us so that all the lying blasts from opposing tongues might only inflame us even more fiercely and not extinguish us. Still, because—for Your name's sake which You have hallowed throughout the earth—our vow and purpose might also find some who would praise it, it seemed like pretentiousness to quit ahead of time, as if making a public profession done before the eyes of all, rather than waiting for the vacation which was now so near. If I had quit then, all who looked on this act of mine and observed how near the time of vintage was which I wished to anticipate, would talk a great deal about me, as if I had desired to appear to be a great man. And how would that have served me, that people should think and debate about my motive and that our "good be evil spoken of" (Rom. 14:16).

Moreover, it had bothered me at first that during this very summer my lungs began to give

215

way because I had pushed myself in my literary work. It was difficult for me to breathe deeply; the pain in my chest made it clear that they were injured, and I had to refuse any full or drawn out speaking. This had troubled me, for it had almost forced me out of necessity to lay down that burden of teaching, or, if I could be cured and recover, at least to suspend it. But when the full wish for free time arose and became settled in me, my God, that I might see that You are the Lord, You know that I even began to rejoice that I had this secondary and uninvented excuse. This excuse might temper the offense taken by those who, for their sons' sake, wished me never to have the freedom of Your sons.

Full then of such joy, I endured that interval of time; it may have been some twenty days. I endured it manfully—I say endured since the covetousness which earlier had carried a part of this heavy business had left me—and I remained alone and would have been overwhelmed, had not patience taken its place. Perhaps some of Your servants, my brothers, may say that I sinned in this, that with a heart fully set on Your service, I allowed myself to sit even one hour in the chair of lies. I would not be contentious about this. But have You not, most merciful Lord, pardoned and forgiven this sin also with my other most horrible and deadly sins through the holy water of baptism?

Verecundus was worn down with care about our blessedness. Being held back by bonds by which he was most strictly bound, he thought that he would be severed from us. He was not yet a Christian, though his wife was one of the faithful;

yet because of this he was more rigidly hindered from the journey which we had now begun than by any other chain. For he would not, he said, become a Christian on any other terms than on those which he could not. However, he courteously offered us the opportunity to remain at his country house for as long as we wanted to stay there. You, Lord, will reward him in "the resurrection of the just" (Luke 14:14), seeing that You had already given him "the lot of the righteous" (Ps. 125:3). When we were absent from him, since we were now in Rome, he was seized with bodily sickness and became a Christian through that, and he departed this life as one of the faithful. Yet You not only had mercy on him, but also on us, lest, remembering the great kindness of our friend towards us, but unable to number him among Your flock, we would have been agonized with intolerable sorrow. (See Philippians 2:27.) Thanks to You, our God, we are Yours. Your inner witness and comfort tell us this. Faithful in promises, You now rewarded Verecundus with the eternal freshness of Your paradise for his country house of Cassiciacum, where we rested in You from the fever of the world. For that, You have forgiven him the sins he committed on earth, in that rich mountain, that mountain which yields milk, Your own mountain.

He, then, had sorrow at that time, but Nebridius had joy. Although he also, not yet being a Christian, had fallen into the pit of that most pernicious error, believing the flesh of Your Son to be a phantom, yet he emerged from there and believed as we

217

did. He was not as yet clothed with any sacraments of Your church, but he was a most ardent searcher of truth. Not long after our conversion and regeneration by Your baptism, he also became a faithful member of the church and served You in perfect chastity and continence among his people in Africa. And after his whole household had first become Christian, You released him from the flesh, and now he lives in "Abraham's bosom" (Luke 16:22). Whatever that place is, which is signified by that bosom, there lives my Nebridius, my sweet friend and Your child, Lord, who was adopted as a freed man. There he lives. What other place is there for such a soul? There he lives, in the place about which he used to ask me much—me, a poor, inexperienced man. Now he does not lay his ear to my mouth, but he puts his spiritual mouth to Your fountain and drinks as much as he can receive, wisdom in proportion to his thirst, endlessly happy. Nor do I think that he is so inebriated with that as to forget me, seeing that You, Lord, whom he drinks, are mindful of us.

This is how we were then, comforting Verecundus who sorrowed, as far as friendship permitted, that our conversion was of the nature it was, and exhorting him to become faithful according to his measure, namely, that of a married estate. We waited for Nebridius to follow us, which, being so near, he was all but doing. So, behold, those days rolled by slowly, for they seemed many and long because I longed for an unhurried freedom, that I might sing to you from my inmost being, "My heart said unto thee, Thy face, LORD, will I seek" (Ps. 27:8).

The day had come when I was indeed to be freed of my rhetoric professorship, from which in thought I was already freed. It was done. You rescued my tongue as You had before rescued my heart. I blessed You, rejoicing, retiring to the villa with my family and friends. What I did there in terms of writing, which was now enlisted in Your service, though it was still, in this resting time, as it were, panting from the school of pride, my books may be a witness. They also reveal what I debated with others and with myself when I was alone before You. My letters bear witness to what I debated with Nebridius, who was absent. And when shall I have time to recount all Your great benefits towards us at that time, especially when I am now hastening on to even greater mercies? For my memory reminds me, and it is pleasant to me, Lord, to confess to You by what inward prods You tamed me and how You had leveled me, lowering the mountains and hills of my lofty imaginations, straightening my crookedness, and smoothing my rough ways (see Isaiah 40:4), and how You also made the brother of my heart, Alypius, submissive to the name of Your Only Begotten, our Lord and Savior Jesus Christ, which he would not at first permit to have inserted in our writings. He would have preferred them to taste of the lofty cedars of the schools which the Lord has now broken down (see Psalm 29:5) than of the wholesome herbs of the church, the antidote against serpents.

With what cries I spoke to You, my God, when I read the Psalms of David, those faithful songs and sounds of devotion which allow no prideful spirit. I was still a catechumen and a novice in Your real love, resting in that villa with Alypius, a catechumen, my mother cleaving to us in female garb with a masculine faith, with the tranquillity of age, motherly love, and Christian piety! What cries did I utter to You in those Psalms, and how was I kindled by them towards You and on fire to proclaim them, if possible, through the whole world, against the pride of mankind! Yet they are sung throughout the whole world, and none can hide himself from Your heat (Ps. 19:6). With what fierce and bitter sorrow was I angered at the Manichees! But I also pitied them because they did not know those sacraments, those medicines, and they raged against the antidote which might have healed them of their madness. How I wished that they had been somewhere near me at that time and that, without my knowing it, they could have seen my face and heard my words when I read the fourth Psalm during that time of rest, and could have seen what that psalm accomplished in me: when I called, the God of my righteousness heard me; in my distress You set me free. Have mercy upon me, Lord, and hear my prayer (Ps. 4:1). I wish that when I spoke these words, they could have heard without my knowing it for fear that they would think that I spoke them only for their sakes! Because I would certainly not speak the same things, nor in the same way, if I perceived that they heard and saw me. Or, if I did speak them, they would not receive them as they would if I spoke by and for myself before You, out of the natural feelings of my soul.

I trembled for fear and I was again kindled with hope and with rejoicing in Your mercy, Father. All these things were reflected in my eyes and my voice when Your good Spirit, turning to us, said, "Oh you sons of men, how long will you be slow of heart? Why do you love vanity and seek after lying?" (See Psalm 4:2.) For I had loved vanity and sought after lying. And You, Lord, had already magnified Your Holy One, raising Him from the dead and setting Him at Your right hand (Eph. 1:20), where from on high He would send His promise, the "Comforter," "the Spirit of truth" (John 14:16–17). He had already sent Him, but I did not know it. He had sent Him because He was now magnified, rising again from the dead, and ascending into heaven. Until then, however, "the Holy Ghost was not yet given; because that Jesus was not yet glorified" (John 7:39).

The prophet cries out, "How long, slow of heart? Why do you love vanity and seek after lying? (See Psalm 4:2.) Know this, that the Lord has magnified His Holy One." He cries out, "How long?" He cries out, "Know this," and because for so long I did not know, I loved vanity and sought after lying. Therefore I heard and trembled because it was spoken to the kind of man that I remembered I had been. In those phantoms which I had held for truths there were vanity and lying, and I spoke aloud many things earnestly and forcibly in the bitterness of my recollection. If only they who still love vanity and seek after lying had heard these things! They perhaps would have been troubled and would have vomited it up, and You

221

would have heard them when they cried to You. For by a true death in the flesh He died for us, He who now "maketh intercession for us" (Rom. 8:34).

I further read, "Be ye angry, and sin not" (Eph. 4:26). How I was moved, my God, I who had now learned to be angry at myself for things past, that I might not sin in times to come! I was justly angry because it was not another nature of a people of darkness which sinned for me, as the Manichees claim, who are not angry at themselves and who "treasurest up...wrath against the day of wrath and revelation of the righteous judgment of God" (Rom. 2:5). The things that I treasured as good were not now external, and they were not sought with the eyes of flesh in that earthly sun. For those who want to obtain joy from external things soon become vain and waste themselves on things that are seen and temporal, and in their famished thoughts they lick their own shadows. If they were only worn out with their famine and would ask, "Who will show us any good?" (Ps. 4:6). And we would say, and they would hear, "The light of thy countenance [is sealed] upon us" (Ps. 4:6). We are not that light "which lighteth every man" (John 1:9), but we are enlightened by You, that having been darkness at one time, we may be light in You (Eph. 5:8).

If only they could see the eternal inner light. Having tasted it, I was grieved that I could not show it to them as long as they brought me their hearts in their eyes which were roving away from You, while they said, "Who will show us any good?" (Ps. 4:6). For when I was angry within myself, in my chamber where I was inwardly pricked, where I had sacrificed, slaying my old man and had purposed to begin a new life, putting my trust in You, there You had begun to grow sweet to me and had "put gladness in my heart" (Ps. 4:7). I cried out as I read this outwardly, finding it to be true inwardly. And I would not be made rich with worldly goods, wasting time and being wasted by time, since I had other corn and wine and oil in Your eternal simple essence (Ps. 4:7).

With a loud cry of my heart I cried out in the next verse, "Oh, in peace. Oh, for the Selfsame!" Why did he say, "I will both lay me down in peace, and sleep" (Ps. 4:8), for who will hinder us when there "shall be brought to pass the saying that is written, Death is swallowed up in victory" (1 Cor. 15:54)? And You are surpassingly the Selfsame, you who do not change, and in You there is rest which forgets all toil. There is none other like You, and we are not to seek those many other things which are not what You are. But You, Lord, alone have made me dwell in hope (Ps. 4:8). I read and was inflamed, but I did not discover what I could do for those who are deaf and dead, like I myself had been, a pestilent person, bellowing bitterly and blindly against those writings which are honeyed with the honey of heaven and luminous with Your own light. I was consumed with zeal against the enemies of this Scripture.

When shall I recall all that happened in those holy days? I have neither forgotten nor will I skip over the severity of Your scourge and the wonderful swiftness of Your mercy. You tormented me with pain in my teeth, and when the pain had intensified to the point that I could not speak, it came into my heart to ask all my friends present to pray for me to You, the God of all manner of health. I wrote this on wax and gave it to them to read. Immediately, as soon as with humble devotion we had bowed our knees, that pain went away. But what pain? How did it go away? I was frightened, my Lord, my God, for from infancy I had never experienced anything like it. And the power of Your decree was deeply conveyed to me, and rejoicing in faith, I praised Your name.

The vintage vacation ended, and I gave notice to the Milanese to provide their scholars with another master to sell words to them. I did this both because I had made my choice to serve You and because my difficulty in breathing and the pain in my chest was not equal to the professorship. By letters I expressed to Your prelate, the holy man Ambrose, my former errors and present desires, begging his advice on what Scriptures I should read to become more prepared and more fit to receive so great a grace. He recommended Isaiah the prophet, I believe, because he, above the rest, more clearly foreshadows the Gospel and the calling of the Gentiles. But I did not understand the first part of my study in Isaiah, and thinking that the whole book was like that, I set it aside, to be resumed when I was more knowledgeable of our Lord's own words.

When the time came when I was to give in my name, we left the country and returned to Milan.

Alypius also wanted to be born again in You along with me, being already clothed with the humility befitting Your sacraments. He would valiantly tame his body, so that, with unusual courage he would walk the frozen ground of Italy with his bare feet.

Also with us was Adeodatus, the son of my body, born of my sin. How well You had made him. He was not quite fifteen, yet he surpassed many grave and learned men in intelligence. I confess to You Your gifts, Lord my God, Creator of all and abundantly able to reform our deformities, for I had no part in that boy but the sin. The fact that we brought him up in Your discipline was Your doing; no one else had inspired us with it. I confess to You Your gifts. There is a book of ours entitled *The Master*; it is a dialogue between Adeodatus and me. You know that everything that is attributed to the person conversing with me is his ideas, in his sixteenth year. I found in him many more things that were even more admirable. His talent struck awe into me. And who but You could be the work master of such wonders? You soon took his life from the earth, and I remember him now without any anxiety, fearing nothing for his childhood or youth or his whole self.

He joined with us, our contemporary in grace, to be brought up in Your discipline. We were baptized, and anxiety over our past life vanished from us. In those days I never grew tired of the wonderful sweetness of considering the depth of Your purposes concerning the salvation of mankind. How I wept during Your hymns and canticles; my inmost being was touched by the voices of Your sweet-tuned church! The voices flowed into my ears, and the truth distilled into my heart, out of which the passions of my devotion overflowed, and tears ran down, and I was happy in all of this.

It was not long before this that the Church of Milan had begun to use this kind of encouragement and exhortation, the brothers zealously joining together in harmony of voice and hearts. It was a year ago, or not much more, that Justina, mother of the Emperor Valentinian, a child, persecuted Your servant Ambrose in favor of her heresy to which she was seduced by the Arians. The devout people kept watch in the church, ready to die with their bishop Your servant. There my mother, Your handmaid, who bore a chief part of those anxieties and watchings, lived for prayer. We, not yet warmed by the heat of Your Spirit, were still stirred up by the sight of the amazed and disquieted city. During that time it was first instituted that, after the manner of the Eastern churches, hymns and psalms should be sung, so that the people would not grow faint through the tediousness of sorrow. From that day to this the custom has been retained, with many, almost all, of Your congregations throughout other parts of the world following suit.

Then through a vision You revealed to Your bishop, Ambrose, where the bodies of Gervasius and Protasius, the martyrs whom You had kept uncorrupted in Your secret treasury for so many years, lay hidden, so that You might in due time produce them to repress the fury of a woman, an

Empress. When they were discovered and dug up and with due honor carried to the Ambrosian Basilica, those who were troubled with unclean spirits, the devils confessing themselves, were cured. Also a certain man who had for many years been blind, a citizen and someone well-known to the city, asked about and heard the reason for the people's confused joy, and jumped up, asking his guide to lead him there. After he was led there, he begged to be allowed to touch with his handkerchief the bier of Your saints, whose death is "precious in the sight of the LORD" (Ps. 116:15). When he had done this and put the handkerchief to his eyes, they were immediately opened. From there reports of the incident spread. From there Your praises glowed and shone. From there the mind of that enemy, though not turned to the soundness of belief, was yet turned back from her persecuting fury. Thanks to You, my God. From where and to where have You led my remembrance, that I should also confess these things to You, which great though they are, I had passed by in forgetfulness? And yet even then, when the odor "of thy good ointments" (Song 1:3) was so fragrant, we did not run after You. Therefore, I wept more during the singing of Your hymns, when I had formerly sighed after You, and at length I was able to breathe You in, as far as the breath may enter into this our house of grass. (See Isaiah 40:6.)

You who make men who are of one mind to dwell in one house, also brought with us Euodius, a young man of our own city who was an officer of the court. He was converted to You and baptized before us. Quitting his secular service, he girded himself to You. We were about to dwell together in our devout purpose. We sought where we might serve You most usefully and were together returning to Africa when, after we had traveled as far as Ostia, my mother departed this life. I am omitting much because I am greatly hastening. Receive my confessions and thanksgiving, my God, for innumerable things of which I am silent. I will not omit whatever my soul brings forth concerning Your handmaid who brought me forth, both in the flesh, that I might be born to this temporal light, and in heart, that I might be born to eternal light.

Not her gifts, but Yours in her, will I speak of, for she neither made nor educated herself. You created her, and neither her father nor her mother knew what kind of woman would come from them. The scepter of Your Christ, the discipline of Your only Son in a Christian house, a good member of Your Church, educated her in Your fear. Yet for her good discipline, she used to credit not so much her mother's diligence as that of a certain older maid who had carried her father when he was a child, as little ones used to be carried on the backs of older girls. For this reason and because of her great age and excellent conversation, she was well respected by the heads of that Christian family. And therefore, the care of her master's daughters was entrusted to her, to which she gave diligent attention, restraining them earnestly, when necessary, with a holy severity and teaching them with a grave discretion. Except at those hours where they were most reasonably fed at their parents' table, she would not permit them, though parched with thirst, to drink even water. Therefore, she prevented an evil habit, and she added this wholesome advice: "You drink water now because you do not have wine in your power, but when you come to be married and are made mistresses of cellars and cupboards, you will scorn water, but the habit of drinking will remain." By this method of instruction, and the authority she had, she restrained the greediness of childhood and even molded their thirst to such an excellent moderation that they would not do what they should not do.

Yet, as Your handmaid told me, a love of wine had crept upon her. When she, as a sober maiden, was asked by her parents, as was customary, to draw wine out of the cask, she sipped a little with the tip of her lips before she poured the wine into the flagon, since her instinctive feelings refused more. She did not do this out of any desire of drink but out of the exuberance of youth which boils over in lighthearted pranks, and which is normally restrained by the gravity of elders. Thus by adding to that daily little amount a little more each day, (for whoever despises little things will fall little by little), she had fallen into a habit of greedily drinking her little cup almost full of wine. Where was that discreet old woman and her earnest revoking then?

Would anything succeed against a secret disease, if Your healing hand, Lord, did not watch over us? Even when father, mother, and guardians are absent, You are present, you who have created us, who call us, who also work out the salvation of our souls through those set over us. What did You do then, my God? How did You cure her? How did you heal her? Did You not out of another soul bring forth a hard and a sharp insult, like a surgical knife out of Your secret storehouse, and with one touch remove all that foul stuff? A maidservant with whom she used to go to the cellar quarreled with her little mistress, as is known to happen, when she was alone with her. The maid taunted her with this fault, and with a most bitter insult, she called her a wine drunkard. The taunt stung her conscience, and she saw the foulness of her fault and instantly condemned it and gave it up. As flattering friends pervert, so reproachful enemies generally correct. Yet You repay them not according to what they do but according to what they had purposed to do. The servant in her anger sought to harass her young mistress, not to correct her, and she did it in private, either because that was simply the time and place of the quarrel or for fear that she herself would also get in trouble for not having disclosed it sooner. But You, Lord, ruler of all in heaven and earth, who turn to Your purposes the deepest currents and the controlled turbulence of the tide of times, did by the very unhealthiness of one soul heal another. You did this so that when anyone reads this, he will not give himself the credit when another, whom he wished to be reformed, is reformed through words of his.

She was brought up modestly and soberly in this manner and was made subject by You to her parents rather than by her parents to You. As soon as she was of marriageable age, she was given to a husband and served him "as unto the Lord" (Eph. 5:22). She diligently tried to win him to You (1 Pet. 3:1), preaching You to him through her pure conduct by which You beautified her, making her respectfully loved and admired by her husband. And she endured his marital unfaithfulness in that she never had a quarrel with her husband on the subject. She looked for Your mercy upon him, that believing in You he might be made chaste. Besides this, he was hot-blooded, not only in his affections but also in anger. However, she had learned not to resist an angry husband, not only in deed but even in word. Only when he was calm and quiet and in a frame of mind to receive it, would she explain her actions, if by chance he had too quickly taken offense.

When many wives, who had milder husbands but who showed evidence of beatings on their faces, would in casual conversation blame their husbands' lives, she would blame their tongues, giving them serious advice in a joking way. She told them that from the time they heard the marriage writings read to them, they should regard them as contracts, by which they were made servants, and that they, remembering their condition, ought not to set themselves up against their lords. And when they, knowing what a quick-tempered husband she endured, marveled that it had never been heard nor was there any evidence that Patricius had beaten his wife or that there had been any domestic difference between them, even for one day, and confidentially asked the reason, she taught them her above-mentioned practice. Those wives who followed it, found good results and returned thanks; those who did not follow it, found no relief and suffered.

She also won over her mother-in-law, who at first was incensed against her by the gossip of evil servants, through respect and persevering endurance and meekness. Of her own accord, she disclosed to her son the meddling tongues by which the domestic peace between her and her daughter-in-law had been disturbed, asking him to correct them. Then, in compliance with his mother and for the well-ordering of the family and the harmony of its members, he disciplined the instigators with whipping, at his mother's request. She promised the same treatment to any who, to please her, spoke evil things about her daughter-in-law to her. No one took that chance, and they lived together with a remarkable sweetness of mutual kindness.

My God, my mercy, You also gave that good handmaid of yours, in whose womb You created me, a great gift: that whenever she was able, she showed herself to be a peacemaker between any disagreeing and conflicting parties. Hearing very bitter things from both sides, such as the belches of undigested irritation when unresolved hatred is breathed out in sour discourses to a present friend against an absent enemy, she would never disclose anything of one to the other but only that which might tend to lead to their reconciliation. This might have seemed a small thing to me, if I did not, to my grief, know numberless people who, through some horrible and wide-spreading contagion of sin, not only disclose to people who are angry with one another things said in anger, but add to them things never spoken. Considering that, to compassionate humanity it ought to seem an easy thing not to incite or increase ill will by harmful words or even to try to quench it by good words. She was like that, and You were her most inward instructor, teaching her in the school of her heart.

Finally, she won for You her own husband towards the very end of his earthly life. After he became a believer, she no longer had to grieve over the things she had endured from him before he was a believer. She was also the servant of Your servants. Whoever knew her, greatly praised, honored, and loved You in her, for through the witness of the fruits of a holy lifestyle they perceived Your presence in her heart. She had been the wife of one man, had honored her parents, had governed her household piously, and was well regarded for her good works. (See 1 Timothy 5:4, 10.) She had brought up children, often travailing for their spiritual birth when she saw them swerving from You. (See Galations 4:19.) Lastly, for all of us Your servants, Lord—whom you allow to speak when on occasion You give good gifts—who, before she fell asleep in You, lived united together, having received the grace of Your baptism, she took care as though she had been the mother of us all; and she also served us as though she had been a child to us all.

The day was now approaching on which she was to depart this life, the day You well knew but which we did not know. And it happened, by Your secret ways so ordering it, I believe, that she and I stood alone, leaning in a certain window which overlooked the garden of the house in which we were now staying in Ostia, and where removed from the noise of men, we were resting from the fatigues of a long journey in preparation for the voyage. We were talking by ourselves very sweetly, and "forgetting those things which are behind, and reaching forth unto those things which are before" (Phil. 3:13). We were discussing with each other in the presence of the Truth, which You are, what the nature of the eternal life of the saints would be like, which "Eye hath not seen, nor ear heard, neither have entered into the heart of man" (1 Cor. 2:9). But still we gasped with the mouth of our heart after those heavenly streams of Your fountain, "the fountain of life," which is "with thee" (Ps. 36:9), that being sprinkled from it according to our ability to receive, we might in some way meditate upon so high a mystery.

And when our discussion was brought to that point that the very highest delight of the bodily senses, in the very purest earthly light, was respecting the sweetness of that life, not only not worthy of comparison but not even of mention, we, raising ourselves up with a more fervent love towards the Selfsame, did by degrees go beyond all bodily things, even the very heaven where the sun and moon and stars shine down from upon the earth. We were soaring higher still by inward musing and reflecting and admiring Your works, and we came to our own minds and went beyond them, so that we might arrive at that region of never-failing plenty where You feed Israel forever (Ps. 78:71) with the food of truth and where life is the Wisdom by which all these things are made— what has been made and what will be made. This Wisdom was not made, but is as it has been, and will forever be. Rather, "to have been," and "hereafter to be," are not in its nature, but only "to be," since it is eternal. "To have been" and "to be hereafter" are not eternal. And while we were discussing and longing after it, we just barely touched on it with the whole effort of our heart, and we sighed. There we left bound "the firstfruits of the Spirit" (Rom. 8:23), and we returned to expressing ourselves through language where the spoken word has beginning and end. And what can be compared to Your Word, our Lord, who exists in Himself without becoming old and makes "all things new" (Rev. 21:5)?

We were saying then: If to anyone the tumult of the flesh were hushed, along with the images of earth and sea and air, and heaven from end to end, the very soul itself, which by not thinking on self rises above itself, plus all dreams and imaginary revelations, every tongue and every sign, and whatever exists only in transition, since if any could hear, all these transitory things would say, "We did not make ourselves, but He who abides forever made us" (see Psalm 100:3), if, then, having uttered this, they too were hushed, having roused only our ears to Him who made them, and if He alone speaks, not by them but by Himself, that we may hear His Word, not through any tongue of flesh nor angel's voice nor sound of thunder nor obscure analogy, but that we might hear Him whom we love through these things, might hear His very self without these things—just like we both now had strained ourselves and in a fleeting thought had touched on that eternal wisdom which abides over all—if this could be maintained, and other visions of a far lesser nature were withdrawn, and this one vision could transport and absorb and wrap up its beholder amid these inward joys, so that life might be forever like that one moment of insight which we now sighed after, would it not be this, "Enter... into the joy of thy lord" (Matt. 25:21, 23)? And when will that be? When we will all rise again, though we will not all be changed? (See 1 Corinthians 15:51.)

Such things I was speaking, and even if not in this exact way and with these same words, yet, Lord, You know that in that day when we were speaking of these things, and this world with all its delights became, as we spoke, contemptible to us, my mother said, "Son, for my own part I have no further delight in anything in this life. What I can do here any longer and for what reason I am here, I do not know, now that my hopes in this world are fulfilled. There was one thing for which I desired to linger for a while in this life, that I might see you a Christian before I died. My God has done this for me more abundantly, that I should now see you also, despising earthly happiness, become His servant. What can I do here?"

What answer I gave her about these things, I do not remember, for barely five days afterward, or not much more, she fell sick with a fever, and in that sickness one day she fainted and lost consciousness for awhile. We hurried to her side, but she was soon brought back to her senses, and, looking at me and my brother[1] standing by her, said to us inquiringly, "Where was I?" And then, looking steadily at us, who were overcome with grief, she said, "Here you will bury your mother." I held my peace and refrained from weeping, but my brother said something to the effect that he wished that she might die not in a strange place but in her own land. When she heard this, she gave him an anxious look and rebuked him with her eyes because he still held on to such things. Then she looked at me and said, "Behold what he says." Soon after, she said to us both, "Lay this body anywhere; do not let the arrangements for it upset you in any way. The only thing I request is that you would remember me at the Lord's altar, wherever you are." And after speaking her wishes in what words she could, she fell silent, overcome with pain because of her growing sickness.

But I, considering Your gifts, unseen God, which You instill into the hearts of Your faithful ones, out of which wondrous fruits are harvested, rejoiced and gave thanks to You. I recalled what I had known before, how careful and anxious she used to be regarding her place of burial, which she had provided and prepared for herself next to the body of her husband. Because they had lived in great harmony together, she also wished—so little can the human mind embrace things divine—to

---

[1] His name was Navigius.

have this addition to that happiness, and to have it remembered among men, that after her pilgrimage beyond the seas, what was earthly of this united pair had been permitted to be united beneath the same earth. When this vanity had begun to cease in her heart, through the fullness of Your goodness, I did not know. I rejoiced, admiring what she had disclosed to me, though indeed during our conversation in the window when she said, "What can I do here any longer?" she did not appear to have any desire to die in her own country.

Afterwards, I also heard that when we were at Ostia, one day when I was absent, she spoke with a mother's confidence with certain friends of mine about her contempt for this life and the blessing of death. When they were amazed at the courage which You had given to a woman and asked whether she was not afraid to leave her body so far from her own city, she replied, "Nothing is far to God, nor do I fear that at the end of the world He will not recognize where He is to raise me up."

Then, on the ninth day of her sickness, and the fifty-sixth year of her life, and the thirty-third of mine, that godly and holy soul was freed from the body.

I closed her eyes, and a mighty sorrow flowed into my heart and overflowed into tears. At the same time, my eyes, by a violent command of my mind, drained their fountain totally dry, and how I battled in my sorrow! When she breathed her last, my son Adeodatus burst out with loud crying, then, checked by us all, held his peace. In the same way, a childish feeling in me, which was, through my heart's youthful voice, finding an outlet in weeping, was checked and silenced. We did not think it fitting to solemnize that funeral with tearful wailing and groaning, for people usually express grief for the departed in this way as though the departed are unhappy or altogether dead. While on the contrary, she was neither miserable in her death nor altogether dead. Of this we were assured on good grounds by the testimony of her good life and her "faith unfeigned" (1 Tim. 1:5).

What was it then that grievously pained me inside but a fresh wound made through the sudden tearing away of that most sweet and dear habit of living together? I joyed indeed in her testimony when in her last sickness, mingling her endearments with my acts of duty, she called me dutiful and mentioned, with great affection of love, that she had never heard me speak any harsh or reproachful sound against her. But yet, my God, who made us, what comparison is there between the honor that I gave to her and her slavery for me? Being therefore deprived of the great comfort I had in her, my soul was wounded and my life was torn in two, as it were, because our lives had merged together as one.

After the boy's weeping was quieted, Euodius took up the Psalter and began to sing the psalm, "I will sing of mercy and judgment: unto thee, O LORD" (Ps. 101:1), with our whole household singing the response. Hearing what we were doing, many brothers and devout women came together. While those whose responsibility it was made ready for the burial, as was customary, I, in a part of the house where I might properly do so, spoke on something appropriate for the moment with those who did not think it fit to leave me. By this balm of truth, I soothed my torment known only to You. They did not know it, and listening intently, thought that I lacked all sense of sorrow. But in Your ears, where none of them heard, I blamed the weakness of my feelings and held back my flood of grief which yielded to me a little, but flowed back again, like a tide. Yet it did not cause me to burst out into tears or to change my demeanor. Still I knew what I was keeping down in my heart. And being greatly displeased that these human emotions had such power over me, which in the due order and appointment of our natural condition must necessarily be experienced, with a new grief I grieved for my grief and was therefore wearied with a double sorrow.

And then, the body was carried to the burial place; we went and returned without tears. I did not weep during those prayers which we poured out to You when the sacrifice of our redemption was offered for her when the corpse was by the grave's side, previous to being laid in it, as is the custom there. Yet during the whole day I was secretly grievously sad, and with an agitated mind I prayed to You, as I could, to heal my sorrow. However, You did not heal it. I believe that through this one instance, You imprinted upon my memory how strong the chains of habit are, even upon a soul which no longer feeds upon deceiving words. It also seemed good to me to go and bathe, having heard that the bath got its name (balneum) from the Greek Βαλανειον, because it drives sadness from the mind. And this also I confess to Your mercy, "father of the fatherless" (Ps. 68:5), that I bathed and was the same as before I bathed. The bitterness of sorrow could not seep out of my heart. Then I slept and woke up again and found my grief had lessened somewhat, and as I was alone in my bed, I remembered those true verses of Your servant Ambrose. For You are the

> Maker of all, the Lord
> > And Ruler of the height,
> Who, robing day in light, has poured
> > soft slumbers o'er the night,
>
> That to our limbs the power
> > of toil may be renewed,
> And hearts be raised that sink and cower,
> > And sorrows be subdued.

Then, little by little, I returned to my former thoughts of Your handmaid, her holy conduct towards You, her holy tenderness and care towards us, of which I was suddenly deprived. I was inclined to weep in Your sight for her and for myself, in her behalf and in my own. And I gave way to the tears which I had held back earlier and let them pour out as much as they desired, resting my heart upon them. And it did find rest in them, for my heart was in Your eyes, not in those of man who would have scornfully interpreted my weeping.

Now, Lord, I confess it to You in writing. Read it, anyone who will, and let him interpret it however he wants. If he finds sin in the fact that

I wept for my mother for a small portion of an hour—the mother who for the time was dead to my eyes, who had for many years wept for me that I might live in your eyes—let him not deride me, but rather, if he is a person of great compassion, let he himself weep for my sins to You, the Father of all the brothers of Your Christ.

But now, with a heart cured of that wound, in which I may deserve blame for succumbing to a worldly sentiment, I pour out to You, our God, on behalf of Your handmaid, a far different kind of tears, flowing from a spirit shaken by the thoughts of the dangers of every soul that dies "in Adam" (1 Cor. 15:22). Although she had been made alive in Christ, even before her release from the flesh, she had lived to praise Your name through her faith and conduct. Yet I dare not say that from the time You regenerated her by baptism, no word came out of her mouth against Your commandment. Your Son, the Truth, has said, "Whosoever shall say to his brother...Thou fool, shall be in danger of hell fire" (Matt. 5:22). But woe even to men who live praiseworthy lives, if You should examine them without mercy. But because You are not exacting in searching out our sins, we confidently hope to find some place with You. But whoever tallies up his real merits before You, what is he counting but Your own gifts? Oh, that men would know themselves to be men. "He that glorieth, let him glory in the Lord" (2 Cor. 10:17).

Therefore, my praise and my life, God of my heart, laying aside for awhile her good deeds for which I give thanks to You with joy, I now appeal to You for the sins of my mother. Listen to me, I beg You, through Him, the Medicine of our wounds, who hung upon the tree and who is now sitting at Your right hand making intercession to You for us (Rom. 8:34). I know that she dealt mercifully, and from her heart forgave her debtors their debts; forgive her debts also (see Matthew 6:12; 18:35), whatever she may have incurred in the many years since her baptism. Forgive her, Lord, forgive, I implore You; "enter not into judgment" (Ps. 143:2) with her. Let Your mercy be exalted above Your justice (James 2:13), since Your words are true, and You have promised mercy to the merciful. You made them to be merciful, You, who will "have mercy on whom [You] will have mercy, and…will have compassion on whom [You] will have compassion" (Rom. 9:15).

And I believe that You have already done what I ask, but accept, Lord, "the freewill offerings of my mouth" (Ps. 119:108). For she, when the day of her death was at hand, did not think of having her body lavishly wrapped or embalmed with spices, nor did she desire a choice monument or to be buried in her own land. She did not command us to do these things but desired only to have her name commemorated at Your altar, which she had served without missing one day. She knew that holy Sacrifice, by whom the handwriting that was against us is blotted out (Col. 2:14), would be administered from it. Through His sacrifice, He triumphed over the enemy, who, summing up our offenses and seeking what to lay to our charge, found nothing in Him (John 14:30), through whom we overcome.

Who will give back to Him His innocent blood? Who will repay Him the price with which He bought us and so take us from Him? Your handmaid bound her soul by the bond of faith to the sacrament of our ransom. Let none sever her from Your protection. Let neither the lion nor the dragon (Ps. 91:13) interfere by force or fraud. She will not answer that she owes nothing, for fear that she will be convicted and seized by the crafty accuser, but she will answer that her sins are forgiven by Him to whom none can repay that price which He, who owed nothing, paid for us.

May she then rest in peace with the husband, before and after whom she had no other, whom she obeyed with patience, bringing forth fruit (Luke 8:15) to You so that she might win him also to You. And inspire, Lord my God, inspire Your servants my brothers, Your sons my masters, whom with voice and heart and pen I serve, so that many who read these confessions may at Your altar remember Monnica, Your handmaid, with Patricius, her onetime husband, by whose bodies You brought me into this life—how, I do not know. May they with devout affection remember those who were my parents in this fleeting light, my kinsmen under You our Father, and my fellow-citizens in that eternal Jerusalem which Your pilgrim people sigh after from their Exodus, to the time of their return there. (See Hebrews 11:10–16.) May they do this so that my mother's last request of me may, through my confessions more than through my prayers, be more abundantly fulfilled for her through the prayers of many.

Book Ten

Having in the former books spoken of himself before he received the grace of baptism, in this book Augustine confesses what he was then, at the time of writing the Confessions. But first, he inquires by what ability we can know God at all, when he enlarges on the mysterious character of the memory, in which God dwells after he is made known, but through which we could not discover Him. Then he examines his own trials under the triple division of temptation: lust of the flesh, lust of the eyes, and pride (see 1 John 2:16), and what Christian self-discipline dictates regarding each. On Christ the only mediator, who heals and will heal all infirmities.

Let me know You, Lord, who know me; let me know You, "as also I am known" (1 Cor. 13:12). Power of my soul, enter into it, and prepare it for You, that You may have and hold it "not having spot, or wrinkle" (Eph. 5:27). This is my hope; that is why I speak, and in this hope I rejoice when I rejoice in a righteous way. Some things in this life ought to be sorrowed over less the more they are sorrowed over, and the more other things should be sorrowed over, the less men sorrow them. For behold, You love the truth (Ps. 51:6), and "he that doeth truth cometh to the light" (John 3:21). This is what I want to do now in my heart before You in confession and in my writing before many witnesses.

From You, Lord, to whose eyes the depth of man's conscience is naked (Heb. 4:13), what could be hidden in me even if I did not confess it? I would only hide You from myself, not myself from You. But now, because my groaning is a witness that I am displeased with myself, You shine out and are pleasing and beloved and longed for, that I may be ashamed of myself, renounce myself, and choose You, and neither please You nor myself, except in You. To You therefore, Lord, I am open, whatever I am. I have already spoken of the results of my confession to you. Nor do I do this with words and sounds of the flesh but with the words of my soul and the cry of my thoughts which Your ear alone knows. When I am evil, then to confess to You is nothing else than to be displeased with myself, but when I am holy, it is nothing other than not to give credit to myself. For You, Lord, bless the godly (Ps. 5:12), but first You justify him who has been ungodly (Rom. 4:5). My confession then, my God, in Your sight, is made silently and yet not silently. In sound, it is silent; in affection, it cries aloud. And I do not utter anything directly to men that You have not earlier heard from me, nor do You hear any such thing from me that You have not first said to me.

What, then, have I to do with men, that they should hear my confessions as if they could heal all my infirmities? Men are quite a race, curious to know the lives of others and lazy to change their own. Why do they seek to hear from me what I am, they who will not hear from You what they themselves are? How do they know whether I speak the truth when they hear about me from me, seeing that no man knows what is in man, but "the spirit of man which is in him" (1 Cor. 2:11)? If they hear from You about themselves, they cannot say, "The Lord lies." What is it for them to hear from You about themselves but to know themselves? Who knows himself and says, "It is false," unless he lies? But because love "believeth all things" (1 Cor. 13:7) among those who are knit together in unity through love, I also, Lord, will confess to You in such a way that men may hear, to whom I cannot demonstrate whether or not I confess the truth. Yet those whose ears are opened to me through love will believe me.

But, my inmost Physician, do make plain to me what fruit I may reap by doing it. For, the confessions of my past sins, which You have forgiven and covered (Ps. 32:1) that You might bless me in You, changing my soul by faith and Your sacrament, stir up the heart when they are read and heard. Then the heart will not sleep in despair and say, "I cannot," but it will awake in the love of Your mercy and the sweetness of Your grace. By this grace, whoever is weak is strong when by it he became conscious of his own weakness. Those who are good delight to hear of the past evils of others who are now freed from them, not because they are evils, but because they used to be but are no longer. With what fruit then, Lord my God, to whom my conscience daily confesses, trusting more in the hope of Your mercy than in its own innocence, with what fruit, I pray, do I in Your presence, through this book, confess to men also what I now am, not what I have been? For that other fruit I have seen and spoken of. But many want to know what I am now, at the very time of making these confessions, those who have or have not known me, and those who have heard from me or of me. But their ear is not at my heart, where I am, whatever I am. They wish then to hear me confess what I am within, where neither their eyes nor ears nor understanding can reach. They wish it, as men ready to believe, but will they know? For love, by which they are good, tells them that in my confessions I do not lie, and charity in them believes me.

But for what reason would they hear this? Do they desire to rejoice with me when they hear how near, by Your gift, I approach you, and to pray for me when they hear how much I am held back by my own burden of sin? To such I will reveal myself. It is no small result, my God, that "thanks may be given [to You] by many on our behalf" (2 Cor. 1:11) and that You may be prayed to by many on our behalf. Let the brotherly mind love in me what You teach is to be loved and grieve over in me what You teach is to be grieved over. Let it be a brotherly mind, not that of a stranger, not that of the "strange children; whose mouth speaketh vanity, and their right hand is a right hand of falsehood" (Ps. 144:7–8, 11). Let it be a brotherly mind, which, when it approves, rejoices for me and, when it disapproves, is sorry for me because whether it approves or disapproves, it loves me. To such men I will reveal myself. They will breathe freely at my good deeds and sigh for my evil deeds. My good deeds are your appointments and Your gifts; my evil ones are my offenses and Your judgments. Let them breathe freely at the one, sigh at the other; let hymns and weeping go up into Your sight out of the hearts of my brothers, Your vessels for incense. (See Revelation 8:3.) And You, Lord, be pleased with the incense of Your holy temple, and have mercy on me according to Your great mercy (Ps. 51:1) for Your own name's sake. In no way forsake what You have begun, and perfect my imperfections.

This is the object of my confessions in which I reveal what I am, not what I have been: to confess this, not before You only in a secret exultation with trembling and a secret sorrow with hope, but also in the ears of the believing sons of men, those who share my joy, and my partners in mortality, my fellow-citizens and fellow-pilgrims, who have gone before or are to follow on, companions of my way. These are Your servants, my brothers, whom You will to be Your sons, my masters whom You command me to serve, if I would live with You and of You. But Your Word would be of little effect if it only commanded by speaking and did not pave the way for my doings. This then I do in deed and word. This I do "under...thy wings (Ps. 17:8); I would be in too great a peril, if my soul were not yielded to You under Your wings and my infirmity not known to You. I am a little one, but my Father always lives, and my Guardian is sufficient for me. The One who begot me is the same One who defends me. You Yourself are all my good, You, Almighty, who are with me before I am with You. To those, then, whom You command me to serve I will reveal, not what I have been, but what I am now and what I still am. But I do not judge myself (1 Cor. 4:3). Therefore, this is the way I want to be heard.

You judge me Lord, because although no man knows "the things of a man, save the spirit of a man which is in him" (1 Cor. 2:11), there are some things in man which not even a man's own spirit knows. But You, Lord, who made him, know all about him. Though in Your sight I despise myself and account myself "dust and ashes" (Job 42:6), yet I know something of You, which I do not know of myself. Truly, "now we see through a glass, darkly," not yet "face to face" (1 Cor. 13:12). Therefore, as long as I am absent from You (2 Cor. 5:6), I am more present with myself than with You. Yet I know that You are in no way subject to transgression, but I do not know what temptations I can resist and what I cannot. There is hope because You are "faithful, who will not suffer [us] to be tempted above that [we] are able; but will with the temptation also make a way to escape, that [we] may be able to bear it" (1 Cor. 10:13). I will confess then what I do know of myself. I will confess also what I do not know of myself. I will do this because what I do know of myself, I know because You shine Your truth upon me, and what I do not know of myself, I will not know until my "darkness be as the noon day" (Isa. 58:10) in the light of Your countenance.

Not with doubting but with an assured knowledge do I love You, Lord. You struck my heart with Your word, and I loved You. Heaven and earth and all that is in them, behold, on every side they call on me to love You. They do not cease to warn everyone, "that they are without excuse" (Rom. 1:20). But You are even deeper than this, for You will have mercy on whom You will have mercy and have compassion on whom You will have compassion (Rom. 9:15), or else the heaven and the earth would speak Your praises in deaf ears. But what do I love when I love You? Not the beauty of bodies, not the fair harmony of time, not the brightness of the light, so radiant to our eyes, not the sweet melodies of musical arrangements, not the fragrant smell of flowers and ointments and spices, not manna and honey, not limbs pleasing to embraces of flesh. I love none of these when I love my God. Yet I love a kind of light and melody and fragrance and food and embrace when I love my God: the light, melody, fragrance, food, embrace of my inner man, where into my soul there shines what space cannot contain, and there sounds what time does not carry away, and there smells what breathing does not disperse, and there tastes what eating does not diminish, and there clings what satiety does not separate. This is what I love when I love my God.

"And what is this?" I asked the earth, and it answered me, "I am not He." Everything that is in it confessed the same. I asked the sea and the deeps and the living creeping things, and they answered, "We are not your God; seek above us." I asked the wind, and the whole atmosphere with his inhabitants answered, "Anaximenes was deceived, I am not God." I asked the heavens, sun, moon, and stars. They answered, "Nor are we the God whom you seek." And I replied to all my bodily senses, "You have told me of my God, that you are not He; tell me something of Him." And they cried out with a loud voice, "He made us." I questioned them in my thinking about them, and their form of beauty gave the answer. And I turned to myself and said to myself, "Who are you?" I answered, "A man." And behold I perceived that I am made up of both soul and body, one outside, the other within. By which of these should I seek my God? I had sought Him in the body from earth to heaven, as far as I could send messengers—the beams of my eyes. But the inner is the better of the two. For to it, as if it were presiding and judging, all the bodily messengers reported the answers of heaven and earth and all things in them, who said, "We are not God, but He made us." My inner man perceived these things by the ministry of the outer. I, the inner man, knew them; I, the mind, knew them through the senses of my body. I asked the whole frame of the world about my God, and it answered me, "I am not He, but He made me."

Is this world not apparent to all whose senses are perfect? Why then does it not speak the same to all? Animals small and great see it, but they cannot question it because they have no reason with which to judge what their senses report. But men can ask, so that "the invisible things of

[God]...are clearly seen, being understood by the things that are made" (Rom. 1:20). However, through an inordinate love of created things, they are made subject to them, and subjects cannot judge. And yet created things do not answer those who question them unless the questioners are able to judge. Nor do they change their voice, i.e. their appearance, if one man only sees, while another both sees and asks, so that they appear one way to this man, and another way to that man. Showing themselves the same way to both men, they are silent to the one, and they speak to the other. Rather, creation speaks to all, but those who understand are the ones who compare creation's external voice with the truth within them. For truth says to me, "Neither heaven nor earth nor any other body is your God." Their own nature says to him that sees them: "They are a mass; a mass is less in part than in the whole." Now, my soul, to you I speak. You are my better part, for you animate the mass of my body, giving it life, which no body can give to a body. But your God is still the life of your life.

What then do I love, when I love my God? Who is He who is above the highest point of my soul? By my very soul I will ascend to Him. I will pass beyond that power by which I am united to my body and which fills its whole frame with life. I cannot by that power find my God. If I could, "the horse" and "the mule, which have no understanding" (Ps. 32:9), might find Him, since it is the same power by which even their bodies live. But there is another power there, by which I not only animate but also infuse my body with sense, which the Lord has framed for me, not commanding the eye to hear and the ear to see, but commanding the eye, that through it I should see and the ear, that through it I should hear, and to the other senses their own particular seats and offices. I, using my one mind, enact these diverse purposes through them. But I will pass beyond this power of mine, for the horse and mule also have this power because they also perceive through the body.

I will pass then beyond this power of my nature, rising by degrees to Him who made me. And I come to the fields and spacious palaces of my memory, where the treasures of innumerable images are brought into it from all sorts of things perceived by the senses. Whatever we think about is stored up, whether by enlarging or reducing or by any other way varying those things which the sense has come to. Whatever else has been committed and laid up, which forgetfulness has not yet swallowed up and buried is also there. When I enter there, I request what I want to be brought forth. Some things instantly come. Others must be sought after longer and be brought in, as it were, out of some inner receptacle. Others rush out in troops, and while I desire and require one thing, they all spring forth, as if to say, "Is it perhaps I?" These I drive away with the hand of my heart from the face of my memory until what I wished for is unveiled and appears in sight, out of its secret place. Other things come up readily, in perfect order, as they are called for. Those in front make way for the rest, and as they make way, they are hidden from sight, ready to come when I want them. All this takes place when I repeat a thing by heart.

In my memory, all things are preserved distinctly and under general subject heads. Each has entered by its own avenue: light and all colors and bodily shapes by the eyes; all sorts of sounds by the ears; all smells by way of the nostrils; all tastes by the mouth; and whatever is hard and soft, hot or cold, smooth or rugged, heavy or light, either outside or inside the body enters by the body through feeling. That great harbor of the memory receives all these in its numberless secret and inexpressible meanderings, to be forthcoming and be brought out at need. Each enters in by its own gate, and there it is stored. The things themselves do not enter in; only the images of the things perceived are there, ready for thought to recall.

Who can tell how these images are formed, even though it is clear by which sense each has been brought in and stored up? For even while I dwell in darkness and silence, in my memory I can produce colors, if I wish, and discern between black and white and whatever others I want to. And sounds do not break in and disturb the image I am reviewing, which was drawn in by my eyes, though sounds are also there, lying dormant and stored apart, as it were. These too I call for, and immediately they appear. And though my tongue is silent and my throat mute, I can sing as much as I want. These images of colors, even though they are there, do not intrude themselves and interrupt when another store of images which flowed in by the ears is called for. So the other things, piled in and up by the other senses, I recall at my pleasure. I discern the breath of lilies from violets, though I am smelling nothing, and I prefer honey to sweet wine, smooth before rugged, though at the time I neither taste nor handle, but only remember.

These things I do within, in that vast court of my memory. Present with me are heaven, earth, sea, and whatever I can think about regarding them, besides what I have forgotten. There I also meet with myself and review when, where, and what I have done, and with what feelings I did a certain thing. There is all that I remember, either from my own experience or through the accounts of others. Out of the same store I continually combine with the past fresh likenesses of things which I have experienced or fresh likenesses of things I have believed in from that which I have experienced. From these I again infer future actions, events and hopes, and all these again I reflect on as if they were present. "I will do this or that," I say to myself, in that great receptacle of my mind stored with the images of many and such great things, "and this or that will follow." "That this or that might be!" "God prevent this or that!" I speak these things to myself, and when I speak, the images of everything I speak about are present, out of the same treasury of memory. I would not speak about any of them, if the images were missing.

Great is the force of memory, excessively great, my God, a large and boundless chamber! Has anyone sounded the bottom of it? Yet this is a power of mine and belongs to my nature, and I myself do not comprehend all that I am. Therefore, is the mind too narrow to contain itself? And where is the part which it does not contain? Is it outside of it and not inside? How then does it not comprehend itself? An astonishing admiration surprises me; amazement about this seizes me. Men go abroad to admire the heights of mountains, the mighty billows of the sea, the broad tides of rivers, the width of the ocean, and the paths of the stars, and they pass themselves by. They do not marvel that when I spoke of all these things, I did not see them with my eyes. Yet I could not have spoken of them unless I then actually saw—inwardly in my memory with the same vast spaces between as if I saw them outside—the mountains, billows, rivers, and stars, which I have seen, and the ocean, which I believe exists. Yet I did not, by seeing them, draw them into myself when I saw them with my eyes. Nor are they themselves with me, but only their images. And I know by what sense of the body each was impressed upon me.

Yet the unmeasurable capacity of my memory does not retain these alone. Here also is all that I learned of the liberal arts and have not yet forgotten, things removed, as it were, to some inner place which is yet no place. They are not images, but are the things themselves. What literature is, what the art of disputing is, how many kinds of questions there are—whatever I know of these—they do not exist in my memory as if I had taken in the image and left the reality outside, or like something that sounds and passes away, like a voice imprinted on the ear by a lasting impression

257

through which it can be recalled, as if it spoke, when it no longer speaks. It is not like a smell, which, while it permeates and evaporates into air, affects the sense of smell by which it conveys into the memory an image of itself, which we renew through memory. Nor is it like meat, which truly has no taste in the belly and yet in a manner of speaking still has taste through the memory. Nor is it like anything which the body perceives by touch and which, when removed from us, the memory still conceives. These things are not transmitted into the memory, only their images are, and with an admirable swiftness, they are caught up and stored, as it were, in wondrous cabinets. They are then wonderfully brought forth by the act of remembering.

But now when I hear that there are three kinds of questions: "Does the thing exist?" "What is it?" "Of what is it made?" I do indeed hold the images of the sounds of which those words are composed, those sounds which have passed through the air with a noise and now no longer exist. But the things themselves which are signified by those sounds, I never encountered with any bodily sense, nor ever discerned them other than in my mind. Yet I have stored them, not their images, in my memory. Let them explain if they can, how they entered into me, for I have gone over all the avenues of my flesh but cannot find any by which they entered. The eyes say, "If those images were of color, we reported them." The ears say, "If they had sound, we gave knowledge of them." The nostrils say, "If they smell, they came through us."

The taste says, "Unless they have a savor, do not ask me." The touch says, "If it does not have shape, I have not handled it; if I have not handled it, I gave no notice of it."

From where and how did these things enter into my memory? I do not know. When I learned them, I did not give credit to another man's mind but recognized them in mine, and accepting them as true, I committed them to it, laying them up, as it were, from where I might bring them forth when I willed. They were therefore in my heart, even before I learned them, but they were not in my memory. Where, then, or why, when they were spoken, did I acknowledge them and say, "So it is; it is true," unless they were already in the memory, but so thrown back, as it were, in deeper recesses, that had not the suggestion of another drawn them forth, I would possibly have been unable to conceive of them?

For that reason, we find that to learn these things, the images of which we do not understand through our senses but which rather we perceive internally, as they are without images, is simply to receive them by conceptualizing them and by taking note to make sure that those things which the memory earlier stored at random and without order, be organized in that same memory where they formerly lay unknown, scattered, and neglected, that they will readily occur to the mind well acquainted with them. How many things of this kind which already have been discovered and organized does my memory bear! If, for some short space of time I were to cease to call to mind these things which we are said to have learned and to have come to know, they would again be buried and glide back into the deeper recesses, so that they must again be thought out from there as if they were newly learned. They have no other home, but they must be drawn together again so that they may be known. That is to say, they must be collected together from their dispersion.

From this the word "cogitation" is derived. For *cogo* (I collect) and *cogito* (I re-collect) have the same relation to each other as *ago* (I do) and *agito* (I do constantly), *facio* (I make) and *factito* (I make often). But the mind has appropriated to itself this word (cogitation), so that, not what is "collected" in any sort of way, but what is "re-collected," i.e. brought together in the mind, is properly said to be cogitated, or thought upon.

The memory also contains principles and innumerable laws of numbers and dimensions, none of which was imprinted by any bodily sense, since they have neither color nor sound nor taste nor smell nor touch. I have heard the sound of the words by which they are signified when they are discussed, but the sounds are different than the things. The sounds are different in Greek than in Latin, but the things are neither Greek nor Latin nor any other language. I have seen the lines drawn by architects, the very finest, like a spider's thread. But the principles are still different; they are not the images of those lines which my physical eye saw. He who, without any conception whatsoever of an object, identifies them within himself, knows them. With all my bodily senses I have also perceived the numbers with which we number things, but those numbers are different than the things. They are not the images of these, and therefore they indeed exist. Let him who does not see this deride me for saying these things, and I will pity him while he derides me.

I remember all these things and how I learned them. I have also heard and remember many things that were argued against them very erroneously. Even if these things are false, it is not false that I remember them. And, I remember also that I have discerned between those truths and these falsehoods argued against them. And I perceive that my present discernment of these things is different than remembering that I often discerned them, when I often thought upon them. I remember, then, that I often understood these things, and what I now discern and understand, I lay up in my memory, that hereafter I may remember that I understood it now. So then, I also remember that I have remembered, in the same way that if later I shall call to remembrance that I have now been able to remember these things, I shall call it to remembrance by the force of memory.

The same memory also contains the emotions of my mind, not in the same manner that my mind itself contains them when it feels them, but far otherwise, according to a power of its own. For without rejoicing I remember that I rejoiced, and without sorrow I recollect my past sorrow. That I once feared, I review without fear, and without desire, I call to mind a past desire. On the contrary, sometimes I remember with joy my past sorrow, and with sorrow, I remember past joy. This is not to be wondered at, as it would be if we were talking about the body, for mind is one thing, body another. If I, therefore, with joy remember some past bodily pain, it is not so extraordinary. But now, the mind sees this very memory itself. For when we command a thing to be kept in memory, we say, "See that you keep it in mind," and when we forget, we say, "It did not come to my mind," and "It slipped out of my mind." We then call the memory itself the mind. This being so, how is it that when with joy I remember my past sorrow, the mind has joy, the memory has sorrow; how is it that the mind is joyful through the joy which is in it, yet the memory is not sad through the sadness which is in it? Does the memory perhaps not belong to the mind? Who will say so? The memory then is, as it were, the belly of the mind, and joy and sadness are like sweet and bitter food. When they are committed to the memory, they are, as it were, passed into the belly where they may be stowed, but cannot be tasted. It is ridiculous to imagine these to be similar, and yet they are not utterly dissimilar.

But, behold, when I say there are four emotions of the mind: desire, joy, fear, and sorrow, I bring them out of my memory. Whatever I can argue concerning them by dividing each into its subordinate class and defining it, I find what to say in my memory. I bring it from memory, yet I am not disturbed by any of these emotions when, by calling them to mind, I remember them. And before I remembered and brought them back, they were there, and therefore they could by recollection be brought from there.

Perhaps, then, as meat is brought up out of the belly by chewing the cud, so by recollection these things are brought out of the memory. Why then does the one who argues and who recollects in this way not taste in the mouth of his musing the sweetness of joy or the bitterness of sorrow? Is this not a fair comparison because both are not in all respects similar? Who would willingly speak of grief or fear if we were compelled to be sad or fearful each time we spoke of them? Yet we could not speak of them if we did not find in our memory not only the sounds of the names, according to the images impressed on us by our bodily senses, but also conceptions of the very things themselves which we never received by any avenue of the body. Rather, the mind itself perceived them through the experience of its own emotions and committed them to memory, or the memory itself retained them without their being committed to it.

But who can readily say whether this occurs through images or not? In this way when I speak of a stone or name the sun, the things themselves are not present to my senses, but their images are present in my memory. I name a bodily pain, yet it is not present with me when nothing aches. However, unless its image were present to my memory, I would not know what to say about it, nor could I, in speaking about it, discern pain from pleasure. I speak of bodily health, being sound in body. The thing itself is present with me, yet unless its image were also present in my memory, I could by no means recall what the sound of this name signifies. Nor would the sick, when health is spoken of, recognize what was spoken unless the same image were retained by the force of memory, although the thing itself be absent from the body. I speak of numbers by which we number, and it is not their images but they themselves which are present in my memory. I name the image of the sun, and that image is present in my memory. I do not recall the image of its image; rather, the image itself is before me, calling it to mind. I talk about memory, and I recognize what I mean. And where do I recognize it but in the memory itself? Is it also present to itself in its image, and not in itself?

When I mention forgetfulness and recognize what I am speaking about, how would I recognize it if I did not remember it? I do not speak of the sound of the name but of the thing which it signifies. If I had forgotten that, I would not recognize what that sound signifies. When I remember memory, memory itself is present with itself through itself, but when I remember forgetfulness, both memory and forgetfulness are present: memory by which I remember, forgetfulness which I remember. What is forgetfulness, but the privation of memory? How then is it present so that I remember it, since when it is present I cannot remember? But if what we remember we hold in memory and, unless we did remember forgetfulness, we could never at the hearing of the name recognize the thing it signifies, then forgetfulness is retained by memory. It is present then, so that we do not forget, and yet when it is present, we forget. It is to be understood from this that when we remember forgetfulness, it is its image, not itself, that is. For if it were present by itself, it would not cause us to remember but to forget. Who now can search this out? Who can comprehend how it is?

Lord, I truly toil in this and I toil in myself. I have become a heavy soil requiring much sweat of the brow. We are not now searching out the regions of heaven or measuring the distances of the stars or inquiring the weight of the earth. It is I myself who remember, I the mind. It is not so extraordinary, if what I am not is far from me, but what is nearer to me than myself? Behold, the force of my own memory is not understood by me, though I cannot so much as name myself without it. What shall I say when it is clear to me that I remember forgetfulness? Shall I say that which I remember is not in my memory? Or shall I say that forgetfulness is for this purpose in my memory, that I might not forget? Both were most absurd. What third way is there? How can I say that the image of forgetfulness—but not forgetfulness itself—is retained by my memory when I remember it? Also, how could I say this, since when the image of anything is impressed on the memory, the thing itself must first be present as the source from which that image may be impressed?

This is the way I remember Carthage, and all the places where I have been, plus men's faces whom I have seen, and things reported by the other senses, and the health or sickness of the body. When these things were present, my memory received from them images, which, being present with me, I might look on and bring back in my mind when I remembered them in their absence. If, then, this forgetfulness is retained in the memory through its image, not through itself, then plainly it was itself once present so that its image might be taken. But when it was present, how did it write its image in the memory, since forgetfulness, by its presence, erases what it finds already recorded? Yet in whatever way, although this way is past comprehension and explanation, I am certain that I also remember forgetfulness itself, by which what we remember is erased.

Great is the power of memory, a fearful thing, my God, a deep and boundless manifoldness! And this thing is the mind, and I am this myself. What am I then, my God? What nature am I? A life various and manifold and exceedingly immense. Look in the innumerable plains and caves and caverns of my memory, innumerably full of innumerable kinds of things, either through images, like all bodies, or by actual presence, like the arts, or by certain thoughts or impressions, like the emotions of the mind, which, even when the mind does not feel, the memory retains, though whatever is in the memory is still also in the mind. Over all these I run, fly, and dive on this side and that as far as I can, and there is no end. So great is the force of memory, so great the force of life, even in the mortal life of man.

What shall I do then, You who are my true life, my God? I will pass even beyond this power of mine which is called memory. I will pass beyond it so that I may approach You, sweet Light. What do You say to me? See, I am mounting through my mind towards You who abide above me. I now will pass beyond this power of mine which is called memory, longing to reach You at that place where You may be found, and to cleave to You there where one may cleave to You. Even beasts and birds have memory, or else they could not return to their dens and nests or to many other things they are used to. And indeed they could not become used to anything except through memory. Therefore, I will pass beyond memory also so that I may arrive at Him who has separated me from "the beasts of the earth" and made me "wiser than the fowls of heaven" (Job 35:11). I will pass beyond memory also, and where shall I find You, You truly good and certain sweetness? And where shall I find you? If I find You outside my memory, then I do not retain You in my memory. And how shall I find You, if I do not remember You?

The woman who had lost her coin and sought it with a light, would never have found it unless she had remembered it. (See Luke 15:8.) When it was found, how would she know whether it was the same one she was looking for unless she remembered it? I remember seeking and finding many things. By this I know that when I was seeking something and was asked, "Is this it?" "Is that it?" I said "No," until the thing which I sought was offered to me. Had I not remembered it, whatever it was, I would not have been able to find it, even though it might have been offered to me, because I would not have recognized it. This is always the case when we seek and find any lost thing. Notwithstanding, when anything visible is accidentally lost from our sight, though not from our memory, its image is still retained within, and it is sought until it is restored to sight. When it is found, it is recognized by the image which is within. We do not say that we have found what was lost unless we recognize it, and we cannot recognize it unless we remember it. This was lost to the eyes but retained in the memory.

But what about when the memory itself loses anything, as happens when we forget and seek to remember? Where, in the end, do we search but in the memory itself? And there, if one thing is perhaps offered instead of another, we reject it until what we seek meets us, and when it does, we say, "This is it." We would not say this unless we recognized it, nor would we recognize it unless we remembered it. Certainly, then, we had forgotten it. Or, if the whole thing had not escaped us, was the lost part sought for by the part which we still held? Did memory, feeling that it did not carry on together all which it was accustomed to, but was maimed, as it were, by the curtailment of its old habit, demand the restoration of what it missed? For instance, we may see or think of someone we know whose name we have forgotten. In trying to remember his name, certain names may come to mind, but none of them will connect with us, because we are not used to thinking of them in relation to him. Therefore each is rejected until that one name presents itself, upon which our knowledge can smoothly come to rest, as on its accustomed object.

From where does that name present itself but out of the memory itself? For even when we recognize it by being reminded of it by another, it still comes from the memory. We do not think of it as something new, but, upon remembering it, we confirm that what was mentioned is correct. If it were utterly blotted out of the mind, we would not remember it even when reminded of it. For we have not yet completely forgotten what we remember that we have forgotten. What, then, we have completely forgotten, though lost, we cannot even seek after.

How then do I seek You, Lord? When I seek You, my God, I seek a happy life. I will seek You so that my soul may live. My body lives by my soul, and my soul by You. How then do I seek a happy life, seeing that I do not have it until I can say, where I ought to say it, "It is enough"? How do I seek it? Do I seek it by recollection, as though I had forgotten it, remembering that I had forgotten it? Or, do I seek it by desiring to learn it as something unknown, either never having known it, or having completely forgotten it, so that I do not even remember that I had forgotten it? Is not a happy life what all men want to have, so that no one does not want it altogether? Where have they known it, that they want it so much? Where have they seen it, that they love it so much? Truly we have it; how, I do not know.

There is a sense in which when one has it, then he is happy, and then there are those who are blessed with hope. These latter have it in a lesser way than those who have it in reality, yet they are better off than those who are neither happy in reality nor in hope. Yet even these would not want to be happy if they did not have the desire for it in some way, and it is most certain that they do want it. How they have known it, then, I do not know; they must have it by some sort of knowledge. What knowledge, I do not know, and I am perplexed over whether it is in the memory. If it is there, then we were once happy, all separately or in that man who first sinned, in whom we also all died (1 Cor. 15:22), and from whom we are all born with misery. I do not now inquire into this, but only ask whether the happy life is in the memory? We would not love it if we did not know it. We hear the name, and we all confess that we desire the thing, for we are not delighted with the mere sound of it. When a Greek hears it in Latin, he is not delighted, not knowing what is spoken. We Latins are delighted, as he would be if he heard it in Greek, because the thing itself is neither Greek nor Latin which Greeks and Latins and men of all other languages long for so earnestly. It is therefore known to all, for if they could be asked in one language if they want to be happy, they would answer without any doubt that they would. This could not be unless the thing itself for which this is the name were retained in the memory.

Is it like one who has seen Carthage remembers it? No, for a happy life is not seen with the eye because it is not an object. Is it like when we remember numbers then? No, for he who has these in his knowledge does not further seek to attain them. But we have a happy life in our knowledge and therefore we love it and yet still desire to attain it so that we may be happy. Is it like when we remember eloquence then? No, for upon hearing this word, some who are not yet eloquent and many who desire to be so call the thing to mind. It therefore appears that it is in their knowledge. Yet they have by their bodily senses observed others to be eloquent, and have been delighted, and desire to be eloquent, though indeed they would not be delighted except for some inward knowledge of it, and they would not wish to be eloquent unless they were delighted in this way. On the other hand, we do not experience a happy life in others through any bodily sense. Is it like when we remember joy? Perhaps, for I remember my joy even when I am sad, like I remember a happy life when I am unhappy. I never did, with any bodily sense, see, hear, smell, taste, or touch my joy, but I experienced it in my mind when I rejoiced. The knowledge of it clung to my memory so that I can recall it sometimes with disgust and sometimes with longing, according to the nature of the things I remember delighting in. For even from foul things have I been immersed in a sort of joy, which, when I now recall, I detest and denounce, and at other times I have rejoiced in good and honest things, which I recall with longing. Perhaps these latter are no longer present, and therefore I recall my former joy with sadness.

Where then and when did I experience my happy life that I should remember and love and long for it? It is not me alone or some few besides, but we all would gladly be happy. We would not want this so strongly unless we knew it through some certain knowledge. How is it, that if two men were asked whether they would go to the wars, one, perhaps, would answer that he would, the other, that he would not; however, if they were asked whether they wanted to be happy, both would instantly, without any doubt, say they would. And, one would go to the wars, and the other would not, for no other reason than to be happy. Is it, perhaps, that as one looks for his joy in this thing, another looks in that? All agree in their desire to be happy, as they would also agree, if they were asked if they wanted to have joy, a joy they call a happy life. Although one obtains joy by one means, another by another, all have one end which they strive to attain, namely, joy. Since joy is something which all must say they have experienced, it is therefore found in the memory and recognized whenever the name of a happy life is mentioned.

Far be it, Lord, far be it from the heart of Your servant who here confesses to You, far be it that, let joy be what it may, I should therefore think myself happy. There is a joy which is not given to the ungodly but to those who love You for Your own sake, whose joy You Yourself are. And this is the happy life, to rejoice to You, of You, for You; this is it, and there is no other. They who think there is another, pursue something else which is not true joy. Yet their will is not turned away from some semblance of joy.

It is not certain, then, that all wish to be happy, since they who do not wish to delight in

You, which is the only happy life, do not truly desire the happy life. Or do all men desire this, but because "the flesh lusteth against the Spirit, and the Spirit against the flesh" (Gal. 5:17), so that they cannot do what they want to, they fall upon that which they can and are content with that? Is this because what they are not able to do they do not desire as strongly as would serve to make them able? I can ask anyone if he would rather delight in truth or in falsehood. They will no more hesitate to say, "in the truth," than they will hesitate to say, "that they desire to be happy." A happy life is joy in the truth, for this means rejoicing in You who are "the truth" (John 14:6), God, "my light" (Ps. 27:1), "health of my countenance" (Ps. 42:11), my God. This is the happy life which all desire; all desire this life which alone is happy. All desire to rejoice in the truth.

I have met with many who would deceive others, but I have met no one who would want to be deceived. Where then did they know this happy life, except where they also knew the truth? They love it also since they do not want to be deceived. When they love a happy life, which is none other than rejoicing in the truth, then they also love the truth which they would not love if there were not some perception of it in their memory. Why then do they not delight in it? Why are they not happy? It is because they are more strongly taken up with other things which have more power to make them miserable than that which they so faintly remember can make them happy. Yet there is a little light in men; let them walk, let them walk, so that the darkness will not overtake them (John 12:35).

But why does truth generate hatred? Why does the Man of Yours, preaching the truth, become an enemy to them (see John 8:40), while at the same time, they love a happy life, which is nothing other than delighting in the truth? How can this be unless truth is loved in such a way, that those who love something else more than the truth would gladly believe that that which they love is the truth, and because they do not want to be deceived, they would not be convinced that they are deceived? Therefore, they hate the truth for that thing's sake which they love instead of the truth. They love truth when it enlightens; they hate it when it reproves. Since they would not want to be deceived and yet they themselves want to deceive, they love truth when it shows itself to them and hate it when it exposes them. (See John 3:20.) For this it will repay them in such a way that those who are not willing to be enlightened by it, will be exposed by it against their will, and yet it itself will not become manifest to them. Thus, thus, does the mind of man, so blind and sick, foul and ill-favored, wish to be hidden, but it does not wish that anything should be hidden from it. The contrary is rendered it, that it itself should not be hidden from the truth, but the truth is hid from it. Yet even though the mind of man is so wretched in this way, it would rather delight in truths than in falsehoods. Happy then will it be when, with no intervening distractions, it will delight in that only Truth by whom all things are true.

See what a territory I have gone over in my memory seeking You, Lord, and I have not found You outside it. Nor have I found anything concerning You but what I have kept in memory ever since I learned of You. For since I learned of You, I have not forgotten You. Where I found truth, there I found my God, the Truth itself, which, since I learned, I have not forgotten. Ever since I learned of You, You reside in my memory, and there I find You when I call You to remembrance and delight in You. These are my holy delights which You have given me in Your mercy, having regard for my poverty.

But where in my memory do You reside? Lord, where do You reside? What manner of lodging have You framed for Yourself? What manner of sanctuary have You built for Yourself? You have given this honor to my memory, to reside in it. I am considering in what part of it You reside. In thinking of You, I passed beyond such parts of it as the beasts also have, for I did not find You there among the images of bodily things. I came to those parts to which I committed the affections of my mind, and I did not find You there. I entered into the very seat of my mind, which is in my memory since the mind remembers itself also, and You were not there. For You are not a bodily image, nor the affection of a living being, as when we rejoice, grieve, desire, fear, remember, forget, or the like. Neither are You the mind itself because You are the Lord God of the mind. All these are inconstant, but You remain unchangeable over all. Yet You have favored me by dwelling in my memory since I learned of You. Why do I now look for the place in which You dwell, as if there were places there? I am sure that You dwell in my memory, since I have remembered You ever since I learned of You, and there I find You when I call You to remembrance.

Where then did I find You that I might learn of You? For You were not in my memory before I learned about You. Where then did I find You that I might learn about You except in You above me? There is no place; we go backward and forward, and there is no place. Everywhere, Truth, You give audience to all who ask counsel of You and You answer all at once, though they ask Your counsel on diverse matters. Clearly do You answer, though all do not clearly hear. All consult You on what they want, though they do not always hear what they want. Your best servant is he who seeks not so much to hear from You what he wants to hear, but rather to want that which he hears from You.

Too late I loved You, Beauty of Ancient Days, yet ever new! Too late I loved You! Behold, You were within me, and I was outside of You. There I searched for You, I who was deformed, plunging amid those beautiful things which You had made. You were with me, but I was not with You. Things held me far from You, which, unless they were in You, would not exist at all. You called and shouted and burst my deafness. You flashed, shone, and scattered my blindness. You breathed aromas, and I drew in breath, and now I pant for You. I tasted You, and now I hunger and thirst. You touched me, and I burned for Your peace.

When I shall cleave to You with my whole self, I shall not have sorrow or labor, and my life will wholly live, being wholly full of You. But now, since You lift up those whom You fill and since I am not yet full of You, I am a burden to myself. Lamentable joys strive with joyous sorrows, and I do not know which side will win the victory. Woe is me! Lord, have pity on me. My evil sorrows strive with my good joys, and which side will win the victory, I do not know. Woe is me! Lord, have pity on me. Woe is me! Behold, I do not hide my wounds. You are the Physician, I am the sick one. You are merciful, I am miserable. Is not man's life upon earth full of trial? (See Job 7:1.)

Who wishes for troubles and difficulties? You command them to be endured, not to be loved. No man loves what he endures, though he loves to endure. Though he rejoices that he endures, he would rather that there were nothing for him to endure. In adversity I long for prosperity; in prosperity I fear adversity. What middle place is there between these two where the life of man is not all trial? Woe to the prosperities of the world: once because of fear of adversity and twice because of the corruption of joy! Woe to the adversities of the world, once, twice, and three times: for the longing for prosperity, because adversity itself is a hard thing, and for fear that it will shatter endurance. Is not man's life upon earth full of trial, without any interval of relief?

And all my hope is nowhere but in Your exceedingly great mercy. Give what You command, and command what You will. You command us to be self-restrained. "When I knew," says one, "that no man can be self-restrained unless God grants it, and this also was a part of wisdom to know whose gift it is." By self-restraint we are bound up and brought back into the One from whom we were dissipated into many. The one who loves anything with You which he loves not for You loves You too little. Oh Love, who always burns and never consumes! Oh Charity, my God, kindle me! You command self-restraint; give me what You command, and command what You will.

Truly You commanded me to restrain myself from "the lust of the flesh, and the lust of the eyes, and the pride of life" (1 John 2:16). You commanded abstinence from promiscuity, and for wedlock itself, You have counseled something better than what You have permitted. And since You gave it, it was done, even before I became a dispenser of Your sacrament. Yet there lives in my memory, of which I have much spoken, the images of such things that my evil custom put there. These haunt me without strength when I am awake, but in sleep they not only haunt me so as to give pleasure, but even to the point where I affirm them, and what is very like reality. The illusion of the image in my soul and in my flesh prevails to the extent that when I am asleep, false visions persuade me to enter into that which when waking, the true cannot.

Am I not then myself, Lord my God? And yet there is such a difference between myself and myself within that moment when I pass from waking to sleeping or return from sleeping to waking!

Where is reason then, which, when awake, resists such suggestions and remains unshaken should the things themselves be urged on it? Is it clasped up with the eyes? Is it lulled asleep with the senses of the body? How is it that often even in sleep we resist and, mindful of our purpose and remaining most chastely in it, yield no assent to such enticements? Yet there is such a difference, that when it happens otherwise, upon waking we return to a clear conscience. By this very difference we discover that we did not do that which we are still sorry was done in us in some way.

Surely You are mighty, God Almighty, so as to heal all the diseases of my soul, and by Your more abundant grace to quench even the impure actions of my sleep! Lord, You will increase Your gifts more and more in me, so that my soul, disentangled from the clinging snare of desire, may follow me to You so that it will not rebel against itself. Even in dreams my soul will not only not commit those debasing corruptions, even to the point of pollution of the flesh through sensual images, but it will not even consent to them. That nothing of this sort should have the very least influence over the pure affections even of a sleeper, not even such as a thought would restrain—to work this, not only during this life but even at my present age, is not hard for the Almighty, who is "able to do...above all that we ask or think" (Eph. 3:20). But what I still am in this manner of my evil, I have confessed to my good Lord, rejoicing "with trembling" (Ps. 2:11) in that which You have given me, bemoaning that in which I am still imperfect, hoping that You will perfect Your mercies in me, even to perfect peace, which my outward and inward man will have with You, when death will be "swallowed up in victory" (1 Cor. 15:54).

There is another evil of the day, and I wish that it were sufficient for it! (See Matthew 6:34.) By eating and drinking we repair the daily decline of our body until You destroy both belly and meat (1 Cor. 6:13) when You will slay my hunger with a wonderful fullness and clothe this corruptible with an eternal incorruption (1 Cor. 15:54). But now the necessity is sweet to me, and against this sweetness I fight so that I will not be taken captive. I carry on a daily war by fasting, often bringing my body "into subjection" (1 Cor. 9:27), and my pains are removed by the pleasure of food. For hunger and thirst are in a manner pains; they burn and kill like a fever unless the medicine of nourishment comes to our aid. Since this medicine is at hand through the comforts of Your gifts, with which land and water and air serve our weakness, our calamity is called a source of pleasure.

You have taught me this so that I should resolve myself to take food as I take medicine. But while I am moving from the discomfort of emptiness to the contentment of being full, in that very passage the snare of desire attacks me. For that path is pleasurable, and there is no other way to pass there where we need to pass. Since health is the reason for eating and drinking, a dangerous pleasure tags along as an attendant. This pleasure generally tries to go on before me, so that I may, for its sake, do what I say I do, or wish to do, for health's sake. And each does not have the same share, for what is enough for health is too little for pleasure. Often it is unclear whether it is for the necessary care of the body that we desire more food or if a self-indulgent, self-deceiving greediness is offering its services. In this uncertainty the unhappy soul rejoices, and in this it prepares an excuse to defend itself. It is glad that what is sufficient for the maintenance of health is not clear, so that under the cloak of health it may disguise its manner of gratification. I daily endeavor to resist these temptations, and I call on Your right hand. I refer my perplexities to You because I have not yet come to a conclusion about this.

I hear the voice of my God commanding us not to let "your hearts be overcharged with surfeiting, and drunkenness" (Luke 21:34). Drunkenness is far from me; You will have mercy so that it will not come near me. But overeating sometimes creeps upon Your servant; You will have mercy so that it may be far from me. No one can be self-controlled unless You grant it. You give us many things when we pray for them, and whatever good we have received before we prayed, we have received from You. We have received it so that we might afterwards know that we received it from you. I was never a drunkard, but I have known drunkards who were made sober by You. It was from You that they who never were drunkards should never be so, and it was from You that they who were drunkards should not be so any longer. And it was by You that both might know from whom it came.

I hear another voice of Yours: "Do not go after your lusts, and turn away from your pleasure." By Your grace I have heard something which I have greatly loved: "Neither, if we eat, are we the better; neither, if we eat not, are we the worse" (1 Cor. 8:8). That is to say, the one will not make me plentiful nor will the other make me miserable. I also heard another:

> For I have learned, in whatsoever state I am, therewith to be content. I know both how to be abased, and I know how to abound...and to suffer need. I can do all things through Christ which strengtheneth me.
> (Phil. 4:11–13)

Behold a soldier of the heavenly camp, not the dust which we are. But remember, Lord, "that we are dust" (Ps. 103:14), and that out of dust You have made man, and that he "was lost, and is found" (Luke 15:32). Nor could the apostle Paul do this in his own strength, because he whom I so loved, saying this through the breathing in of Your inspiration, was made of the same dust. "I can do all things," he said, "through [Him] which strengtheneth me" (Phil. 4:13). Strengthen me so that I can do all things. Give what You commanded, and command what You will. The apostle confesses to have received it, and when he glories, he glories in the Lord (1 Cor. 1:31). I have heard another begging in order to receive. "Take gluttony away from me," he said. Therefore, it appears, my holy God, that You give when men do what You command to be done.

You have taught me, good Father, that "unto the pure all things are pure" (Titus 1:15), but that "it is evil for that man who eateth with offence" (Rom. 14:20), and that "every creature of God is good, and nothing to be refused, if it be received with thanksgiving" (1 Tim. 4:4), and that "meat commendeth us not to God" (1 Cor. 8:8), and that "no man [should] judge [us] in meat, or in drink" (Col. 2:16), and that he who eats, "let not him... despise him that eateth not; and let not him which eateth not judge him that eateth" (Rom. 14:3). I have learned these things, thanks be to You, praise to You, my God, my Master, who knock at my ears, enlightening my heart. Deliver me out of all temptation.

I do not fear the uncleanness of meat but the uncleanness of lust. I know that Noah was permitted to eat all kinds of animals that were good for food (Gen. 9:3), that Elijah was fed with meat (1 Kings 17:6), that John, gifted with an admirable abstinence, was not polluted by feeding on living creatures, the locusts that he ate (Matt. 3:4). I know also that Esau was deceived by lusting for lentils (Gen. 25:34), and that David blamed himself for desiring a drink of water (2 Sam. 23:15–17), and that our King was tempted, not concerning meat, but bread (Matt. 4:3). Therefore, the people in the wilderness also deserved to be reproved, not for desiring meat, but because, in their desire for food, they murmured against the Lord (Num. 11:1).

Placed, then, amid these temptations, I strive daily against craving food and drink. For it is not the kind of thing that I can resolve to cut off once for all and never touch afterward, as I could of promiscuousness. The bridle of the throat, then, is to be held in control between slackness and stiffness. And who is he, Lord, who is not transported a little beyond the limits of necessity? Whoever he is, he is a great one; let him make Your name great. But I am not such, "for I am a sinful man" (Luke 5:8). Yet I, too, magnify Your name, and He who has "overcome the world" (John 16:33) "maketh intercession" (Rom. 8:34) to You for my sins, numbering me among the weak members of His body (1 Cor. 12:22), because "Thine eyes did see my substance, yet being unperfect; and in thy book all...[shall be] written" (Ps. 139:16).

I am not very concerned about the allurements of smells. When they are absent, I do not miss them; when they are present, I do not refuse them, yet I am ever ready to be without them. So I seem to myself; perhaps I am deceived. That is also a mournful darkness, by which the abilities within me are hidden from me, so that my mind, making inquiry into itself regarding its own powers, does not easily risk believing itself. Even what is in it is mostly hidden unless experience reveals it. And no one ought to be overconfident in this life, the whole of which is called a trial (see Job 7:1), so that he who has been able to go from worse to better, may not likewise go from better to worse. Our only hope, only confidence, only assured promise, is Your mercy.

The delights of sound had at one time firmly entangled me, but You loosened them and freed me from them. Now, in those melodies into which Your words breathe life, when sung with a sweet and melodic voice, I do take some pleasure, not to the degree that I am held by them, but only to the point that I can disengage myself from them when I want to. But along with the words which are their life, and by which they find admission into me, they seek in my affections a place of some estimation, and I can scarcely assign them one suitable. Sometimes, I seem to give them more honor than is appropriate, thinking that our minds are more holy and fervently raised to a flame of devotion by the holy words themselves when they are sung well than when they are not. The various emotions of our spirit, by a sweet variety, have their own proper melodies in the voice and singing by some hidden correspondence with which they are stirred up. But this contentment of the flesh, to which the soul must not be given over to be made frail, often beguiles me when the sense does not wait upon reason, following it patiently, but, having been admitted merely for reason's sake, it strives even to run before it and lead it. Thus in these things I sin unaware, but afterwards I am aware of it.

At other times, when I over-anxiously shun this very deception, I err in having too great a strictness—sometimes to the degree that I wish to have the whole melody of sweet music which is used to accompany David's Psalter banished from my ears and the church's also. It seems to me that the safer style is the one used by Athanasius, Bishop of Alexandria, which I remember often hearing about. He made the reader of the psalm utter it with a slight inflection of voice that was nearer to speaking than singing. But still, when I remember the tears I shed at the songs of Your church, in the beginning of my restored faith, and how I am now moved, not with the singing, but with the things sung, when they are sung with a clear voice and a very suitable modulation, I acknowledge the greater use of this practice. Thus I fluctuate between the peril of pleasure and acceptable wholesomeness. I am rather inclined, though not as if I were pronouncing an irrevocable opinion, to approve the custom of singing in the church, so that through the delight of the ears, weaker minds may rise to a feeling of devotion. Yet when it happens that I am more moved with the voice than the words sung, I confess that I have sinned in a way that deserves punishment, and then I would rather not hear music.

See what a state I am in now. Weep with me, and weep for me, you who govern your feelings within in such a way that good action ensues. For you who do not act in this way, these things do not move you. But You, Lord, my God, listen to me, and look, and see, and "have mercy" and "heal me" (Ps. 6:2), You, in whose presence I have become a problem to myself, and "this is my infirmity" (Ps. 77:10).

There remains the pleasure of these eyes of my flesh, on which to make my confessions in the hearing of the ears of Your temple, those brotherly and devout ears. So I conclude the temptations of the lust of the flesh which still assail me, groaning and "earnestly desiring to be clothed upon with [my] house which is from heaven" (2 Cor. 5:2). My eyes love beautiful and varied forms and bright and soft colors. Do not let these occupy my soul; let God who made these things good, very good indeed (Gen. 1:31), occupy it instead. He is my good, not they. These affect me while I am awake, the whole day. No rest is given me from them as there is given me in silence from musical voices and sometimes from voices. For this queen of colors, the light, bathing all which we see, wherever I am through the day, gliding by me in varied forms, soothes me when I am engaged on other things and not observing it. So strongly does it entwine itself in my life, that if it is suddenly withdrawn, I seek it, longing, and if it is absent long, it saddens my mind.

Oh Light, which Isaac saw when his fleshly eyes were heavy and closed by old age and it was granted him, not knowingly, to bless his sons, but by blessing to know them. (See Genesis 27:1–40.) Light which Jacob saw, when he also, blind through old age, with illumined heart shed light on the different races of future peoples foreshadowed in the persons of his sons, and laid his hands, mystically crossed, upon his grandchildren by Joseph—not as their father corrected them by his outward eye, but as he himself inwardly discerned. (See Genesis 48:11–22.) This is the Light. It is One, and all who see and love it are one.

But that physical light of which I spoke seasons the life of this world for its blind lovers with an enticing and dangerous sweetness. But they who know how to praise You for it, All-creating Lord, take it up in Your hymns and are not taken up with it in their sleep. I want to be this way. I resist these seductions of the eyes, for fear that my feet with which I walk upon Your way will become ensnared, and I lift up my invisible eyes to You that You would "pluck my feet out of the net" (Ps. 25:15). You do now and always pluck them out, for they are ensnared. You do not cease to pluck them out, while I often entangle myself in snares on all sides, because You who "keepeth Israel shall neither slumber nor sleep" (Ps. 121:4).

What innumerable trifles, made either by art or manufacturing, in our apparel, shoes, utensils, and all sort of works, in pictures also with various images—and these far exceeding all necessary and moderate use and all pious meaning—have men added with which to tempt their own eyes. They outwardly follow what they themselves make and inwardly forsake Him by whom they themselves were made and destroy that which they themselves have been made!

But, my God and my glory, I also accordingly sing a hymn to You, and I consecrate praise to Him who consecrates me because beautiful patterns, which through men's souls are conveyed into their cunning hands, come from that Beauty which is above our souls, which my soul day and night longs after. The framers and followers of outward beauties derive from them the rule for judging them, but not for using them. He is there, though they do not perceive Him, so that they might not wander but keep their strength for You and not scatter it abroad upon pleasurable weariness. And I, though I speak and see this, still entangle my steps with these outward beauties; but You pluck me out, Lord, You pluck me out because "thy lovingkindness is before mine eyes" (Ps. 26:3). For I am caught miserably, and You pluck me out mercifully. Sometimes I do not perceive it, when I have only lightly lighted upon them; other times I perceive it with pain because I am stuck fast in them.

To this we can add another form of temptation, more manifoldly dangerous. Besides the lust of the flesh, which consists of the delight of all senses and pleasures, in which its slaves who go "far from thee shall [waste and] perish" (Ps. 73:27), the soul has, through the same bodily senses, a certain vain and curious desire veiled under the title of knowledge and learning, not of delighting in the flesh but of making experiments through the flesh. This is based on the appetite for knowledge, and sight is the sense chiefly used for attaining knowledge; therefore, it is called in divine language "the lust of the eyes" (1 John 2:16). To see belongs properly to the eyes, yet we also use this word for other senses when we employ them in seeking knowledge. We do not say, "Listen how it flashes," or "Smell how it glows," or "Taste how it shines," or "Feel how it gleams"; for all these are said to be seen. And yet we not only say, "See how it shines," which the eyes alone can perceive, but also, "See how it sounds," "See how it smells," "See how it tastes," "See how hard it is." And so the general experience of the senses, as was said, is called "the lust of the eyes," because the office of seeing, in which the eyes hold the prerogative, the other senses take to themselves in the form of an analogy when they search after any knowledge.

But by this it can be more clearly seen in what particular ways pleasure and curiosity are the objects of the senses. Pleasure seeks objects that are beautiful, fragrant, savory, and soft; however, curiosity, for the sake of experimentation, seeks the contrary, not in order to suffer annoyance but out of the desire to experience and know them. What pleasure is there in seeing a mangled corpse that will make you shudder? Yet if it is lying near, people flock there to be made sad and to turn pale. Even in sleep they are afraid to see it, as if when awake, someone forced them to see it, or some report of its beauty drew them there! It is the same way also in the other senses, but it would take a long time to go through them all. From this disease of curiosity all those strange sights are exhibited in the theater. Therefore, men go on to search out the hidden powers of nature, which is beyond our purpose, in order to know that which does not profit, and of which men desire nothing but to know. Curiosity, also, is what causes people to inquire into the magical arts, spurred on by their desire to gain perverted knowledge. Consequently, in religion itself, God is tempted when signs and wonders are demanded of Him, and these are not desired for any good end but merely for an experiment.

In this vast wilderness full of snares and dangers, see how many of them I have cut off and thrust out of my heart, as You have enabled me, "O God of my salvation" (Ps. 27:9). Yet when do I dare say, since so many things like this buzz on all sides about our daily life, when do I dare say that nothing of this sort engages my attention or generates an idle interest in me? True, the theaters do not now carry me away, and I do not care to know the courses of the stars, nor did my soul ever consult departed ghosts. I detest all sacrilegious mysteries. By what artifices and suggestions does the enemy deal with me to desire some sign from You, Lord, my God, to whom I owe humble and single-hearted service! I beg you by our King, and by our pure and holy country, Jerusalem, that as any consent to asking You for a sign is far from me, so may it ever be further and further. But when I pray to You for the salvation of anyone, my purpose and intention are far different. You give and will continue to allow me to follow You willingly, doing what You will.

Notwithstanding, in how many extremely petty and contemptible things is our curiosity daily tempted, and who can recount how often we give way? How often we begin as if we were tolerating people telling vain stories, for fear that we might offend the weak; then by degrees we take interest in them! I do not now go to the circus to see a dog chase a hare, but if I see this as I am walking past a field, that chase perhaps will distract me even from some weighty thought and draw me after it. It does not make me turn my horse in order to look at it, yet still I incline my mind there. Unless You, having made me see my infirmity, quickly admonished me, either to rise towards You through the sight itself by some contemplation, or to despise and pass it by altogether, I would stand stupidly looking at it.

What if, when I am sitting at home, a lizard catching flies or a spider entangling them as they rush into its web often captures my attention? Is the activity different because they are only small creatures? I go on from them to praise You, the wonderful Creator and Orderer of all, but this does not first draw my attention. It is one thing to rise quickly to You, another not to fall. Of such things my life is full, and my one hope is Your wonderful great mercy. For when our heart becomes the receptacle of such things and is clogged up with multitudes of these abundant vanities, then our prayers are also thereby often interrupted and distracted, and while in Your presence we direct the voice of our heart to Your ears, this very great concern is broken off by the rushing in of I do not know what idle thoughts. Will we then consider this also to be among things of little concern, or will anything bring us back to hope, except Your complete mercy, since You have begun to change us?

And You know how far You have already changed me, You who first healed me of the lust of justifying myself, so that You might forgive all the rest of my iniquities and heal all my infirmities and redeem my life from corruption and crown me with mercy and pity and satisfy my desire with good things (Ps. 103:3–5), You who curbed my pride with Your fear and tamed my neck with Your yoke. Now I bear it, and it is light to me (see

Matthew 11:30) because You have promised thus and have made it so. Truly, it was so, but I did not know it when I was afraid to take it.

Lord, You alone are without pride because You are the only true Lord, You who have no lord. Has this third kind of temptation also ceased for me, or can it ever cease through my entire lifetime, this wish, namely, to be feared and loved by men for no other reason except that we may experience a joy from it which is not real joy? What a wretched life that is, and a foul boastfulness! Because of this especially, men neither purely love nor fear You. Therefore You "resisteth the proud, but giveth grace unto the humble" (James 4:6; 1 Pet. 5:5). You thunder down upon the ambitions of the world, and the foundations of the mountains tremble (Ps. 18:7).

Because certain positions in human society make it necessary for some to be loved and feared by men, the adversary of our true blessedness constantly bombards us, everywhere spreading his snares of "Well done, well done!" He does this so that, greedily grasping at these words, we may be taken unawares and sever our joy from Your truth and set it in the deceitfulness of men, and so that we will be pleased with being loved and feared, not for Your sake but in Your stead. Then, having made us like himself in this way, he may have us for his own, not in the ties of love but in the chains of punishment, he who purposed to set his throne in the north so that in a dark and chilly place, we might serve him who pervertedly and crookedly imitates You. (See Isaiah 14:12–14.)

But we, Lord, behold, we are Your "little flock" (Luke 12:32); possess us as Yours. Stretch Your wings over us, and let us fly under them. Be our glory; let us be loved for Your sake, and let Your word be feared in us. Whoever wants to be praised by men when You find fault with him, will not be defended by men when You judge, nor be delivered when You condemn. But when it is not the case where a sinner is praised in the desires of his soul or an ungodly man is blessed, but rather, a situation in which a man is praised for some gift which You have given him, and he rejoices more at the praise for himself than in the fact that he has the gift for which he is praised, he is also praised while You reproach him. Better is he who did the praising than he who is praised. For the one took pleasure in the gift of God in man; the other was more pleased with the gift of man than of God.

We are assaulted daily by these temptations, Lord; without ceasing we are assaulted. Our daily furnace is the tongue of men. (See Proverbs 27:21.) In this way also You command us to be self-disciplined. Give what You command and command what You will. You know the groans of my heart and the flood of tears from my eyes concerning this matter. I cannot discern to what extent I have been cleansed from this plague, and I greatly fear my secret sins (Ps. 19:12), which Your eyes know but mine do not. For in other kinds of temptations I have some way of examining myself; in this temptation, I have scarcely any. In holding back my mind from the pleasures of the flesh and idle curiosity, I see how much I have attained when I do without them, either by forgoing them voluntarily or by not being able to have them. Then I ask myself how much more or less troublesome it is to me not to have them. Riches are desired so that they may serve one, two, or all three of the lusts. (See 1 John 2:16.) If the soul cannot discern whether, when it has them, it despises them, they may be cast aside so that it may prove itself. But to be without praise, and to try our powers in that, must we live evil lives, so abandonedly and atrociously that no one could know us without detesting us? What greater madness can be said or thought of? But if praise accompanies and ought to accompany a good life and good works, we ought not to forgo its company rather than a good life itself. Yet I do not know whether I will do well or badly without something, unless it is absent.

What then do I confess to You in this kind of temptation, Lord? What, except that I am delighted with praise, but I am more delighted with truth than with praise. For if it were proposed to me whether I would rather be praised by men and delirious through error on all things, or be blamed by all while being consistent and very settled in the truth, I know which I would choose. Yet I cheerfully wish that the approval of another would not also increase my joy for any good in me. Yet I admit, it does increase it, and not only that, but condemnation also diminishes it.

When I am troubled at my misery in this, an excuse occurs to me. Of what value this excuse is, You, God, know, for it leaves me uncertain. Since

You have commanded us not only to have self-restraint, that is, have commanded us from what things to withhold our love, but have commanded righteousness also, that is, on what we are to bestow our love, You have willed us not only to love You, but our neighbor also. Often, when I am pleased with intelligent praise, it seems to me that I am pleased with the proficiency or progress of my neighbor. Or I am grieved at his error when I hear him condemn either what he does not understand or what is good. Sometimes I am grieved at my own praises, either when those things which I do not like about myself are praised or when lesser and inconsequential good qualities are valued more than they ought to be. But again, how do I know whether or not I am influenced in this way because I do not want he who praises me to differ from me about myself, not because I am influenced by concern for him but because those same good things which please me in myself please me more when they please another also? Somehow I am not praised when my own judgment of myself is not praised, either when those things which displease me are praised or those which please me less are more praised. Am I then doubtful of myself in this matter?

Behold, in You, Truth, I see that I ought not to be moved by my own praises for my own sake, but for the good of my neighbor. Whether it is so with me, I do not know. For in this matter I know less of myself than You do. I implore You now, my God, to show me myself so that I may confess to my brothers, who are to pray for me, where I find myself weak. Let me examine myself again more diligently. If, when I am praised, I am moved by the good of my neighbor, why am I less moved if another is unjustly condemned than if it is myself? Why am I stung more by reproach cast upon myself than at that cast upon another, right in front of me, with the same injustice? Do I not know this either? Or in the end is it that I deceive myself (Gal. 6:3; 1 John 1:8) and "do not the truth" (1 John 1:6) before You in my heart and speech? Put this madness far from me, Lord, unless my own mouth be to me the sinner's oil to make fat my head (Ps. 141:5). "I am poor and needy" (Ps. 109:22), yet I am better while I am offended with myself and seek your mercy in hidden groanings, until what is lacking in my defective state is renewed and perfected to that peace which the eye of the proud does not know.

Yet, because of a love of praise, words that are spoken and deeds that are known to men bring with them a most dangerous temptation. Through our love of praise, we want to establish a certain renown of our own, and so we seek and collect men's approval. It tempts me even when I reprove it on the very ground that it is reproved. Often a man glories with more vanity in his very contempt of conceit, and so it is no longer contempt of conceit in which he glories, for he does not condemn when he glories.

Within us also is another evil, arising out of a similar temptation. By this, men become vain, pleasing themselves in themselves, though they do not please or displease others or do not care to please others. But pleasing themselves, they displease You greatly, not only by taking pleasure in things that are not good but which appear good, but also by taking pleasure in Your good things that they see as their own. Even if they see them as Yours, they still see them as a reflection of their own merits. Or, even if they see them as coming from Your grace, they do not receive them with brotherly rejoicing, but envy the same grace in others. In all these and similar perils and travails, You see the trembling of my heart, and I would rather feel that my wounds are cured by You than that they are not inflicted by me.

Where have You not walked with me, Truth, teaching me what to beware of and what to desire, when I related to You what I could discover here below and consulted You? With my outward senses, as much as I could, I surveyed the world and observed the life which my body has from me, and from my senses. From there I entered the recesses of my memory, those numerous and spacious chambers, wonderfully furnished with innumerable stores. I considered them and stood aghast, being able to discern nothing of these things without You, and finding none of them to be You. Nor was it I who discovered these things, who went over them all and labored to distinguish and to value everything according to its dignity, taking some things on the report of my senses, questioning others which I felt were mingled with myself, numbering and distinguishing the reporters themselves, and in the large treasure-house of my memory, musing on some things, storing up others, drawing out others. I was still not myself when I did this, that is, it was not my power through which I did it; neither was it You, for You are the abiding Light which I consulted concerning all these things, whether they were, what they were, and how they were to be valued. I heard You directing and commanding me. This I often do; this delights me, and as far as I may be freed from necessary duties, I take refuge in this pleasure.

In all these things which I review, consulting You, I cannot find any safe place for my soul except in You, where my scattered members may be gathered and from whom nothing of me may depart. Sometimes You allow me to experience a very unusual feeling, in my inmost soul, which reaches to a strange sweetness, and which, if it were perfected in me, I do not know what in it would not belong to the life to come. But through my miserable encumbrances I sink down again into these lower things, and I am swept back by former habit and am held. I greatly weep, but I am greatly held. So much does the burden of a bad habit weigh us down. Here I can stay, but I do not want to; there I would stay, but I cannot; in both ways I am miserable.

In this way I have therefore considered the sicknesses of my sins in that threefold lust (see 1 John 2:16), and I have called on Your right hand to help me. With a wounded heart I have gazed on Your brightness, and, thrown back by it, I said, "Who can attain to it? 'I am cut off from before thine eyes'" (Ps. 31:22). You are the Truth who presides over all. In my covetousness I would not completely abandon You, but along with You I wanted to possess a lie, as no man would speak falsely in such a manner that he himself becomes ignorant of the truth. So, then, I lost You because You do not stoop to be possessed with a lie.

Whom could I find to reconcile me to You? Was I to have recourse to angels? By what prayers? By what sacraments? Many who have endeavored to return to You, but were unable to on their own, have, I hear, tried this and have fallen into a lust for strange visions and have been considered worthy to be deluded. They, being high-minded, sought You by the pride of learning. They sought You with swelled heads rather than by beating their breasts, and so, with the approval of their hearts, they drew to themselves the princes of the air (Eph. 2:2), the fellow-conspirators of their pride, by whom, through magical influences, they were deceived. They were seeking a mediator by whom they might be purged, and there was none. The Devil transformed himself "into an angel of light" (2 Cor. 11:14). It greatly enticed proud flesh that he had no body of flesh. For they were mortal and sinners, but You, Lord, to whom in their pride they sought to be reconciled, are immortal and without sin. But a "mediator between God and men" (1 Tim. 2:5) must be something like God and something like men, for fear that being too much like man, he would be far from God, or if too much like God, too unlike man, and so not be able to be a mediator. That deceitful mediator then, by whom, in Your secret judgments, pride deserved to be deluded, had one thing in common with man: sin. He wished to seem to have something else in common with God; not being clothed with the mortality of flesh, he would boast that he was immortal. But since "the wages of sin is death" (Rom. 6:23), he has this in common with men, that with them he should be condemned to death.

The true Mediator, whom in Your secret mercy You have revealed to the humble and sent to them so that by His example they also might learn that same humility, that "mediator between God and men, the man Christ Jesus" (1 Tim. 2:5), appeared between mortal sinners and the immortal Just One: mortal with men, just with God. Because the wages of righteousness are life and peace (compare Romans 6:23), He was able, by a righteousness joined together with God, to nullify the death of sinners now made righteous, which He willed to have in common with them. Therefore, He was revealed to holy men of old, so that they, through faith in His passion to come, might be saved as we have been saved. For as man, He is the Mediator, but as the Word, He is not in the middle between God and man because He is equal to God, and God with God, and together one God (John 1:1–2).

How You have loved us, good Father, who "spared not [Your] own Son, but delivered him up for us all" (Rom. 8:32)! How You have loved us, for whom He who "thought it not robbery to be equal with [You]" was made subject "unto death, even the death of the cross" (Phil. 2:6, 8), He alone, "free among the dead" (Ps. 88:5), having "power to lay [His life] down, and...power to take it again" (John 10:18). For our sake He is to You both victor and victim. Because He was the victim, he is therefore the victor. For our sake He is to You priest and sacrifice. Because of his sacrifice he is therefore our priest, making us Your sons instead of servants by being born of You and by serving us. For this reason, my hope is strong in Him, that You will heal all my diseases (Ps. 103:3) by Him who sits at Your right hand and "maketh intercession for us" (Rom. 8:34), or else I would despair. Many and great are my infirmities, many they are and great, but Your medicine is mightier. We might imagine that Your Word is far from any union with man and despair of ourselves unless He had been "made flesh, and dwelt among us" (John 1:14).

Frightened over my sins and the burden of my misery, I had agonized in my heart and had purposed to flee to the wilderness, but You prevented me and strengthened me, saying, "that [Christ] died for all, that they which live should not henceforth live unto themselves, but unto him which died for them" (2 Cor. 5:15). See, Lord, I cast my care upon You (Ps. 55:22; 1 Pet. 5:7) that I may live and "behold wondrous things out of thy law" (Ps. 119:18). You know my lack of knowledge and my infirmities; teach me, and heal me. He, Your only Son, "in whom are hid all the treasures of wisdom and knowledge" (Col. 2:3), has redeemed me with His blood. "Let not the proud oppress me" (Ps. 119:122), because I meditate on my redemption and eat and drink and share it, and, being poor, I desired to be satisfied from Him among those who eat and are satisfied: "they shall praise the LORD that seek him" (Ps. 22:26).

Foxe's Book of Martyrs
John Foxe

They were people who triumphantly donned the armor of God—the helmet of salvation, the shield of faith, the sword of God's Word. They faced torture and death in their fight of faith, willing to stand for their beliefs regardless of the price. The faithfulness of such historical figures as William Tyndale and Martin Luther will create courage in anyone facing the trials of life and is sure to inspire you to live for Christ today. This best-selling classic is a must for every Christian's library!

ISBN: 0-88368-095-5 • Pocket • 416 pages

The Autobiography of George Müller
George Müller

What can be accomplished through an ordinary
man who trusts in an extraordinary God? George
Müller discovered the endless possibilities! Share his
experiences in these thrilling excerpts from his diary.
Enter into his struggles and triumphs as he establishes
orphanages to care for thousands of English children,
calling on God to supply all their needs daily. Müller's
unwavering, childlike dependence upon the Father
will inspire you to trust the God of the impossible
in every area of your life.

ISBN: 0-88368-159-5 • Pocket • 240 pages

WHITAKER
HOUSE

www.whitakerhouse.com